UNMASKED

Unmasked

Exposing the Cultural Sexual Assault

By Jim Anderson

With Heidi Karlsson

Lifeline Ministries
P.O. Box 8071
Spokane, WA 99203

www.lifeline-ministries.org
info@lifeline-ministries.org

Cover photography by Hannah Robinson
www.worldsapartphotography.com

Cover design by Sarah Mejia and Lee Watson

Unless otherwise indicated, all Scripture quotations are taken from the
New American Standard Bible, © 1960, 1962, 1963, 1968, 1971, 1972,
1973; Creation House, Inc. Used by permission.

ISBN 978-0-9828642-0-3

DEDICATION

I dedicate this book to my wife Lisa, the love of my life, my friend, my help meet, and the mother of our eight children. You are the heart of our family, our home, and our ministry. This book was possible because of you, and I thank God for the gift you are to me.

Acknowledgements

This book would not have been possible without Heidi Karlsson's labor of love in taking a year of her life to compile all my notes and sermons into the initial manuscript. God bless you, Heidi. I believe your work will bless many, many people.

Many thanks to our computer gurus, "Doctor" Chuck Boren and James Bishop, who are so faithful to help us every time we have a technological crisis. Thank you, Noreen Bechard, for all your editing work and for answering our questions so graciously every time we called with yet another question. I am also thankful for the insights Larry Alberts and Dr. Lance Wonders gave me on the manuscript.

I am grateful for the creative young people God has brought into our lives who have contributed to this project. They include Hannah Robinson (www.worldsapartphotography.com), who took the original picture for the cover, Sarah Mejia, and our son-in-law, Lee Watson, who patiently worked with us on the cover design. Thank you for using your gifts to serve and help us!

I would like to acknowledge the long-term, faithful support I have received from the following members of the Lifeline Clergy Council: Ed Cain, Sonny Clemmer, Dan Henshaw, Barry Hill, John Macpherson, and Doug Malott. Most of these men have stood with me for years.

I have felt supported and encouraged by many discipleship school directors: Tom Hardebeck, Marco Prado, Kevin McCuen, Gerald Evans, and Tim Ainley. The message of this book developed and expanded, in part, as you encouraged me to teach and minister in your schools year after year.

Many thanks to our intercessors who, for years, patiently put up with prayer requests from us to "get the book done." Our collective prayers have been answered. It is finally done!

Endorsements from Ministry Leaders

Jim Anderson has written a clear exposé of the enemy's plan and how to be totally free from it through his new, future best seller, *Unmasked*. It is not only a "must read" for every Christian, it has the secret antidote for the poison that is destroying us. That antidote will help save our lives, families, and nation!

God chose us in Him before the foundation of the world that we would be holy and blameless before Him, for without holiness, no man will see God. We are the temple of the living God. God needs holy vessels through whom He can bring His kingdom on earth as it is in Heaven. As a result, Satan's biggest trick is to seduce God's children into sexual compromise. **Thank God for this timely, prophetic masterpiece** that clearly and practically exposes the enemy's plan and gives God's glorious revelation for victory!

Bob Weiner
Weiner Ministries International

Through *Unmasked*, Jim Anderson offers us a considerable and substantial "read" that is radical, real, relevant, revelatory—and, yes, revolutionary, if heeded and applied. This brother clearly loves God's daughters and has been given much divine wisdom on how husbands, fathers, brothers, and pastors—men in general—can and should care for, and be protective of, their sisters' needs. Though controversial and radical in some places, Jim's book is a much-needed corrective for the non-Biblical, culture-dominated "traditions" we so-called "Christians" have been following in recent generations. *Unmasked* **is lucid, liberating, life-enhancing, and a breath of fresh hope in an atmosphere increasingly characterized by despair.**

Larry J. Alberts
Senior Elder, Way of the Lord Church
Apostolic team leader of Fathers and Families Together Network
Minneapolis, Minnesota

Unmasked is not just another book on spiritual discernment or family living. The truths enunciated in the pages of this book have a quality of spiritual fire that can set ablaze a generation. **Truly, this book has the potential to help create a context for the greatest move of God this world has ever witnessed—a third Great Awakening.** Jim Anderson contends for our daughters and sons, indeed entire families, for breakthrough for the impossible. I have no doubt *Unmasked* will change your life, set your daughters free, and become a tool in your spiritual arsenal.

Bob Brasset
Extreme Healing Ministries
Victoria, British Columbia, Canada

Jim Anderson's book, *Unmasked*, is nothing short of profound. **Jim understands the heart of a woman like no one else I've ever read.** He has masterfully captured the essence of God's loving intentions for all human relationships. **This is a must read for every pregnancy center worker** who wants to sincerely understand and help the women who come to pregnancy centers. With the insights of this book, they will be better equipped to provide the meaningful help and hope that women desperately need.

Paula Cullen, R.N.
Pacific Northwest Regional Representative, Care Net
Founding Director, Life Services of Spokane (1991-2009)

Though *Unmasked* is written as a book, it would be incorrect to say it is only a book. It is more like an exposé, a manifesto, a manual of war. **Jim Anderson is a cultural warrior, and *Unmasked* is a well-crafted weapon and tool intended not for the destruction of nations but for their healing.**

The sexual revolution is no longer a problem "out there." The worship of sex has extracted a high price inside the church as well. Jim Anderson is not a novice in facing this giant. For years, he has effectively defined the issues we face and with great effect, provided liberating solutions.

As a pastor whose ministry is built on the joining of the generations, I have seen firsthand the devastating fruit of the worship of sex. Jim has come to us year after year to share the truth contained in this book. Each year we experienced the same result—countless lives set free from shame, guilt, and brokenness, the results of sexual sin. This book is not written in the hope of setting captives free. The truths contained herein have already been setting captives free.

Norm Willis
Senior Pastor, Christ Church Kirkland

There are sad but true stories of small communities poisoned by contaminated drinking water. Sickness, disease, and premature death continue until the problem is discovered, the water supply is cleansed, and health returns. We live in a culture that, in many ways, is sick and dying. *Unmasked* uncovers the destructive forces working to destroy our loved ones and our culture.

Every pastor, parent, and young adult should read this book. Within its pages, the plans of the enemy are exposed. **Unmasked has the answers that will restore health back to our families and to our culture.**

Craig Lotze
Senior Pastor, Victory Faith Fellowship
Spokane, Washington

Unmasked is a scholarly, yet extremely practical, outworking of a Biblical approach to upholding women in their proper place. He provides a working model of "a better way" that honors the differences between men and women, yet views them as fully equal in God's sight and purposes.

Men, if you want a book that helps you to understand women, look no further!

And, ladies, if you have mourned the fact that men just "don't get" what you are all about, or if you yourself have lost your way and feel you no longer know who you are in the midst of all of society's deceptions, here at last is a heaven-sent magnifying glass that makes the truth obvious even to those often unwilling to face it. *Unmasked* is a one-of-a-kind approach to one of today's most important subjects.

Buy one to read and three to give away!

Dr. Lance Wonders
Dean, ACTS International Bible College
Blaine, Minnesota

Gideon was afraid to destroy the high places, so he did it at night. **Jim, through *Unmasked*, is openly destroying the high places** we have allowed to take root in our culture and even in our own homes. I dare you to join us in exposing this cultural sexual assault and then to walk in radical purity, rendering powerless every weapon formed against us.

Steve Weber
Regional Director CIS
Christian Broadcasting Network Worldreach

For the past few years, I have been given the incredible opportunity to call a young generation to radical devotion to Jesus Christ. I have seen firsthand that the concentrated and relentless assault against sexual purity is one of the enemy's main strategies in his attempt to render this army ineffective. **In *Unmasked*, my friend Jim Anderson helps move us forward in the revelation of sexual purity and freedom.** I especially want to encourage the younger generation, as well as those called to father them, to lay hold of these principles, as I believe they will help them navigate through the cultural landmines of sexual immorality that have been set up to destroy and steal the destiny of so many. May this book be spread far and wide as a voice God uses to both heal and empower a generation!

Rick Pino
Fire Rain Ministries

***Unmasked* is truly a book of healing.** It not only speaks healing to daughters who have been injured, but to sons and fathers who, through repentance, can become the men God has called them to be. The enemy attacks our families. His goal is to move the next generation away from God's plan of what a family should become.

This book is a call to restore the hearts of fathers to their children so the children's hearts can be restored back to their fathers.

Cal Pierce

Director, Healing Rooms Ministries

My good friend Jim Anderson is a true prophet with a strategic message for the Body of Christ. *Unmasked* represents the best of all the wisdom he has gained from the Lord through many years of faithful Kingdom service. *Unmasked* gives us revelation that is key to our mission to reform the Church and transform our world. **I am making this book mandatory reading for all of our leaders and all of our churches.** Whole nations can be impacted through *Unmasked*, and I look forward to being one of those leaders who will make sure this message reaches tens, even hundreds, of thousands!

George Bakalov

Founder and Overseeing Apostle

Apostolic Reformed Church

Sofia, Bulgaria

Have you ever wondered why we are so messed up and broken sexually— even in the church? How can we do the work of the Lord when we are plagued with sexual bondage, addictions, dysfunction, and shame few people are willing to bring into the light? *Unmasked* addresses these topics and much more. Ephesians 5:11 tells us to . . . *have nothing to do with the fruitless deeds of darkness, but rather expose them.* Wherever Jim ministers, he does just that.

It is time to turn on the lights and liberate the church with the unique, yet divine, perspective the Lord has entrusted to Jim. **He is willing to address and tackle sexual issues most of us don't talk about in the church—** things we think about and deal with constantly, things that are secretly destroying and distorting us as a church and as a society. It's time to come out of the bondage of this world and be liberated sons and daughters of the Most High. The message of *Unmasked* is a pathway to that reality.

It is an honor and a joy to know Jim Anderson and to see how he so effectively walks out this message as a true, healing and liberating father to this young generation. I highly recommend him, his message, and this book. It is a true labor of love that has come into fruition for such a time as this. Jim has not just written a book but he passionately and consistently has lived this message for decades, and because he lives it, he can now give it away!

Scott MacLeod
Founder and Director of Provision International & Thunder School

We are at a critical moment in history. Perversion, sexual brokenness, shame, violence and death have pervaded our culture. There is a global crisis, a desolation of generations of men and women, boys and girls, and parents and children who suffer from poverty of mind, soul and spirit. **Jim Anderson has masterfully fashioned *Unmasked* as a weapon to combat moral poverty and strategically release the Isaiah 61 movement of healing, deliverance and restoration to broken generations through the heroic love and power of God.** Thank you, Jim, for being such a servant of the Revolution!

Shawn Foster
President, LIFE Alliance/YouthStorm
youthstorm.org

Endorsements from Discipleship School Directors

There are books that come and go, and then there are books that transform cultures and nations. Jim Anderson's *Unmasked* is a culture-and-nation-transforming book. A sexual assault has been loosed upon our young people. Our nation must change, and for that change to occur, we need the revelations from *Unmasked* about a daughter's heart and the role of a father in her life. **Jim's message has transformed the life of our congregation, set our ladies free, and equipped our men to take their proper place.** A generation stands in need of the answers this book holds. It's a "must read"!

Pastor Tom Hardebeck
Director of Generational Leadership
Tom serves under Ed Pohlreich, senior pastor, Generational Hope
Christian Center
Maple Valley, Washington

The message of *Unmasked* regarding the sexual assault we have endured for the last 50+ years in our society is absolutely vital for the healing and revival of this generation. Jim Anderson's firsthand experience in ministering healing to thousands of men and women devastated by sexual sin enables him to speak with authority and to provide real answers for one of the most urgent societal problems we face today. Jim's ministry to this assaulted generation has brought freedom from the shame and guilt of sexual sin to many, and now they can face their future with confidence. *Unmasked* **is "must read" for everyone!**

Pastor Kevin McCuen
Director of The Master's Commission
Kevin serves under Norm Willis, senior pastor, Christ Church Kirkland
Kirkland, Washington

This world's system has been telling our sons and daughters who they are their whole lives. The result has been confused identities, broken sexuality, and destroyed marriages. **Finally, a voice, through *Unmasked*, that will stand against the tide of this cultural onslaught and speak truth and healing into the hearts of this generation!** Jim Anderson's message is one I will always make place for in our school. He carries the Father's heart in warring for the lives and destinies of our sons and daughters. On behalf of the hundreds of young adults I have personally seen healed through your ministry, thank you, brother, for your courage, truth, and love.

Tim Ainley
Director, Foundations School of Discipleship
Visalia, California

When I think of Jim Anderson, my first thought is that he is a prophet like Jeremiah. In *Unmasked*, he trumpets a call to holiness and exposes the high places of idolatry and sexual worship in our midst. It is a message needed in every church in our nation. Jim has ministered the message of *Unmasked* in our church and our discipleship school for the last 14 years and has given a life-changing impartation to hundreds of people. **The lives of those who hear the message and obey will be changed forever.** Western Canada is being changed one disciple at a time, in part, due to Jim's ministry and message.

Gerald Evans
Director of Master's Commission
Gerald serves under Lorne Lueck, senior pastor, City Life Church
Chilliwack, British Columbia, Canada

It is hard to overstate how important Jim Anderson's message in *Unmasked* is. Every woman lives under the pressure of a culture that worships her sexuality (whether she understands it or not). Every man needs to understand a woman's heart and that he is called to protect her and honor her. *Unmasked* contains the rare, clear message that releases freedom. In our mentoring program, we have seen this message heal, transform, and restore the broken hearts of both men and women. Over the years, we have seen many relationships begin and thrive as a result of this teaching. We are seeing hurting young people, who lived under the fear that they had thrown away all hope for a "happily ever after," walk down the aisle on their wedding day completely restored and white as snow. **Our lives, our church, and our nation are forever changed by the message found within this book.**

Pastor Keri Harvey
Assistant Director, The Master's Commission
Keri serves under Lorne Lueck, senior pastor, City Life Church
Chilliwack, British Columbia, Canada

Jim Anderson is a man born for this age. His life message uncovers the major forces at work to undermine godly sexuality, the family unit, and the hearts of sons and daughters. He is a true father to this generation and a partner to all of us fighting for revival in our depraved culture. Every time Jim ministers to students in our international Table Internships, an absolute transformation happens in the identities and values of our young adults. **After experiencing 10 years of Jim's ministry, I can truly say his message reveals the keys for giving us a plan to overcome and shine in the darkest of days ahead.**

Marco Prado
Pastor/International Director, The Table
Marco serves under Francis Anfuso, senior pastor, Rock of Roseville
Roseville, California

CONTENTS

FOREWORD

BY LOU ENGLE – THE CALL, CO-FOUNDER & PRESIDENT

There are moments in history when a door for massive change opens. Great revolutions for good or for evil occur in the vacuum created by these openings. It is in these times that key men and women, and even entire generations, risk everything to become the hinge of history — that pivotal point which determines which way the door will swing.

Elijah was such a man. Born into one of the darkest times in Israel's history, where only 7,000 out of a nation of ten million had not bowed their knees to Baal, Elijah's calling was to turn an entire nation back to God. At that time, King Ahab and his heathen wife Jezebel seemed on a personal mission from hell to stamp out what righteousness remained in Israel. They served the vile Canaanite idols, Baal and Ashtoreth, demonic principalities who, in their fertility rituals, demanded sexual immorality, perversion, and the blood of innocent babies. In a rampage against righteousness, Jezebel built pagan altars and murdered the Lord's prophets, replacing those spiritual leaders with more than 800 cultic priests, soothsayers, and temple prostitutes. Israel, a nation with godly roots and heritage, belonging to the Lord, had sunk into its deepest moral morass. The influence of the demonic power operating through Jezebel was so great, that out of ten million Israelites, only 7000 were considered to be faithful to the Lord. Jezebel had caused them to forsake their covenant with God and was responsible for corrupting an entire nation. Welcome to America!

However, in the midst of this spiritual seduction, Elijah strode onto the scene to confront Ahab and Jezebel and their legions of pagan sorcerers. Surrounded by unspeakable depravity, Elijah stood as a solitary voice for righteousness, and his spiritual revolution overthrew Ahab's regime, turned many back to the Lord their God, and began a generational movement that shifted history.

The good news is that the very same "Elijah revolution" is promised once again before the return of the Lord. *Behold I will send you Elijah the prophet . . . and he will turn the hearts of the fathers to the children and the hearts of the children to their fathers* (Malachi 4:5-6). It is with that Elijah revolution in view that God raised up TheCall — a prayer movement that has gathered hundreds of thousands of young people to "Mount Carmel" flashpoint moments, calling forth the fires of revival with fasting and prayer. But Mount Carmel is not enough to turn a nation. We need the "fast burn" of revival, but we must also have the "slow burn" that comes with fathering the next generation. I hear the whisper on the top of a mountain, "Go anoint Elisha."

The book you are about to read is not just a whisper. It is a shout, and it thrills my heart. It is evidence and a witness that this Elijah revolution is now at hand in the darkest days of America. In *Unmasked* you will hear the roar of a prophet, an Elijah war cry, as it describes a prophetic panorama of our sexually broken and death-dominated present-day culture. It is the weeping of a dad, a weeping filled with intimate care and burning jealousy for the protection of his daughters. It is the thunder of Abba exposing the ravenous wolves of America's sex culture that seek to devour the beloved ones. It is the holy rage of God the Father who erupts with warning, "Don't you dare touch my little sparrows!" It is a war manual for fathers and leaders who are not content with a casual and peaceful coexistence with the altars of sex and abortion on which the sons and daughters of America are ravaged.

For years, I've known Jim Anderson as a pillar and holy prayer activist from the beginning days of the pro-life movement. He has not allowed his heart to grow bitter and has remained oiled with prayer. He has stood in the trenches ministering to thousands of young people, primarily young women. Young people's testimonies of freedom, of deliverance, and of supernaturally finding their identities in Christ are spreading across the nation. A dear friend of mine from California just called to tell us of the powerful effect Jim's ministry has had recently on the sons and daughters in his own ministry school.

In our major gatherings, TheCall calls forth "Carmel's fire." Jim Anderson's ministry is Elijah stretching himself out face to face, eye to eye, mouth to mouth, heart to heart over the sexually and emotionally

orphaned youth of America and raising them from the dead. Before
Elijah could raise a nation from the dead, he raised just one dead child.
Jim's ministry is where the rubber meets the road in hand-to-hand
spiritual combat for the individual soul. This book proclaims spiritual
freedom through the love and power of Jesus Christ, and it is manifested
through a father who weeps and wars over the young generation with a
wisdom distilled through years of "Elijah ministry." I am so glad that
you, Jim Anderson, wrote this book. It gives me hope that the revolution
is still on and is mightily in progress.

Introduction

It has taken over fifteen years of teaching in ministry training schools, discipleship schools and Bible schools with names as diverse as Thunder School, S.O.L.D. Out, Foundations, Generational Leadership, The Master's Commission, School of Leadership, Table Internship, and YouthStorm to develop the message of this book. Those programs were birthed out of the dream of my generation to disciple the next generation in the things of God. They were birthed by a generation who had "slain their thousands" but wanted to see their sons and daughters "slay their ten thousands." The Malachi mandate—turning the hearts of the fathers to their children and the hearts of the children to their fathers—was an impetus behind these schools and programs. As a leader who has had the privilege of ministering on a yearly basis in these schools, my desire is to see young people have an experience with Jesus that results in lifelong change in their lives.

I have coined two terms I believe are necessary ingredients in the discipleship of young people: "prophetic urgency" and "strategic longevity." Prophetic urgency marks a lot of our ministry to young people — a sense of urgent mission that encompasses everything from mission trips, 24/7 prayer, and fasting to healing, prophecy, and "treasure hunts." It involves worship, intercession, and words of wisdom. In some circles, it represents speaking in a prayer language, having your hands or body shake in God's presence, spiritual dreams, or heavenly visions — the manifestation of the supernatural in our midst.

It is vitally important that our sons and daughters experience the supernatural presence of God. Apart from those experiences in God's presence, they will be drawn to the "secondary realities" of drugs, alcohol, sex, extreme experiences, materialism, and addictive hobbies. However, I believe we are doing our young people a disservice if we give them supernatural experience alone. We need to move beyond "prophetic urgency" to include "strategic longevity."

Let me explain. When a young person "experiences" God with the supernatural manifestation of His felt presence, I am excited for them. However, I want to ask them the "strategic-longevity question" and marry it to their "prophetic-urgency experience." In other words, I want to say, "God's presence touched you in the meeting last night, but did that same presence move you to take the garbage out for your mom?"

Let me give you another example. When a young person tells me they saw an angel in a prayer meeting, I am thrilled for them. I have never seen an angel. However, I want to ask the strategic-longevity question, "How awesome that you saw an angel in the meeting last night, but are you *being* an angel with the opposite sex?" We see a need to marry the practical with the supernatural in our training of the next generation. As leaders, we need to give them both. The excitement of the supernatural needs to translate into an intimacy with God that causes their roots to go down deep so that their "spiritual tree" can grow and bear long-term fruit that affects the everyday, practical areas of their lives. In other words, if we just give them an experience in a meeting or at the altar but do not equip them to be able to have marriages that will last, we are not being the spiritual moms and dads we ought to be.

In the midst of the cultural sexual assault, two of the best ways we can strategically disciple our young people are to:

- Provide healing from the effects of sexual sin.

- Help them know how to relate to the opposite sex in a way that honors God.

Down the road, both will help them secure lasting marriages and stable families — for ultimately, that is the "stuff" of the Kingdom that matters most.

Our prayer is that this book will speak to different groups of people. We pray that it will bring revelation and understanding to a generation of young women and older women. We pray that it will help them understand that there has been a global, demonic assault against them persuading them to adopt an identity of sexuality that causes them to forfeit their God-ordained identity. We pray that the revelation in this book will create a longing in them to reclaim their true identity.

We pray that the truth in this book will teach men of all ages how to take significant steps into authentic manhood. We long to have young men and older men take their rightful place in this war against women that has been loosed by the powers of darkness. In order to do so, they need two revelations:

- The revelation (understanding) of the heart of a daughter.
- The revelation (understanding) of the demonic hatred for what is in the heart of a daughter and the knowledge that women have been targeted for destruction by the powers of darkness in every nation of the earth.

I have seen these two revelations change men's battle for personal purity. These revelations also help men take their proper place as protectors of the women in their lives.

A final group we have targeted is church leaders. We believe the revelations this book contains concerning the heart of a woman, authentic manhood, and God's gift of sexuality can become a blueprint to create an atmosphere in churches to provide healing, deliverance, and restoration. *Unmasked* has been written in the spirit of the mandate Paul gave the church. *Have nothing to do with the unfruitful deeds of darkness, but rather expose them* (Ephesians 5:11). We have seen in school after school and church after church that the simple, yet powerful, commitment to talk about and expose the enemy's cultural sexual assault is the first step in the positive work of reformation we are called to do. Jeremiah's mandate was to uproot, overthrow, cast down, and destroy. Then he was called to build and plant. I have seen that a simple willingness on the part of leaders to begin to speak of such things is the first, essential step in seeing the enemy's power, plan, and influence dismantled. It is my prayer that the truths in this book will be foundational building blocks for sermons, teachings, and messages to be sown into the heart of a generation.

The church of Thyatira in Revelation 2 was rebuked by God for *not* dealing with the woman Jezebel, for tolerating her in their midst, and for allowing her to lead God's people into sexual immorality. Our prayer is that the truths here cause us to rise above such toleration and rid our churches of the "Jezebel spirit" of immorality, to allow purity to be released in our midst. Then, I believe, we will be in position to receive the promise of Revelation 2:26, *And he who overcomes, and he who keeps My deeds until the end, to him I will give authority over the nations.* A pure church, complete with healed and whole individuals, marriages, and families, is positioned to have authority and to bring healing and wholeness to nations.

And, finally, I believe the message of this book speaks to the current "hot-button issue" of sex slavery. I have observed trends over the last 20 years, and one of my concerns is that we will do the same thing to the sex-slavery issue that we did to the abortion issue in the 1990s—and sadly, still do today. We put abortion into an "ideological ghetto." We told ourselves that the women who were touched by the issue of abortion will help the women who are being hurt now, and it really doesn't have anything to do with the rest of us. It didn't take us long to realize this was religious hogwash! The only difference between the women who went to the abortion clinics and the ones who didn't was that the ones who went to the clinic thought they were pregnant or were pregnant. Everything else in their lives was the same. The sexualization of the culture affected them all in the same way. The negative messages of the culture — equating their value and worth with their sexuality—had the same influence on both groups. The depersonalizing images of women in every magazine, on every television show, and on every billboard continually bombarded all of them.

We tend to have similar thoughts with the issue of sexual slavery. I can already hear the conversations in America, Europe, and Asia: "These are the girls who are caught in sex-slavery trafficking. These are the people who are going to help girls be rescued from this horror and see them restored. But, it doesn't really affect the rest of the women in our culture." Again, hogwash! That is one of the reasons I have written this book. Just as we did with the issue of abortion in the 1990s, we tend to put sex slavery in a neat, little box that doesn't relate to us, into another "ideological ghetto." We do this, either because we are unable to see how those issues are related to the broader issues of sexuality in our culture, or we do not want to face the fact that all of us are influenced by the cultural mindsets that allow such moral injustices to occur.

We need revelation to understand how these issues are related to the broader issues of sexuality in our culture. We need to connect sex slavery to the junior-high hallway. We need to connect sex slavery to the philosophy of the television show *Sex and the City*. What do I mean by that? Let me explain. The roots of sex slavery can be found in our junior-high hallways. We see those roots by observing the effects of the negative messages of our culture on the identity of our daughters. The roots of sex slavery are also seen in popular entertainment that enshrines those same values. We have allowed our daughters to be sexualized, depersonalized, and objectified, creating an atmosphere in which sexual predators thrive. This objectification and sexualization of our daughters leads to the creation of a pornography industry, which, in turn, feeds a sex-slavery industry. When we permit the message that the primary value of a woman is her sexuality to pervade our entire culture, how can we be shocked when people act on that indirect invitation and partake of what is being offered to them? The appetite of the western nations for sex slavery is a direct result of this alteration of identity, this identity theft on a generation of young women. When we no longer tolerate the philosophy of *Sex and the City* in our midst, only then will we begin to see inroads made into the war against the sex-slavery trade. Otherwise, we are asking the fox to guard the hen house in a society that boldly declares (and lives) the philosophy that no one is allowed to limit our sexual experiences or sexual expression. I pray that the truths in this book will give us insight into the nature of our battle against these issues and lead us to victory over the forces of darkness so profoundly affecting our sons and daughters, our homes, our marriages, and as a result, our very culture and nation.

Read the testimony of a young woman I will call Emily. It is for the healing and restoration of young women like Emily and the young men who were her "friends" that I want this book to go forth.

EMILY'S TESTIMONY

Not long ago, I was shooting up painkillers, working double shifts, and making sure I had enough pills on hand to get up and do it again the next morning. There were times when I went to bed shaking, thinking, for sure, I had taken too many pills, not sure if I was going to wake up in the morning. I was a lost, hopeless and broken 22-year-old woman with no sense of self worth or value. I was full of shame, regrets and guilt.

Sometimes I took shower after shower because I felt so disgusting on the inside, like I could never get that clean feeling back again. Growing up, I found my identity in being a sports star until my sophomore year of high school, when I gave up sports to become the "party girl" or "somebody's girlfriend." I didn't have any self control when it came to drugs, drinking, or boys. There were times I woke up not knowing who I was sleeping next to — or how I got there. Relationships became a game to me, and I started "selling" myself for nothing. Going out for a "good night" was always a gamble as to what was going to happen, what guy I would go home with, what kind of drugs we would take, or if I would even be alive the next day.

At age 16, I found out I was pregnant and was planning to have the baby, even though I had a lot of pressure to get an abortion. I stopped partying and was secretly hoping this was going to be my way out — that having a baby was going to fill the deepest desires of my heart. At four-and-a-half months, I miscarried. At this point, I was completely empty and hopeless on the inside and tried even more desperately to find something to fill the emptiness. Pain killers soon became my best friend. I went through detox twice to try get off OxyContin but always returned to self-medicating in order to deal with my pain. I had so much shame and felt so filthy on the inside that I couldn't stand living in my own body without some kind of pain killer or medication.

I did everything the world told me to do in order to be happy. My parents had money, so I had nice things. I spent my time trying to look like the media image of what a woman should look like, even to the extent of having plastic surgery. Yet I always felt as though I hadn't obtained perfection. I was popular. I had the job I had always wanted, and I had the boy all the other girls wanted. In the midst of it all, I wore a mask that said everything was fine. Under that mask, I was dead, broken, desperately searching for answers and fulfillment, confused, and hopeless to the point of considering suicide. The more I searched for answers, the more the world just kept sucking every bit of life out of me. Inside, I was screaming for an answer, but the world just kept lying to me. I had even started to accept the "fact" that I might be bisexual.

At this point, a friend led me to the Lord. I cried out to God, "OK, God, I am going to try You this time. I am giving You a chance to show me You are real!" At that moment, I surrendered my life to God, and He became the great "I Am" in my life. I entered a year-long discipleship program. Worshipping Him became my "fix." He became the father I needed, and He filled the emptiness in my heart. He breathed life into me and gave me a supernatural peace. He gave me mental clarity and a sense of worthiness. He gave me an understanding of life, a purpose, and a destiny. Through seeking Him and coming to know Him in a deeper, more intimate way, He healed the deepest wounds of my heart. My pain, shame, regrets, and guilt that had constantly haunted me and led me to self medicate are gone. I am completely free, satisfied and complete in Him. His amazing grace has broken my chains. He has redefined my reality. I am truly a new creation and have been born again. God has given me a new way of thinking and a hope for my future. I will never be the same.

Because of my obedience in surrendering to God, I began to pave the road for my family to meet Him. Since that day my mom, my dad, and my 20-year-old brother have given their hearts to the Lord and have been filled with the Holy Spirit. God is restoring my relationship with my dad. He has been sending me text messages in the morning telling me I am beautiful and that he loves me. He even brought me flowers the other day because of the teaching Jim Anderson and my school director have given to the fathers in our church.

A year ago, I didn't see any reason to get married because I watched everyone around me getting divorced. Now, I can't wait to get married. I can't wait to court my husband and have a pure, God-centered relationship. I can't wait to have the family that God is strategically planning for me — and to raise my kids to love God. I am so grateful that my family line has turned from darkness to light. My kids and my brother's kids are not going to have to go through the hell we went through. They will have a testimony of the keeping power of God. The generational curse of addiction has been broken off my family bloodline by the blood of Jesus Christ. Praise God!

God peeled off my mask and gave me a new identity in Christ. I am now holy and set apart, and I am a daughter of the King. He has washed me white as snow, and I am a princess. My price tag reads, "Priceless!" I know I am loved by the King, and it really makes my heart want to sing.

God has given me the gift of discernment and a heart for the lost and
broken. I am now privileged to have answers for the lost and to be able
to look into the eyes of broken women and tell them that they are worth
everything and were bought at a great price. I have finally found what I've
been desperately searching for all my life, my *Abba*-Father, Jesus Christ!
Now all I want to do is praise Him, live in His will for my life forever,
and let my life glorify His name!

~ ~ ~ ~ ~ ~

Testimonies like Emily's are what we live for. They are the evidence
of revival and reformation, one person at a time. They demonstrate the
marriage of the supernatural wonder of God's presence in the life of a
shattered daughter to the practical building blocks of truth that allow for
permanent change to occur in her life on a long-term basis. In Emily's
words, we hear hope, the one element missing in a battered, confused
generation. Hope for restoration, hope for purity, hope for marriage,
hope for family, hope for a wonderful future, hope for the healing of our
nation, and hope for the healing of the nations of the earth. These things
are the heart-cry of a generation. May this book unlock that heart-cry.
We pray that restored heart-cry of a generation will be music in our ears
as an older generation, and may it be a delight in the ears of our Father in
heaven!

Prologue
The Healing of a Skeptic

I sat leaning back with my head tilted to one side, my eyes progressively narrowing. I was suspicious of this Pastor Jim Anderson, the "Daughter, Flower, Princess" preacher. I had heard him speak briefly before, and to be honest, I didn't think I was the kind of person who needed to hear his message. I wasn't the girl with "the past" — the tall, beautiful woman with long, shimmering, blonde hair who had had men beating down her door her whole life; the lady with the "men on her face" — who had been through many immoral relationships; one who suffered from the shame of divorce, abuse, or an abortion. That wasn't me. I didn't want to hear about flowers or princesses. I sat back and looked at him doubtfully. He wasn't going to get to me. At least that is how it started.

He wrote two words on the white board: "flirting" and "abortion." He drew a line between them and said, "I'm going to connect these two words for you this week."

He wrote two words on the white board: "flirting" and "abortion." He drew a line between them and said, "I'm going to talk about our culture, and I'm going to connect these two words for you this week."

That's ridiculous! I'd like to see you try! I thought. I had no idea what he was talking about, but something pulled me in when he drew that line. I knew most people lived with deep pain. I had always had a feeling there was some major conspiracy in our culture, some hidden thing lurking and lying to us, but since we were unaware of its existence we had to participate in it, and there was nothing we could do to stop it or escape. I found myself hanging on every word. I needed to hear the end of the connection—hoping to hear for the first time what I had felt crushed by but had never been able to identify.

Growing up, my life was a pretty happy sequence of sports, school, homework, practicing piano, trying to remember not to sing at the dinner table, and playing with my older brother and younger sister. There were no real tragedies to speak of, but there was this one thing that was constantly with me. It was voice, maybe a feeling. At first, it lingered in the corner of my mind and poked at me. In elementary school, it was a familiar whisper that told me there was something wrong with me, that I was weird and the other kids couldn't like me. It proceeded to attack my character, my femininity, my appearance, and my heart. In high school, despite many friends and teachers who seemed pleased enough with me to call me a leader and a great example for others to follow, I heard that I was utterly unlikeable; that no one truly wanted to be my friend; that they were all just pretending to put up with me. A voice yelled into my consciousness that if these people really knew me and discovered how terrible I was, they would cover their faces and run away. I didn't know what they would be terrified by. I just believed they would run. By the time I graduated from university, the voice was screaming constantly, "There's something really wrong with you. You are untouchable and shameful!"

It's hard to explain how things were so terrible inside at times and so normal and fine at other moments. On the one hand, I knew God's call was on my life, that I was different in a good way. On the other hand, however, I believed there was a unique set of oppressive rules and limits especially assigned to me for my life. I thought that if I tried to be open and beautiful, people would laugh and think it was a joke. I was always afraid of getting in trouble, always afraid I was doing something wrong. I wanted to please, but perfection eluded me. I lived in fear, but I acted as though I was afraid of nothing and no one. I fooled a lot of people, but never myself. There was so much pressure inside. If anyone had asked, "Heidi, what is so terrible about you that you feel you have to hide and be ashamed?" I would not have been able to answer. All I knew was a familiar voice that fed me a constant diet of fear and discouragement, and I had nothing with which to fight back.

THE ENEMY DOESN'T CARE HOW
IT'S DONE, BUT FROM THE VERY
BEGINNING, HE WANTS EACH ONE
OF US TO REJECT THE TRUTH
ABOUT GOD AND ABOUT OURSELVES.

So there I sat, staring at this man as he created a crazy combination of words, arrows, circles, names, places, stories, and Scripture on a white board. Piece by piece, I began to see this cosmic conspiracy against every son and daughter on the earth come together. The enemy doesn't care how it's done, but from the very beginning, he wants each one of us to reject the truth about God and about ourselves. By the end of the week, I had listened enough to Pastor Jim to realize I had permission, for the first time in my life, to just *be* and know I was OK. It was OK to be a daughter; OK to be strong *and* sensitive; OK for me to sing and then shoot hoops; OK for me to want to be beautiful; OK for me to admit I needed help, protection, affection, and acceptance. It was OK. I was OK. The enemy had his conspiracy, but God had His truth and His plan for me. I might not have been the typical candidate for a "Daughter, Flower, Princess" message, yet it was just what I had been waiting for.

I jumped in. I pursued the message. I pursued the Andersons. I took a couple of overseas trips with Pastor Jim and had many conversations and fired-up arguments about protection, beauty and submission. I worked through some relationships and did a lot of difficult looking into the mirror of my heart, mind and life, bit by bit reducing the impact the enemy had on my life and destiny through his lies. I also worked at opening myself up the Holy Spirit to let Him challenge many of my assumptions, to let Him teach me who He is and what kind of young woman I could be. I spent time with the Andersons, discovering that these are everyday people holding tenaciously on to a truth they discovered that brings freedom to themselves and others. It costs them, and, as much as I am willing to participate in this message of truth, I have found it costs me, too. But the freedom it brings, and the clarity, truth, and peace I have now are incomparably greater than the prison of fear, frustration, and dread I lived with before.

Nearly eight years after first hearing the message, I am now a wife and mother. It's difficult, if not impossible to say how and in what ways I have been impacted by Pastor Jim's life and message. I think, see, and believe differently. I feel different because I am changed. I have truth to fight off the lies that were crippling me. I know what I am up against, and I know that there is a way out.

I HAVE SOMETHING PRICELESS TO GIVE TO MY CHILDREN — A MORE HEALED AND TRUTH-FILLED VERSION OF MYSELF, SOMEONE I NEVER WOULD HAVE BEEN IF IT HAD NOT BEEN FOR GOD'S INTERVENTION IN MY LIFE THROUGH THIS MESSAGE.

My relationship with my parents is different. After the healing we all went through as a result of my opening my life up to them, they were able to participate with me on the way to my marriage rather than be shut out by my independence. The whole process was a treasure we all could share, and it was a blessing for my husband to participate in something so wholesome, open and protective. My parents' lives and relationship have been changed as a result of seeing the transformation I went through. My marriage and how I view my husband is built on a completely different foundation than I had before. Who knows how I would have handled this beautiful part of my life had it not been for the healing deep inside my heart? Not only that, I have something priceless to give to my children — a more healed and truth-filled version of myself, someone I never would have been if it had not been for God's intervention in my life through this message. It is incredible to walk in the light of truth and revelation after being haunted and hurt by lies for so long.

For much of my life, I've thought I would like to write a book that exposed a fundamental conspiracy that was at work in our culture, one that was destroying everyone, but one that everyone was blind to. The only trouble was, I didn't know what the conspiracy was. When I was in Russia on a trip with Pastor Jim, as I was looking at the white board where he had been outlining the message in his unique way, a thought came to me, "There's your conspiracy! Why not write about *that*?" I felt it was God. A few years later I quit my job, raised some support, and spent a year or so gathering Jim's message from sermons, tapes, notes, conversations, and anywhere else I could get them in order to work with Jim and Lisa in getting this revelation into a book so other people can find the freedom I have found. Now, here it is. It's one of my ways of saying, "Thanks," to God, "Thanks," to the Andersons, and a way to reach my hand out and pull just a few more people off the path of destruction. I am grateful for the depth of understanding and peace God has worked in my life and the doors He has opened for me, my family, and my children because of this message.

Heidi Karlsson
Surrey, British Columbia
Canada

CHAPTER ONE

THE SOURCE OF TRUE BEAUTY

Warm August sunshine streamed through the giant French windows into the lofty, old, law school classroom. It was my first time to teach in Russia. Tall, empty ceilings hung over the 50 or so women and the handful of men as they sat at tables in row after row. I looked at the women's faces and noted such a variety of ages — 19-year-olds seated next to grandmotherly *babushkas*. In preparation for my trip, I had learned the average woman in the former Soviet Union had six abortions and that 80-85 percent of their women had been touched by abortion. It was their main method of birth control. The young women of that nation watched their mothers and grandmothers go through countless men and multiple abortions, learning that the same fate, future, and pain would undoubtedly be theirs also.

I had a wonderful three-point sermon prepared, "The Three Roles of the Church in Dealing with Abortion," and I was ready to deliver it.

1. The church needs to preach that abortion is sin, but we need to do so with a broken heart.

2. The church needs to provide an atmosphere of healing and restoration for those touched by abortion.

3. The church should then take the truth about abortion into the culture, again, with a broken heart.

Everything went well until I got to the middle of my first point, and several women around the room started to cry. To be honest, it kind of bothered me. It was distracting, and I was not sure what to do. I continued to preach. Inside, however, I began a micro-conversation with God. "Lord, the ladies are starting to cry, and I don't think I'm going to be able to finish my talk!"

"I DON'T CARE ABOUT YOUR SERMON," THE LORD REPLIED. "I'M CHANGING YOUR MINISTRY."

"I don't care about your sermon," the Lord replied. "I'm changing your ministry."

I was shocked. "Lord, what do you mean? What do you mean You are going to change my ministry?" I started to get nervous.

"I want you to tell the ladies that today I am going to heal them and restore their broken hearts from abortion and immorality," I felt the Lord say.

That made me even more nervous. "Lord, if I tell them You are going to heal them today, You are going to have to do something right away!" What had been an idyllic setting was now awkward and uncomfortable for me. The initial excitement I had for my sermon began to wane, but I continued to preach.

Some of the women started to sob. The men just sat there. Obviously, they had an interest in the abortion issue or they wouldn't have been in the room. However, I am sure, like me, they had never witnessed anything like this.

My micro-conversation with the Lord continued. "Maybe You don't know it, but in America, men don't do this. Men don't deal with the private areas of a woman's life, especially abortion and morality issues. All the Crisis Pregnancy Centers in America are staffed by women. Women are the ones who counsel and pray for women who come into the clinics. You need to understand, Lord, I am a man, and You are asking me to break all the rules. Men just don't work with women in this arena!"

DO YOU THINK THE BROKEN HEART OF A DAUGHTER COULD BE HEALED BY THE TOUCH OF A FATHER?

The Lord gently responded, "Do you think the broken heart of a daughter could be healed by the touch of a father? That is what I am going to release you to do."

As the Lord and I dialogued, I persisted in preaching my sermon, but since my first excuse had been undone by God, I was extremely uneasy. If things continued in the direction they were heading, pretty soon I would have to stop my sermon and ask the women to come forward for healing, and I was not ready for that. "Lord," I protested, "I cannot insult these women by telling them they are going to get healed today. These are deep wounds some of them have been carrying for a long time. It will take at least a 12-week Bible study to deal with this. It would be an insult to promise instantaneous healing."

The Lord asked me another question, "Do I have your permission to be a supernatural God? If I want to open heaven, and in a moment in time, touch the heart of a daughter and supernaturally break all the darkness, shame, and torment in her life, may I do that?"

He had me. "Well, yes, Lord," I said, "I give you permission to do that." More women had begun to cry, and as I continued to speak, their weeping grew louder and more desperate. It was time to obey the Lord. I stopped my sermon and said, "We are going to do something different. Whoever would like healing from abortion and immorality, please come forward."

Simultaneously, 45 chairs were pushed back. The aisle was immediately filled with women, all of them crying. They stood with their arms folded tightly across their chests, tears coursing down their cheeks, a mixture of hope and fear in each of their faces. It was as though they were communicating with their eyes and the creases of pain etched in their expressions, "Is it really going to happen? Is the pain really going to end? I want it to end. I'm so tired of the lies and the torment I have carried for so long."

I first prayed for Stella. Lena, our translator, told me her name meant "star." I asked the Lord, "What should I say to her?"

"Tell her she is a bright star for Me — not a dull star."

I turned to her, looked directly into her eyes, and said, "Stella, you are a bright star for God. You are not a dull star." Her face contorted into an expression of hope mingled with fear. She began to weep uncontrollably at the realization that perhaps it was true that God loved her, that He was not ashamed of her. The truth that God did not hate her began to sink in. The prophetic declaration I had just made was already breaking the darkness over her life. "What else do I say, Lord?"

TELL HER EVERY DAUGHTER OF A KING IS A PRINCESS, AND IF JESUS IS THE KING OF KINGS, THEN SHE IS HIS PRINCESS.

"Tell her she is a princess. Tell her every daughter of a king is a princess, and if Jesus is the King of Kings, then she is His princess. Tell her I love it when she comes into My courts and into My presence. I am not ashamed of her." I told Stella everything God said to me. She began weeping so heavily she could no longer stand. She collapsed to the floor and curled into a ball like a little girl, sobbing profusely. I had not finished praying for her, and I did not know what else to do, so the translator and I knelt down on the floor beside her, and we continued to speak truth into her darkness. I told her the following: The Lord is the only One who could put the petals back on the flower the enemy had torn off; He would take her and plant her in His garden in a very special place reserved just for her; she was not relegated to the wilted-flower section, but He had reserved a special place in the garden just for her.

The Lord said, "Tell her she is a daughter. Tell her she is My special daughter, and I love it when she runs to Me, just as you love it when your Maggie runs to you. She is My daughter, and I love it when My little girls run to Me. I never point My finger in their faces and ask, 'What are you doing here?' I always open My arms to them and hold them next to My heart."

THE LORD IS THE ONLY ONE WHO COULD PUT THE PETALS BACK ON THE FLOWER THE ENEMY HAD TORN OFF.

I said, "Stella, He loves it when you run to Him. He loves to look at you with His big eyes of approval, hold you next to His heart, break the darkness and shame, and tell you everything is going to be all right." Stella stayed on the floor and continued to cry as the Lord came with His truth. I kept speaking. "When my girls run to me with an *owie* on their finger, I look at them and I say, 'May I kiss your owie?' When they say 'Yes,' I kiss their owie, and they smile and skip away. The Lord loves it when His daughters run to Him with their hurts. He loves to kiss them with His presence and break all the darkness, hurts, lies, shame and torment."

We cancelled the subsequent session, and for the next several hours, we continued to pray for all of the ladies. From that day on, I began to release God's healing to those who had been wounded by abortion and immorality, preaching that the broken heart of a daughter can be healed by the touch of a father.

A Hug a Day

We have a saying at our house, "A hug a day keeps the bad boys away." Every day, I make sure I find each of my daughters, look them in the eye, speak value to them, and hug them. Girls who have not received similar words and attention from their fathers are vulnerable to the attention of "bad boys" because their needs have not been met.

We have a saying at our house, "A hug a day keeps the bad boys away."

Let me explain my use of the term, "bad boys." Young men, apart from the heart-changing work of the Holy Spirit, tend toward predatory sexual behavior with young women. I am not saying every young man is evil incarnate. However, many might be described as "bad" in terms of the influence and the sexual pressure they put on young women, often because of their own brokenness.

When young men say, "Hey baby, you're looking pretty good," a girl who has not had hugs from her dad is vulnerable and tempted to turn toward the alternative source of attention and affection. Women are fueled by love; speaking words of love and affirmation over her are like filling up her gas tank. When a daughter's heart is full of words of love and affirmation from her dad and her Heavenly Father, she does not need to respond to the inappropriate advances of young men. Fathers fill the hearts of their daughters with words of love, the pure touch of love, and eyes of love. Words of love are like honey to a daughter's heart; words go straight into the heart of a woman. Pure, non-sexual touch directly touches a daughter's soul. Daughters also receive love from a father's loving eyes. A father looks into a daughter's eyes with a pure look, and that look fills up her heart.

A FATHER-DAUGHTER RELATIONSHIP IS THE GOD-ORDAINED BIRTHPLACE OF TRUE BEAUTY IN A YOUNG WOMAN.

A father-daughter relationship is the God-ordained birthplace of true beauty in a young woman. Just as God spoke words into a formless void and the world came into being at creation, a father's words create beauty, security, and confidence in a daughter. When words of blessing, looks of love, and pure touch have gone forth from a father and done their work in a daughter's spirit, she is not drawn to the other voices that may want to lure her. She is not dependent on those other voices to validate her because she has already been securely validated in her beauty through her father.

Unfortunately, there are countless daughters whose hearts have not been filled and whose needs have not been met. Possibly, their fathers are totally absent from their lives, or are present but have failed to meet their daughter's needs. Those daughters, desperate to have their needs met, may easily fall into immoral relationships.

Let's look at a father-daughter relationship in the book of Esther to see a faithful father at work and observe the wonderful fruit it bore in the life of his daughter.

THE ROYAL BEAUTY CONTEST

King Ahasuerus held a great banquet to which he invited all the government and military leaders of the country. The party lasted 180 days and was followed by a subsequent seven-day party for all the commoners in the capital city of Susa. The queen held a separate banquet at the palace for all the women. At the end of the feast, the king requested that his beautiful queen make an appearance. He wanted to display her beauty to all the people. Queen Vashti decided she was not in the mood and refused the request of the king. Enraged and embarrassed, the king consulted his advisors, and after some quick deliberation, deposed the queen of her position. Thus ended the reign of Vashti.

Now, King Ahasuerus needed a successor. Almost immediately, a search was started to find the next queen from among all the beautiful young maidens of the land. I assume, because he was king, Ahasuerus had had his pick of beautiful women in his first marriage, and that Vashti had been the most beautiful woman he could find. I wonder if, the second time around, he might have been looking for more than just a pretty face in his new queen. Perhaps there was a longing in his heart to find a woman of true beauty with whom he could share an intimacy and oneness he had not known with Vashti.

I BELIEVE THE KING WAS SEARCHING FOR WHAT EVERY MAN LONGS FOR — TRUE INTIMACY.

I believe the king was searching for what every man longs for — true intimacy. As leader of the most prominent empire in the known world, King Ahasuerus had everything he wanted. The harem existed to satisfy his sexual desires. He had found the most beautiful, sensual woman he could find in Queen Vashti. However, in spite of her beauty and sensuality, his relationship with her left him unfulfilled. Today, many men, having adopted the prevailing cultural value that equates physical sexuality with true intimacy, settle for a one-dimensional view of intimacy that leaves them with a similar emptiness. Many have initiated their own "beauty contests" in an attempt to populate their personal modern-day harems with beautiful, sensual women. They have failed to realize, however, that they are in search of something that cannot be found in the physical act of sex alone. True intimacy consists of spiritual oneness, soul/friendship oneness, and physical/sexual oneness.

Our story continues

Meanwhile, in the capital city of Susa, a man named Mordecai was raising his orphaned niece, Esther. Regarding their relationship, the Bible says, . . . *when her father and mother died, Mordecai took her as his own daughter* (Esther 2:7). We know nothing about Mordecai's family, or if he was married and had other children. What we do know is that he recognized the void in Esther's life and became a father to her. Both Mordecai and Esther become prominent players in this story.

> *It came about when the command and decree of the king were heard and many young ladies were gathered to Susa, the capital, . . . that Esther was taken to the king's palace into the custody of Hegai, who was in charge of the women* (Esther 2:8). The beauty contest began. Exceptionally attractive women from all over the kingdom were gathered. Esther, who was *beautiful of form and face* (Esther 2:7), was among them. We know from the Biblical account that Esther was chosen queen and in that position was instrumental in saving her people from destruction. Scripture also tells us Esther found favor in the eyes of all who saw her, even in the eyes of her competitors.

So, what was the source of her beauty that caused her to find favor and win the king's heart? Let's examine the sources of true beauty that positioned Esther to be a deliverer for her people.

Every Day Dads

I love the phrase, "her hand given in marriage." It implies a father figure who has a loving influence and authority in his daughter's life. He literally and figuratively holds her hand and watches over and protects her right up until the moment she stands at the altar. He then takes her hand and gives it to another to hold, transferring to that man the authority over her life and the responsibility to protect and provide for her — a seamless transition. Ideally, there is not one moment in her life when she is not protected, watched over, or cared for in a way that is a blessing to her. I believe that is God's provision for His daughters. Under this kind of care, a young woman can grow in true beauty and freely release her beauty and nurturing spirit into the nations of the earth.

Mordecai was one such father in Esther's life. His presence in her life, the words he spoke, and the kind of covering and care he gave her while she was growing up stored up such inner strength and confidence inside her that she had the courage it took to be a deliverer for her entire nation. The presence of a loving, faithful father in the life of a daughter is one of God's intended means of producing true beauty in the heart of a woman.

EVERY DAY, MORDECAI WALKED BACK AND FORTH IN FRONT OF THE COURT OF THE HAREM TO LEARN HOW ESTHER WAS AND HOW SHE FARED.

Every day, *Mordecai walked back and forth in front of the court of the harem to learn how Esther was and how she fared* (Esther 2:11). I can picture him asking the gatekeeper daily, "How is Esther today? Tell her that Mordecai is here to see her." He waited to see if she could come and speak with him. Whether or not he was actually able to visit with her, he faithfully inquired, hoping to receive a report of her welfare and to leave a message of his care and concern for her — every day. Before a young lady could appear before the king, she had to complete one full year of beauty preparations. That didn't deter Mordecai. Every single day, he made it a priority to know what was going on in her life, in her heart. His consistency, presence, and communication conveyed value and importance to Esther.

Esther knew she was special in Mordecai's eyes. She wasn't desperate to become the queen of Persia as she was already the royal princess-daughter in the home and life of Mordecai. When we "princess" our daughters with our words, our non-sexual touch, and our attention, they will not want to be enthroned in the life of some other modern-day "king" they hardly know. Instead, they will be secure in our love until the right kind of man comes into their lives. Mordecai protected Esther from the influences the harem would bring to bear on her. His love and attention put something in her she would take with her wherever she went—a spiritual "force field" that protected her from the values, dictates, and cultural expectations of an immoral harem.

A SPECIAL DATE

One day, years ago, I arranged to take one of my daughters on a date. Although I was 15 minutes late, she knew I would arrive. There she was, my little, 8-year-old Maggie Joy, all ready in her shiny black shoes and red coat. I walked into the house and said, "Excuse me. I know I am a little late, but I am looking for a Maggie Joy. Is that you? Is this a good time for you? I think we have a very special appointment."

She tilted her head to look at me, "Dad, of course I'm Maggie. I've been waiting for you. You're late." I opened the door for her, and we got into the car.

"I think the place is still open," I said, "and I think they have a special spot just for us. You can order anything you want, Maggie." She ordered a big cup of hot chocolate, and we sat down to visit.

IF YOU WANT TO FIGHT HELL AND THE POWERS OF DARKNESS THAT SEEK TO DESTROY THE HEARTS OF OUR DAUGHTERS, I KNOW A TYPE OF SPIRITUAL WARFARE THAT CREATES VALUE IN A DAUGHTER'S SPIRIT.

There has been a lot of talk about spiritual warfare in recent years. If you want to fight hell and the powers of darkness that seek to destroy the hearts of our daughters, I know a type of spiritual warfare that creates value in a daughter's spirit. It is called "Taking your Daughter out for Tea" or "Going to Her Soccer Game," and it works in direct opposition to the agenda of hell and darkness that wants to destroy their lives. They need our time, attention, questions and interest. I was just a dad with my daughter Maggie Joy at the coffee shop, but I was fighting hell, warring against that destroying spirit that wants to whisper lies into her ear. I was warring against the demonic spirits that want to induct her into the modern-day harems of our age. I was doing what a dad was designed to do in his daughter's life.

INSIDE-PRETTY AND OUTSIDE-PRETTY

As a father of six daughters, I am an expert on beautification techniques. Each night, I watch as, one by one, my daughters' heads are bent over the sink in the bathroom. After washing and drying their faces, they apply special lotions and creams. When Molly was 12, I would see her in there, and I'd say, "Little Moll, you do beauty work too?"

She would roll her eyes at me and say, "Aw, Dad."

THERE ARE TWO KINDS OF PRETTY... INSIDE-PRETTY AND OUTSIDE-PRETTY.

I would continue, "Julie-roo, now beautiful Julie is doing it. By now you are an expert at it. Rachel and Maggie, you are just waiting around the corner!" I enjoyed doing that because it was a time for me to bless them and speak words of truth into their spirits. "Hey, Molly! There are two kinds of pretty, Moll, inside-pretty and outside-pretty. Which one's most important? Make sure you don't forget. I love how pretty you are. You've got that beautiful heart, too, don't you?!" She nodded while I spoke value to her spirit and encouraged her. I rehearsed the difference between inside-pretty and outside-pretty over and over again with my daughters as they were growing up. Now we are starting to do so with our granddaughter and will continue to do so with our future granddaughters.

A BEAUTY BORN OF SORROW

I believe Esther learned the difference between inside-pretty and outside-pretty from Mordecai. It is obvious she cultivated both kinds of "pretty" in her life. In addition to beauty that came from Mordecai's love for her, I believe she also possessed a beauty born of sorrow—a type of beauty that can only be created in the life of one who has walked through the valleys of hardship. We remember Esther as the young woman who faced death and bravely declared, *If I perish, I perish* (Esther 4:16). She is also remembered as the one to whom Mordecai inquired, *And who knows whether you have not attained royalty for such a time as this?* (Esther 4:14). However, these famous depictions of Esther have eclipsed another time in her life, a time of great suffering. *Now the young lady was beautiful of form and face, and **when her father and her mother died,** Mordecai took her as his own daughter* (Esther 2:7, emphasis mine). Esther was an orphan; she lost both parents. Most likely, they died before her eyes. I wonder what her prayers were like between the death of her first parent and the death of her second parent. Our response in such times of deep trial determines what kind of person we become. Our choices determine if we become a person of bitterness and hardness of spirit or a person with depth of character and a profound trust in God. Rightly responding to seasons of suffering can produce beauty of soul and character, resulting in a countenance that is "other-worldly" — from heaven. Part of this process in Esther's life meant she had to go to a distant relative named Mordecai and choose to open her heart to him, allowing him to function as a father in her life. Esther had "question marks" in her life for which there were no answers this side of heaven. She did not hold God hostage with those question marks, demanding an answer from Him. Because of her beauty of character, we know she did not surrender to bitterness or harden her heart. I imagine Esther and Mordecai had long talks about God and faith as she worked through her sorrow and grief at losing her parents. The attentive love of Mordecai as a listening father in her life undoubtedly helped bring her to a place of restored trust in God. A depth and beauty of character was born in her as she found that place of trust.

ESTHER HAD "QUESTION MARKS" IN HER LIFE FOR WHICH THERE WERE NO ANSWERS THIS SIDE OF HEAVEN.

The older I get, the more question marks I encounter in my own life. My question marks involve growing up with an alcoholic mother, seeing my father divorce my mother after a long, rocky marriage, and the breakup of a church I was part of for 21 years. I have learned to take difficult things to the foot of the cross and leave them there. I then declare to God that He is worthy of my life, and no matter what happens in my life, I am going to give Him praise. It is not a robotic, unthinking praise I offer. I choose to honor God for *who He is* no matter the difficulty or testing.

Today, there is a beauty from heaven waiting to be born in the lives of modern-day Esthers who are willing to offer their question marks to God. It is in that very costly offering that deep beauty is born.

What are some of those question marks that rightly responded to, have the potential to create otherworldly beauty in us? The divorce. The alcoholic parent. The death of a friend. The betrayal by a family member. The sexual assault. The loss of a home. The sexual abuse as a child. The unplanned pregnancy. The physically abusive father. The breakup of a church. The cancer. The bankruptcy. The loss of purity. The secret sin. The abortion. All are tragedies, which when offered to God in surrender, can produce a depth and beauty of character that can position us to be people of influence — as Esther was.

THE HAREM

The beauty contest had begun. In modern-day beauty contests, all the contestants volunteer to compete for the exalted position of queen. Promises of scholarships and speaking engagements abound for the one selected to represent beauty to her generation.

The contest in ancient Persia was a little different. Young women were probably conscripted into the king's harem, especially if the report of their beauty reached the palace. Participation in the king's "beauty contest" was not voluntary. Word of the royal decree went out over the whole empire to gather every beautiful young virgin to the harem. Esther . . . *was beautiful of face and form* (Esther 2:7). It was only a matter of time before the soldiers doing the king's bidding knocked on Mordecai's door and took Esther to the palace. There she would either become the queen or a prisoner in the harem for the rest of her life—a concubine. If not chosen as queen, she would never leave the harem, and she would never marry. Her life would change forever as a result of her one night with the king. It was a gamble with high stakes and long odds for any young woman "invited" to the harem.

Imagine with me the atmosphere of the harem and the mentality of each woman preparing for her night with the king. Have you ever been around women who wanted the same thing or the same man? Have you ever witnessed a "catfight" between two young women warring over a young man? The competitive spirit in women who want the same man can cause the less attractive attributes lying dormant in a woman's spirit to take over. Battle does not usually involve hand-to-hand combat, but the battle is very real nonetheless and is often waged with sharp tongues and spiteful spirits.

It was into such an atmosphere that Esther was thrust. The women prepared themselves by undergoing 12 months of preparation—*six months with oil of myrrh and six months with spices and cosmetics* (Esther 2:12). The preparation obviously emphasized outward beauty. I am certain most of the women were also depending on sexual expertise and sensuality as the key to winning the king's favor. I can picture one woman with a dance-hall girl persona thinking, *Hey, King, I am getting ready for my night with you, and it's really going to be something else! You aren't going to forget me!*

The king senses her spirit as she walks into his chambers and immediately says, "Next." He dismisses her before the evening even begins. Remember, he already has access to all the sex and outside beauty he wants.

Another young woman, more sultry and seductive than the first, prepares for her turn. "Hello, King, I will be the one coming to see you tonight." Her practiced enticements are fully employed. "I promise you an evening you will always remember."

Again, the king's response, "Next." He is tired of superficial, external beauty that is only skin-deep. He already had that with Vashti.

What was it about Esther that captured the king's attention and heart? I believe part of her favor came because she chose to embrace the counsel of Hegai, the eunuch in charge of the harem, rather than the predominant spirit of the harem. *Now when the turn of Esther . . . came to go in to the king, she did not request anything except what Hegai, the king's eunuch who was in charge of the women, advised* (Esther 2:15). Note here that Hegai, the king's servant in charge of all the women, was a eunuch — a man with no sexual drive or sexual capacity. Perhaps he had been made a eunuch for the safety of the women in the king's palace.

Whatever the reason, the reality was that any advice he gave the women would probably not have been based on their sexual performance. His council would, undoubtedly, have been about other issues, possibly about the heart or character. There are two kinds of counsel in the world — that of Hegai, which I believe was God's counsel, and the contrasting counsel, that of the "spirit of the age." The two voices speak to women constantly. The counsel of a Hegai says, "Cultivate the inner person, and it will give you favor and good standing before the king."

THE WORLDLY COUNSEL SAYS, "GIVE YOURSELF TO SEDUCTION."

The worldly counsel says, "Give yourself to seduction. Watch the films and read the magazines; model yourself after them. Then you will surely be appealing and get what you desire."

In a harem full of outwardly beautiful daughters vying for the attention of one man, the potential for backbiting, competition, envy, and hatred would have been enormous. Yet the Bible says that Esther *found favor in the eyes of all who saw her* (Esther 2:15). Even though she so impressed Hegai that he gave her seven choice maids and elevated her to the best place in the harem, Scripture says she found favor in the eyes of everyone, even her competitors. In other words, she was the hands-down choice, not only to be chosen queen, but for the prize for Miss Congeniality. Her character, the inner person of her heart, had been cultivated with a spirit of graciousness and understanding. She was inside-pretty and outside-pretty. She rejected the counsel of the world, and she instead submitted her beauty to God and cultivated a true beauty of the heart. She was loving, kind, selfless, humble, and others-centered, so much so that all the women she was competing with, the very ones who could have hated her and been threatened by her, liked her, even favored her.

ONE-NIGHT STAND

Women in the harem had one night, one meeting, a single opportunity to make an impression on the king. A woman left for the palace in the evening and returned the following morning to the second harem to wait for word as to whether or not she had pleased the king. If the king delighted in her, he summoned her by name. If not, the contest was over for her, and the young contestant was sent to the second harem to join the ranks of the king's concubines for the remainder of her life.

TODAY, THE HAREM SPIRIT IS ALIVE IN OUR CULTURE.

Today, the harem spirit is alive in our culture. It invites our daughters to participate in the cultural beauty contest where the prize is commitment from a "king" — a young man. Permanent commitment is the deepest longing and desire of a young woman's heart. Many women are convinced that if they gamble their purity, they will be rewarded the prize. "One night with the king thinking" pervades our culture. Daughters are seduced into believing that one moment or one sexual experience will endear the heart of the "king" to them and assure them the permanence they long for. All too often their gamble fails; their purity is lost; the king doesn't choose them; and they are dismissed into the spiritual and psychological prison of the harem as a modern-day concubine. They take their place alongside his other ex-girlfriends in the modern-day harem/prison of damaged emotions, broken dreams, and sexual dysfunction.

The women of ancient harems never married. The mark of the modern-day harem on our daughters is often a future of damaged relationships and marriages. Some women never marry. Some resign themselves to settling for any young man who will have them. They "hook up." They move in with a "nice guy." They believe they are not worthy of a decent man or a good marriage. They see themselves as damaged goods. Today's daughters languish in the shame of the harem, waiting for a call from an "ex." If he does call, she thinks, "Oh, he is having second thoughts about me and misses me." She will try to win him again with another "night with the king." Sadly, he is only there for one thing. She will return to the harem of broken dreams, lost purity, and distrust of men that pervades the atmosphere of our modern-day dating environment.

Sadly, the harem is alive and well in today's culture.

TRUE BEAUTY WINS THE DAY

Not only did all Esther's rivals favor her, the king also *loved Esther more than all the women, and she found favor and kindness with him more than all the virgins* (Esther 2:17). King Ahasuerus had already experienced outside-beauty once; it had been extremely dissatisfying to him. There had been something missing between Queen Vashti and him, something he longed for. I believe that missing ingredient was intimacy. I believe all men long for something more, but when they attempt to find it through the pursuit of mere sexuality, they are left with a hollow counterfeit. I am sad for the Russian men, in spite of the fact that their women have a reputation for being some the most seductive and sensual women on earth. In fact, I am sad for the men in every nation in which women are viewed as sexual objects, where their personhood has been separated from their sexuality. The result is that men get women who will give them sex, but those women are wounded, disconnected from their own hearts, and often, hardened and harsh. God designed sexual intimacy to be the blending of physical, emotional, and spiritual oneness — a complete and inseparable package. In other words, when a woman is fully loved, not just because of what she can give a man physically, he gets to experience true intimacy in which a woman gives herself completely. When a woman is loved the way God intended, she can bless her husband with the fullness of her mind, will, emotions, and body. All the blessing of her being is fully released; nothing is held back. Most men know nothing of that full blessing; all they are getting is sex.

WHEN A WOMAN IS LOVED THE WAY GOD INTENDED, SHE CAN BLESS HER HUSBAND WITH THE FULLNESS OF HER MIND, WILL, EMOTIONS, AND BODY.

I believe the king yearned for a woman of inner beauty who would give herself fully to him. It is not surprising the king loved Esther more than all the others. She was beautiful, but her outer beauty did not alienate others from her, nor was it the only thing that attracted people to her. She was wise and humble enough to understand submission. After one encounter, the Bible says, *the king loved Esther more than all the women* (Esther 2:17). The Hebrew word for love here is rarely used to mean sexual relations, but rather is used to describe the non-sexual parts of a marriage or the relationship between a parent and child. Based on her character, it can be assumed the king valued her, delighted in her, and connected with her as a whole person. In other words, his attraction to her was not solely a sexual one but a loving and valuing of her whole being.

Esther was given access to the king at a time when her people, the Jews, were set for destruction. When a conspiracy arose to destroy the Jews in all of the king's provinces, Esther, at the urging of Mordecai, interceded for her people before the king. Her relationship with the king, combined with her courage to speak out, resulted in the preservation of all the Jews living in that nation. Esther was beautiful in form and face but was most famous for her intercession, fasting, prayers, and courage on behalf of a people set for destruction by the powers of darkness. As we set ourselves before God in submission as His bride, submit our beauty to Him, and develop a heart of intercession, we become like Esther and can be used of God to deliver others slated for death. What a contrast, indeed, to those who use their beauty merely for selfish gain!

So, was God condoning the morals of the Persian Empire by allowing Esther to be inducted into the king's harem? Not any more than we are by allowing our daughters to grow up in the increasingly sexualized cultures of our modern nations. It used to trouble me that it appeared Esther was forced to give up her purity during her night with the king. Are we to believe God would ask a daughter to compromise one of His most sacred and holy standards, that of sexual purity, to position her to bring deliverance to a nation under a decree of death? Does God ever require a compromise of His standards to achieve His perfect will on the earth? I think not. As I have prayed and meditated on this story, I have come to some conclusions. I don't believe she slept with the king or violated God's sexual boundaries. King Ahasuerus was not desperate for sex. As I said earlier, he had all the sex he wanted. I believe it is much more likely the king was captured by her purity and beauty of spirit and was fully willing to delay a sexual union until after their marriage. Considering Esther's godly submission of spirit, I am certain the king was more than willing to honor her request in this regard.

ESTHER SUE

Another Esther understood true beauty and intercession. Her name was Esther Sue. She was a grandma who decided to "adopt" me when I became her son's friend. I was a 15-year-old, needy, young man from a broken, alcoholic home. Esther Sue's true beauty gave her access to the King, and from the day she met me until the day she died 32 years later, Esther Sue interceded for me. She never won an earthly beauty contest but she won the heart of the King of Kings and found a place before Him in her intercession. She prayed me into salvation, into a godly marriage, and into a ministry. She knew the secret of true beauty and the place of influence it gave her before the King. She could have given in to that other spirit, the spirit that says that life is all about *me*, the spirit that never finds time to cry out to God on another person's

WHEN YOU ARE A "GODDESS," THE WORLD REVOLVES AROUND YOU, AND YOU DRAW ALL ATTENTION TOWARD YOU.

behalf. When you are a "goddess," the world revolves around you and you draw all attention toward you. However, when you are a daughter of the King, all attention goes to God and to others, and all praise goes to Him. A daughter who surrenders her beauty to God gains access and has influence with the King. Her intercession before Him can save a nation. I believe God wants to deliver daughters from the bondage of the cultural beauty contest and position them as intercessors for the deliverance of individuals and nations.

CONCLUSION

I want to see our daughters safe, beautiful and radiant. I want to see their hearts filled with the knowledge that they are loved and special. That is their protection from the advances of young men who want to take advantage of them sexually. However, daughters like that don't just happen. As men, it is our job to be like Mordecai — to care for and inquire daily about the condition and well-being of our wives, mothers, daughters, and sisters. It means breaking the sound barrier by speaking words of love and affirmation to them. It requires spending time with them and listening to them. It involves breaking through the awkwardness to give them the hugs and the pure touch they need.

> ## AS MEN, IT IS OUR JOB TO BE LIKE MORDECAI — TO CARE FOR AND INQUIRE DAILY ABOUT THE CONDITION AND WELLBEING OF OUR WIVES, MOTHERS, DAUGHTERS, AND SISTERS.

If we do so, God will release something through them. We, as men, can help create an Esther generation of women who will bless the nations, whose cries of intercession will make a difference in the heavens and, subsequently, on the earth.

Women, also, have a part to play in seeing true beauty birthed in their hearts. It is their responsibility to choose a right response to their seasons of testing and trial. Their choices determine if they become hardened and bitter, or if they learn to trust God. Women need to choose to resist the spirit of the world that relentlessly presses them to focus on outside-pretty instead of inside-pretty. And as Esther did, they need to learn to allow natural and spiritual fathers to speak into their lives and minister to them.

CHAPTER TWO

THE WORSHIP OF SEX

Some years before her death, Mother Teresa was invited to speak at the National Prayer Breakfast in Washington, D.C. Leaders from all over the world attended the great event. I can just imagine the event organizers thinking, *Everything is perfect. Mother Teresa will talk about the phenomenal work she is doing in India with the poor and the outcast. She will motivate us to noble service — to care for the marginalized in our society. What an inspiration she's going to be!* And yes, Mother Teresa did talk about the marginalized and forgotten ones, but they were not the "ones" the event organizers had in mind. Mother Teresa centered her entire talk squarely on abortion — the most politically incorrect of all topics to discuss!

ANY COUNTRY THAT ACCEPTS ABORTION IS NOT TEACHING THE PEOPLE TO LOVE, BUT TO USE ANY VIOLENCE TO GET WHAT THEY WANT.

I feel that the greatest destroyer of peace today is abortion. It is a war against the child, a direct killing of the innocent child, murder by the mother herself. If we accept that a mother can kill even her own child, how can we tell other people not to kill one another?

How do we persuade a woman not to have an abortion? As always, we must persuade her with love. We remind ourselves that real love requires a willingness to give until it hurts. Jesus gave His life to love us. The mother who is considering abortion should be helped to love — that is, to give until it hurts her plans or her free time in order to respect the life of her child. The father of that child, whoever he is, must also give until it hurts. Abortion does not teach a mother to love, but to kill even her own child to solve her problems. Abortion teaches the father that he does not have to take any responsibility for the child he has brought into the world. That father is much more likely to place other women into the same position. Abortion leads to more abortion. Any country that accepts abortion is not teaching the people to love but to use any violence to get what they want. That is why the greatest destroyer of love and peace is abortion.

Mother Teresa shocked those attending the prayer breakfast by addressing the taboo topic of abortion. She understood the connection between abortion and the downward spiral in our nation and was compelled to speak out.

Every year 1.2 million children lose their lives in America before they make it out of their mother's womb, far outnumbering deaths from all other unnatural causes. Arguably, the most dangerous place in America is in the womb of a mother.

The Necessary Elements in the Worship of Sex

Mother Teresa's insight into the relational and societal issues surrounding abortion relates to the broader issue, the worship of sexuality in the nations, or simply said, the worship of sex. She referred to some of the elements involved in abortion and the inner conversations of both the young woman and the young man as they make the choice to end the life of their baby. Let's take a closer look at the necessary elements involved in the worship of sex.

Necessary Element #1: Abortion

I spent years working in the pro-life movement in the United States, initially getting involved in national events which later led to my local and regional involvement. We were "those people" on television, engaging in peaceful, non-violent protests, and getting arrested at abortion clinics. In fact, 30,000 people were arrested at those pro-life events. Compare that with only the 6,000 arrested in the entire Civil Rights Movement (even though our activities were much less publicized or acknowledged). After a series of protests and repeated arrests, I began to ask, "God, why can't we break the back of this thing? Why, with all the time and energy we have spent laboring to stop abortion, does nothing change?" God began to show me that we had depersonalized the issue of abortion. We had made it an objective issue, a topic of debate, a historical Supreme Court decision, and a term-paper topic for English classes. We had forgotten that abortion is *not* an impersonal issue. It has always been about someone's daughter, wife, sister, or mother. Abortion is not just about taking the life of children.

ABORTION IS ABOUT THE WORSHIP OF SEX.

Everywhere we gathered, radical homosexuals were standing opposite us, fighting for abortion rights. I thought, *They can't get pregnant. Why are they fighting so hard for something that seems to have nothing to do with them?* Then it dawned on me. **Abortion is about the worship of sex.** The fight over abortion is not simply about the killing of innocent children or the so-called "freedom of choice." Rather, it is an attempt to remove any restrictions, boundaries, or limitations on sex — homosexual or heterosexual — period. When sex is worshipped, there has to be abortion. The resultant children must be eliminated because their presence will wreak havoc on the whole system. The presence of a child demands a family, commitment, and permanence. Therefore, in order for sex to continue without restrictions, the children must be silenced.

LOGICALLY SPEAKING, ABORTION IS AT THE END OF A CONVEYOR BELT IN A CULTURE THAT WORSHIPS SEX.

Comfort, ease, convenience, material security, and reputation are 95-98 percent of the reasons couples list for having an abortion. Abortions are rarely done solely for the health of the mother. Abortion silences the voice of a child who asks with its very being, "Where is my mother? My father? My family?" Abortion erases the consequences of uncommitted, recreational sexuality. That little voice demands responsibility from the young man who, possibly, never even liked the gal he "hooked up" with. There is a good chance their relationship was all about him and his pleasure. It makes sense for him to silence the little voice that will demand responsibility or commitment. The suddenly pregnant young lady also rejects the consequences of her actions, thinking, "It's not the right time. I have plans and dreams. I'm not sure if my boyfriend is committed. I need to finish school or college. I don't have money to support myself — let alone someone else." An abortion ensures these very real limits on sexuality remain unchallenged. However, in the process, the father of the child violates a part of his manhood, the essence of what a father is. The mother also suppresses her maternal spirit and takes life rather than giving life. Abortion directly assaults the God-given design of both men and women. Abortion is not a stand-alone issue that involves only the death of a child. It involves so much more. Logically speaking, abortion is at the end of a conveyor belt in a culture that worships sex.

NECESSARY ELEMENT #2: CHANGING THE ROLE OF A MAN

God designed men to take risks — to be watchmen, guardians, and defenders willing and able to fight for and protect those they care for. Men are designed for honor, to do what is right instead of what is easy. They are designed to uphold a righteous standard, to fight evil, and to maintain what is good. That explains their willingness to go to war and lay down their lives in the service of their country and in defense of their families.

The "Ephesians mandate" outlines what a husband's relationship with his wife should look like when it says, *Husbands, love your wives, just as Christ also loved the church and gave Himself up for her* (Ephesians 5:25). I believe this is one of the most radical Scriptures the church can preach. It should be one of the foundational truths of the blueprint missionaries use when building the church in the nations of the earth. We often miss the essence of that verse that seems so clearly to outline our role as men in serving our wives. Ephesians directly confronts those husbands and men who are harsh, abusive, or "mini-tyrants" in their households.

GOD WANTS TO TAKE THE STRENGTH OF THE MALE QUALITIES CURRENTLY UNDER ATTACK IN OUR FEMINIZED CULTURE AND EMPLOY THEM IN THE DEFENSE AND PROTECTION OF THE WOMEN IN THEIR LIVES.

How are we supposed to love our wives? We are supposed to love our wives as Christ loved the church and gave Himself for her.

How did Christ love the church? He laid down His life for her. He suffered for her. He served her, guarded her, protected her, honored her, communicated with her, defended her, and died for her. A husband's mandate is to serve his wife and sacrifice himself for her. God wants to take the strength of the male qualities currently under attack in our feminized culture and employ them in the defense and protection of the women in their lives. The enemy, on the other hand, wants to pervert those male qualities and loose them in the culture in such a way that men become predators instead of protectors.

PRINCIPLES HIDDEN IN THE OLD TESTAMENT

The Old Testament contains some interesting laws concerning sexual assault. Just as in Chapter 7 we will discover hidden principles in the obituaries of the kings, we will also discover hidden principles in the Old Testament sexual assault laws. Let's take a closer look at one of these sexual assault laws: *If there is a girl who is a virgin engaged to a man, and another man finds her in the city, and lies with her, you shall bring them both out to the gate of that city, and you shall stone them to death; the girl, because she did not cry out in the city, and the man, because he has violated his neighbor's wife . . . But if in the field the man finds the girl who is engaged, and the man forces her and lies with her, then only the man who lies with her shall die. You shall do nothing to the girl . . . When he found*

her in the field, the engaged girl cried out, but there was no one to save her
(Deuteronomy 22:23-27). If the rape occurred in the city, both the man
and the woman were guilty, but if the rape occurred in the country, only
the man was held guilty. What was the reason for the delineation? In
the case of the rape in the country, the assumption was that even if the
woman had cried out with all her might, there simply would not have
been anyone around to rescue her. So, the woman was innocent; only
the man was punished. However, in the city, people were nearby. A rape
victim's cries would have been heeded, and she would have been rescued.
If a sexual assault was carried through to completion in the city, it was
assumed the woman had not cried out for help. In that case, both the
woman and the man were considered guilty.

What can we learn from this story? My first question is, who would
rescue a woman under assault? The Hebrew police force? Good guess.
However, there was no Hebrew police force then. There were only temple
guards. So, who would respond to the cries of a woman under assault?
Who would go? A father? A brother? I firmly believe every responsible
man in that culture would have responded to the cries of a daughter
under assault. In the face of injustice, a man's responsibility is to respond;
a man's responsibility is to rescue those in danger; a man's responsibility
is to hear the cry and respond.

To apply this story to the current assault being perpetrated against
daughters, I believe it is the responsibility of fathers to rescue their
daughters from the effects of the cultural sexual assault. However, only
fathers who are alive with God's Spirit will find themselves positioned
and willing to respond to such a call.

INSTEAD OF FUNCTIONING AS PROTECTORS OF THE WOMEN IN THE CULTURE, MEN HAVE GIVEN WAY TO THEIR LOWER NATURE AND MORE OFTEN FUNCTION AS PREDATORS OF THE VERY WOMEN THEY ARE CALLED TO PROTECT.

Note that Deuteronomy talks about an assault in the country, an uninhabited place. No one was available to rescue a daughter under attack. Unfortunately, today even our cities have become places where our daughters can regularly be assaulted, and yet no one rescues them. When the lies assault her, beguiling her to change her nature and identity, God's design is that fathers or pure-hearted sons hear her cry and respond immediately with a sense of personal responsibility that says, "I will put a stop to this!" However, the enemy has worked hard to change the man's role from protector to predator. Instead of functioning as protectors of the women in the culture, men have given in to their lower nature and more often function as predators of the very women they are called to protect. Instead of walking in self control and purity, they seek easy, uncommitted sexual encounters. In our "hook-up" culture, young men do not even have to pretend to offer commitment and permanence. They expect, and readily receive, sexual gratification with absolutely no responsibility attached to it.

GOD IS VERY CLEAR THAT THE RESPONSIBILITY FOR THE BEHAVIOR OF THE WOMEN IN THE CULTURE IS BEING LAID AT THE FEET OF THE MEN.

In Hosea, God reprimanded the men of the culture for what was happening with their daughters. *I will not punish your daughters when they play the harlot or your brides when they commit adultery, for the men themselves go apart with harlots and offer sacrifices with temple prostitutes; so the people without understanding are ruined* (Hosea 4:14). God is very clear that the responsibility for the behavior of the women in the culture is being laid at the feet of the men. The men of the culture were answerable to God. While it is true their daughters were involved in sexual sin, God was not going to hold them responsible for their actions because the men — the fathers and sons — were the ones who allowed, cultivated, and perpetuated this evil in the culture. It is obvious God expects the men to be the "culture creators" and "atmosphere maintainers." There is a sense that the women take their cues from the values that are allowed to become dominant in the culture through the men.

I am not saying women are not accountable for their sins, but in examining Jesus' dealings with women, His accountability was accompanied with much tenderness and mercy. More than once, He sided with a prostitute in the face of the powerful religious people of His time. I think it was because Jesus knew the men of that community had long ago failed in their responsibility to be protectors. In fact, some of those men had probably sought that prostitute's favors and had themselves functioned as predators. If we look at any culture, we will see that women are the reflection of what the men have cultivated and allowed in that culture. If the men want sexuality and seduction, the women become sensual and seductive. If the men walk in purity, their women will be chaste and pure. The oppression we have allowed our daughters to experience in our North American and Western societies is an indictment against us men. Men love risk, adventure, "the fight," the contest, and the struggle. God put those things in us so that we will fight evil. We are supposed to use our often-misunderstood male virtues in the fight against those things which destroy what is in the hearts of our women. In doing so, we reclaim the essence of authentic manhood.

WOMEN CAN ONLY BE VICTIMIZED AND TAKEN ADVANTAGE OF IF THE MEN ALLOW IT TO HAPPEN.

In his book, *Her Hand in Marriage,* Doug Wilson gives us insight into another telling, Old Testament, sexual-assault law. If a young woman was found not to be a virgin after she had been given in marriage to a man, the law stated that . . . *they shall bring out the girl to the doorway of her father's house, and the men of her city shall stone her to death* (Deuteronomy 22:21). Since, in most other cases, people were stoned at the city gates, this command indicates moral responsibility on the part of the father for failure to keep his daughter a virgin. It was *his* job to watch and care for her, to ensure her virginity. She was put to death for her sin, but shame and responsibility were attached to her father. The symbolism in the location of the woman's execution — in front of her father's home — should not be missed. The responsibility for the moral state of a culture is laid at the doorstep of the men of that culture. Women can only be victimized and taken advantage of if the men allow it to happen.

In the story of Lot, in Genesis 19, a bizarre exchange takes place. One day Lot happened across some visitors to his city who were planning to sleep in the town square for the night. Knowing the depravity of the citizens of his city, Lot insisted the men stay in the safety of his home. When the neighbors and townspeople heard about the visitors, the men of the city went to Lot's home and banged on his door, threatening him and demanding that he release the visitors to them so they could violate them sexually. Lot tried to placate the men with an offer. *"Please, my brothers, do not act wickedly. Now behold, I have two daughters who have not had relations with man; please let me bring them out to you, and do to them whatever you like; only do nothing to these men, inasmuch as they have come under the shelter of my roof"* (Genesis 19:7-8). The visitors, who turned out to be two angels, struck the crowd with blindness so they couldn't find the door. The crowd eventually left Lot and his household alone.

Elements of this story remind me of our generation. The culture is pounding on the doors of our homes. In the place of a sodomite, rapist crowd is a value system that guarantees unhappiness, diseased bodies, destroyed dreams, and broken hearts through the current dating system. Despite all that, we insist the dating system is not broken. In our case, *we* are the ones who are blind, willingly giving our daughters to the world's system of relationships that will destroy and take advantage of them — a culture that devalues women and views them as sexual objects. We naively allow our daughters to spend time with young men we (and/or they) barely know. If we were honest with ourselves, we would admit we have entrusted our daughters into the hands of young men we wouldn't even trust with the keys to our car! We give our daughters to this system, unprotected and totally vulnerable. We are no different than Lot. It horrifies us to think Lot would sacrifice his daughters' purity and safety. It is no less horrifying to risk our own daughters' purity and safety by blindly giving them to the world's system of relationships.

NECESSARY ELEMENT #3: CHANGING THE HEART OF A WOMAN

The worship of sex instigates and releases a wholesale assault against women. In order for women to participate in the worship of sex, not only must there, of necessity, be abortion, which ensures the absence of consequences (at least the illusion of their absence) or responsibility, there also must be a change in the heart of a woman. It is not in the God-given nature of a woman to sacrifice the life of her child to meet her own selfish needs or desires. Quite the contrary! God put a strong maternal instinct into women that causes them to go to great lengths to sacrifice *for* their children. It is also not natural for a woman to sacrifice her purity in an atmosphere which lacks commitment and security. Women are created to need safety, security, permanence, and commitment. These are the things that allow them to smile at the future, as is said of the woman in Proverbs 31. The powers of darkness come to coax our daughters into trying to obtain their dreams of safety, security, permanence, and commitment by means of an identity and behavior that separate their personhood from their sexuality. In other words, Satan convinces them to focus solely on the sexual part of their being, to the exclusion of the other beautiful aspects of their nature, to lure a man. The enemy seeks to objectify them, to convince daughters to build their lives around an altar of charm and beauty in an attempt to get their needs met. As always, the enemy's ultimate agenda is to steal, kill, and destroy. He knows if he can convince daughters to go against their God-ordained nature, they will be destroyed.

IN ORDER FOR WOMEN TO PARTICIPATE IN THE WORSHIP OF SEX, NOT ONLY MUST THERE, OF NECESSITY, BE ABORTION ... THERE ALSO MUST BE A CHANGE IN THE HEART OF A WOMAN.

Charm is deceitful, and beauty is vain, but a woman who fears the Lord, she shall be praised (Proverbs 31:30). This Scripture indicates that God designed every daughter on the face of the earth to be praised and to be noticed in the right way. God promises that when a woman fears Him, when she positions herself in that right place before Him, the result will be appropriate attention, praise, and value. However, charm is deceitful. Charm says, "Get attention your own way. Use your sensuality to draw attention to yourself." The word, charm, implies a spell. It has a connotation of magic, seduction, and allurement to it. It lies, though. It cannot deliver on its promises; it will not fill a woman up, it will not meet her needs in a way that truly satisfies. Attention that comes through charm separates a daughter's heart from her personhood and the true beauty God has given her. A culture of charm calls for attention to vain, physical beauty. It causes a daughter to make herself the center of the universe, leaving her empty and focused on herself.

OUR CULTURE WOULD LIKE US TO BELIEVE THAT EVERYTHING BETWEEN A MAN AND A WOMAN CAN BE REDUCED TO SEX.

Our culture would like us to believe that everything between a man and a woman can be reduced to sex. And I have to admit, they do a pretty convincing job of making life appear as though it really is all about sex, sex, and more sex. The movies, billboards, advertisements, television shows, and Internet are full of such propaganda. We do, however, encounter some problems with this concerted focus on sex. Men are getting sex but missing out on the true intimacy God designed for them to experience. And, in the midst of all the sex, women are sorely disappointed by the lack of relationship and permanence they receive — the very things they yearn for. That's the heart of a daughter.

A woman who lives with a guy is on tiptoes in her spirit asking, "Is this permanent? Do you value me? Are you going to commit to me?" Every daughter, with her "power to attract," is always asking, "Do you value me for me, or is it just something on the outside that grabbed your attention?" The rich widow faces a similar dilemma — never knowing for sure why people like her or why they go to visit her. In the back of her mind she wonders, *Do you want my inheritance? Do you want me to give you some money? Are you my friend? Do you love me just for me?* In our culture, every daughter asks that same kind of question in the deepest part of her spirit.

Unfortunately, the demonically inspired, prevailing message is this, "You better give yourself to this seductive image. You better learn to walk a certain way, talk a certain way, look a certain way, and give yourself away because everyone else is doing it, and, if you don't, no man is ever going to want you." Their constant bombardment with this message, combined with their fear of a future alone, causes many daughters to give in. They then focus on and develop their sexual identity to the exclusion of the other parts of their being, denying their deepest needs and desires, and risk everything in the hope that those needs will be met by giving themselves to men. It is all part of the assignment of the powers of darkness to change the heart of a woman and destroy her spirit. In fact, the woman, in doing such things, becomes an accomplice to the destruction of her own dreams.

> ## MARRIAGE PROVIDES THE ONLY ARENA IN WHICH A WOMAN IS SECURELY PROTECTED BY LOVE AND A COVENANT AND, THEREFORE, IS ABLE TO FULLY GIVE HERSELF IN A SEXUAL WAY.

I am not saying women are not sexual. I am saying they are primarily relational and secondarily sexual. In other words, in the sexual arena, a woman's greatest need is that a man commits to her, and then out of that place of safety and security, she can fully and unreservedly give herself to him sexually. A daughter needs to know a man has made a commitment to her, not just for her body, but because of her personhood (the entirety of who she is). That is God's design and purpose for relationships. Marriage provides the only arena in which a woman is securely protected by love and a covenant, and therefore is able to fully give herself in a sexual way. In that one relationship, God releases her to express her sexuality. Apart from the marriage relationship, she is not meant to relate to men sexually. In all other relationships with men, she is to relate as a sister, daughter, or mother. The lie perpetrated by the enemy leads her to believe she needs to relate on a sexual level with all men. In the process, her heart is altered, her nature compromised, her dreams trampled on, and her future destroyed. Only in the covenant of marriage is a woman's sexuality released in a way that is a blessing to her. As I said earlier, you cannot worship sex without instigating and releasing a wholesale assault against the woman. In order to have a willing participant, you first must change the heart of a woman. And only then, out of deception, brokenness, and destruction, will a daughter become someone God never intended her to be.

During former President Bill Clinton's first term in office, he was caught in a sexual affair with a young White House intern, Monica Lewinsky. The scandal made headlines all over the world. In the report containing the investigation of the whole affair, information came to light regarding her conversations with the President. (Watch both for the deception in which she found herself and the aforementioned elements found in a daughter's heart.) In the midst of the affair, she said, "I think I've fallen in love with the President." Because daughter's hearts are integrated, Ms. Lewinsky was not thinking solely about sex as a man would, but about her future with a man — and a host of other related issues. Love, for her, held the promise of permanence and commitment. When a man touches a woman's body, he is not just touching her body. It goes much deeper than that for a woman. He is touching parts of her soul — parts as diverse as to how she feels about being a grandmother someday, what is her favorite ice cream, how much she loves her pet, and her opinions of how the current President is governing. The man wants a sexual encounter, and love is far from his mind; she desires permanence, commitment, safety, and security. As with Monica, though, there is a level of wounding in her spirit that allows her to dream about permanence in her relationship with the President. That is an illogical deception, albeit a deception to which many women fall prey. Countless women have affairs with married men, thinking those men will make a permanent commitment to them, even though the men are violating their prior commitment to their spouses in having an affair.

> ## "I ASKED HIM, 'WHY DO YOU NEVER ASK ME ANY QUESTIONS ABOUT MYSELF?' AND 'IS THIS JUST ABOUT SEX, OR DO YOU HAVE SOME INTEREST IN ME AS A PERSON?'"

The next questions Monica asked unveiled the essence of every daughter's heart, questions that every woman asks in every relationship, whether or not they are ever verbalized. She must have taken the risk to ask them when she began to doubt his motivation toward her. *I asked him, 'Why do you never ask me any questions about myself?' and 'Is this just about sex, or do you have some interest in me as a person?'"*

I can only imagine the look on Mr. Clinton's face.

God designed his daughters to be valued and communicated with, to be honored, and to be cherished. When they are wounded and lies of the enemy have altered their woman's heart, only then do they become willing to trade their daughter-heart for an illicit relationship with a man. Or, as in the case of some Japanese teenagers, trade their daughter-heart for a perverted moment with a father figure.

Many Japanese girls have fathers who are emotionally and physically absent from them because of the fathers' long hours of work. Some girls will post their cell-phone numbers on a website and agree to meet, have lunch, and talk with older businessmen, only to allow the men to take advantage of them fifteen minutes later in some hotel room, receiving "mall money" in payment. Why would young teens do that? The men are looking for a sexual encounter, but the girls are not simply looking for money for new clothes or a sexual experience — such desires are not resident in the true heart of a woman. I believe those girls, in a culture where their fathers are emotionally and physically absent in their lives, are desperate for genuine male attention.

NO WOMAN WILL BE SATISFIED IN HAVING A MAN KNOW HER ONLY ON A SEXUAL LEVEL.

What do I mean when I say the enemy tries to separate a woman from her personhood and make her relate on a solely sexual level in her relationships to men? By personhood, I mean the entirety of who she is — her body, mind, will, and emotions. No woman will be satisfied in having a man know her only on a sexual level. Women want the men to whom they give themselves to know everything about them. They want someone with whom they can share their most private dreams, desires, and hopes. They want someone with whom they can share their fears, failures, and insecurities — and know they will still be accepted. Women want to be listened to, comforted, and prayed for when they are going through a hard time. They want to know someone will commit to them and stay with them, even if they get sick, gain weight, or lose their youthful beauty. They want someone to grow old with. For a woman to settle for anything less, that woman must first deny her God-designed heart.

DESPERATION AND THE ADULTEROUS WOMAN

Proverbs 30 uses the illustration of an adulterous woman to teach us about the desperation in a woman whose needs have not been met. *This is the way of an adulterous woman: She eats and wipes her mouth, and says, "I have done no wrong"* (Proverbs 30:20). This symbolism expresses a daughter's hungry heart in terms of eating, and eating in the sense of consuming another man's life — his relationship with his wife, his marriage, and his family. There is such a hunger in this woman's life, such a desperate desire in her heart for someone to connect with her, that she disregards all the destruction she is about to cause and refuses to consider what she would feel like if she were that man's wife. Because of all the brokenness and pain in her life, all she cares about is herself and having her needs met. Then she wipes her mouth and says, "I have done nothing wrong."

HER DESPERATION AND PERSISTENT SEDUCTION POINT TO THE FACT THAT HER BUFF, MACHO, CAPTAIN-OF-THE-BODYGUARDS HUSBAND WAS PROBABLY NOT MEETING HER NEEDS.

We see that same desperation in Potiphar's wife in the story of Joseph in Genesis 39. Scripture says that day after day she said to Joseph, "Lie with me." Her desperation and persistent seduction point to the fact that her buff, macho, captain-of-the-bodyguards husband was probably not meeting her needs. Knowing the heart of most women, I doubt she was looking for a sexual experience. She was probably looking for the true intimacy she was not receiving from her husband.

THINGS THAT SHAKE THE EARTH

The author of Proverbs lists four things that shake the earth — that shake the foundations stable civilizations must have in order to continue to exist. *Under three things the earth quakes, and under four, it cannot bear up: under a slave when he becomes king, and a fool when he is satisfied with food, under an unloved woman when she gets a husband, and a maidservant when she supplants her mistress* (Proverbs 30:21-23).

The first cause for shaking is political — a slave who becomes king. He undoubtedly operates out of insecurity and a low self-image, which then characterizes the way he governs. Such is the story of tyrants who shed the blood of millions, sometimes of their own people, in order to secure their reign, such as Hitler, Stalin, Idi Amin, and Pol Pot. Their tyrannical rule shook the earth.

The second cause of earth-shaking is economic — a fool who is satisfied with food. This reminds me of economic systems like communism or any other social-welfare system that robs people of personal initiative and responsibility. It is not difficult to see how politics and economics gone awry can "shake" the earth.

You might assume the next two causes of earth shaking would involve scientific or technological issues. Surprisingly, the last two causes of earthquakes deal with the heart of a woman — an unloved woman who gets a husband and a maidservant who takes the place of her mistress.

THE UNLOVED WOMAN WHO GETS A HUSBAND

Imagine a little girl looking forward to being married. Her father has not met her needs, and she dreams that the man who becomes her husband will be a prince and treat her like his princess. What happens when, not too long into the marriage, she discovers he doesn't love her or cherish her as she has longed to be loved and cherished? "Unloved" means to be alienated and includes in its meaning anything from simple opposition to intense hatred. It is the way someone should feel toward an enemy, not his own wife!

Picture this husband. He comes home, eats the meal she has prepared, reads the paper, watches the news, and then wants a sexual relationship. She knows, without a doubt, that her husband's heart is elsewhere. He has not shared himself with her or looked into her eyes to see what is in her spirit. She feels violated because he wants sex but is not meeting her relational and emotional needs. Such a violation of a woman's nature sets in motion some things that can cause the earth — marriage, families, societies — to "shake."

Consider this. Before the women's liberation movement gained momentum in our culture, a woman's identity was most often an extension of her marriage and family, which are the foundational building blocks of a nation. I would argue, however, that the impetus of the feminist movement, which led to a mass exodus of women from their homes, in part, did not actually begin with women. Among other causes, I believe some of the impetus for the movement began when a husband became unwilling to meet the basic needs of his wife's heart, or when a father refused to acknowledge or meet the needs of his daughter's heart, either through ignorance, busyness, or selfishness. The result was unfulfilled, frustrated, empty-hearted daughters and wives crying out for meaning, purpose, and satisfaction. They attempted to find those things in places outside of God's design, apart from their husbands and the home. Uncherished and undervalued, women began to seek identity outside their marriages, families, and homes, and a revolution took place that has shaken society.

With her new identity being forged outside the home and an ever-increasing amount of time spent in the workplace, things got complicated. Women encountered other men in the workplace, and men encountered other women in the workplace. Empty-hearted women, uncared for and undervalued, suddenly discovered there were men at work who appreciated them. They talked to her, asked her opinions, and made her feel important. As men and empty-hearted women spend time together with those who are not their spouses, a spirit of betrayal and infidelity is easily birthed. The empty-hearted woman has an affair and gets pregnant. For the sake of reputation and secrecy, she gets an abortion. Often, both partners divorce their spouses and marry each other. The resultant earthquake sends devastating shockwaves through both their homes. Men's, women's, and children's lives are destroyed in the process. I know this may sound simplistic and that there are other contributing factors for the breakdown of the family, but I am convinced that empty-hearted women who have been hurt by men are one of the driving forces behind the women's rights movement. Furthermore, empty-hearted women, in seeking to have their needs met, have

Anything that threatens the health and stability of marriages and families threatens the health and stability of societies and nations.

contributed to the rise of divorce and abortion, which have slowly eroded the stability of society until the earth "shakes" and nations begin to disintegrate from within. Anything that threatens the health and stability of marriages and families threatens the health and stability of societies and nations.

A Maidservant When She Supplants Her Mistress

A maidservant who supplants her mistress also causes the earth to shake. Supplant means to seize, take possession of, drive away, dispossess, or occupy. When the female head of the house discovers her maidservant or "another woman" has won the heart of her husband, the order of the home is destabilized and the earth "shakes." I believe the "other woman" need not necessarily be literal. Many times the maidservant is simply a career, hobby, sport, or even a ministry. After years of neglect and suffering, a husband, occupied with things other than his wife, can expect to hear her say, "I cannot live in this state of emotional starvation any longer. Choose between me and your maidservant!" Years of pain and neglect force her to speak the reality of a daughter's heart, "I was not designed to have something or someone replace me. I can't live this way." The earth is shaken because a woman, designed by God to be loved, is not having her needs met.

She Smiles At Her Future

She smiles at the future (Proverbs 31:25). It is such a small little phrase and yet full of implications and reflections on a daughter's heart. If you consider how God designed a daughter, and how some of her deepest needs center around the issues of safety and security, you can understand that when those needs are met, a genuine smile is generated in the deepest part of her heart.

GOD ALSO WANTS TO REMIND YOU THAT HE KNOWS HOW YOU FEEL WHEN YOU'VE GIVEN YOURSELF TO SOMEONE AND HE THROWS YOU AWAY LIKE A PIECE OF PROPERTY.

Contrast this with Daniella, a beautiful, southern-European, dark-eyed waitress who happened to be serving my table at a restaurant in Bulgaria. I am not a man who makes a habit of looking for such things, but she was wearing the shortest pair of shorts I had ever seen in my life and an extremely tight shirt. There was something in her face and eyes that disturbed me. Her beauty was overridden by a haunting sense of sorrow and fear that seemed to say, "Nothing is going to change. I have a horrible feeling that the things I have experienced in my past are only going to be repeated in the future." By the end of the meal, I had a strong urge to be a dad and tell her some things her daughter-heart needed to hear. The Lord prompted me to give her a tip three times the actual cost of the meal. I knew that would give me her attention. As I gave her my tip, I said, "Daniella, this is for you. God told me to give this to you. It is a reminder that God loves you, that He cares for you, that He has a plan for you, and that you are important to Him. Oh, and, Daniella, God also wants to remind you that He knows how you feel when you've given yourself to someone and he throws you away like a piece of property. God never wanted you to feel like that. He never designed a daughter to feel that much pain. He knows how you feel when that happens."

WHEN A DAUGHTER GIVES HERSELF AWAY AND IS BETRAYED TIME AND TIME AGAIN, YOU SEE THE MEN ON HER FACE.

Something broke through into her heart, and she began to weep. She put her hand over her mouth and ran out of the restaurant into the kitchen. She was like many 21st century daughters — sophisticated, independent, and isolated — who appear to have it all together. However, by barely scratching that veneer of sophistication, the reality of her heartbreak spilled out. To coin a phrase, "I could see the men on her face." When a daughter gives herself away and is betrayed time and time again, we see the men on her face. The compounded hurt, betrayal, and lies she has experienced in relationships are etched into her heart and are evident in her hopeless expression. Daniella had lived through hell, was living through hell, and hell was all she could conceivably look forward to. Fear causes people to recoil in fear for their future. Daughters were not designed to be full of fear and wary of every potential relationship. I hate seeing that pain. God designed women to thrive in an atmosphere of trust and safety. We need God's perfect love to come and cast out fear and fill the heart of every daughter with safety and security so she can literally smile when she thinks about her future.

END OF THE CONVEYOR BELT

As horrible as abortion is, we have learned that abortion is not an isolated issue. If abortion is truly on the end of a conveyor belt in a nation that worships sex, it would behoove us to look closely at the factors in society that contribute to abortion. In order to effectively deal with abortion, we first need to address the enemy's assault against the heart of a woman and the God-ordained role of men. Only as we seek to understand and undo this assault will be we successful in our fight to see abortion end.

CHAPTER THREE

TWENTY-SIX HOT SPOTS

I landed in the Heathrow International Airport on my way home from a fruitful ministry trip to Latvia. As I walked through the multitudes of shops and booths at the airport mall, I came across an Urban Decay cosmetics shop where a perky little 20-something British clerk stood waiting to serve me. I could just imagine her looking at me and thinking, *Aw, now look, here's a father who is going to buy nail polish for his daughters. How wonderful!* I walked up to her and asked about new product lines they might be carrying. I had already been citing many of their nail polish and product names in my sermons and was looking for another example. Excited by my inquiry and, perhaps by the fact that I wasn't British, she took me to one of their product displays and gestured widely with both hands, as if to say, "Ta da! Here they are!"

Wondering what new names they had come up with, I asked, "And what is the name of this new product?"

"*Hot Pants,*" she declared — a proud salesperson.

I had been teaching in a Latvian Bible school about confronting cultural lies around the area of sexuality and had concluded by praying for students who had been wounded by sexual sin. I was tired — excited and positive — but really tired, and probably a little dangerous. Everything I had just been teaching and the pain in the faces of the young people I had just prayed for were fresh in my spirit. I looked at her and said light-heartedly, "*Hot Pants.* Is that about standing too close to the stove?"

Confusion filled her face while she quickly tried to decide if this American was short a few marbles or if she had a pervert on her hands. My determined stare back into her eyes told her I was neither. I gestured to the lip gloss and tried again. "Let me ask the question in another way.

IF MY 15-YEAR-OLD DAUGHTER LIVED THE LIFESTYLE OF HOT PANTS, WOULD IT ENSURE THAT ALL HER DREAMS WOULD COME TRUE, OR WOULD IT GUARANTEE THAT EVERY DREAM SHE HAS EVER HAD WOULD BE DESTROYED?

If my 15-year-old daughter lived the lifestyle of *Hot Pants,* would it ensure that all her dreams would come true, or would it guarantee that every dream she has ever had would be destroyed? Which one?" She couldn't answer my question. I suspected it was because the young lady was already living the lifestyle of *Hot Pants.* Maybe she couldn't answer me because she had already seen a good many, if not all of her dreams stripped away and destroyed. She excused herself and went to get the manager.

Almost immediately, a middle-aged woman appeared and asked if there was a problem. I looked straight into her eyes and told her I was ashamed and saddened to encounter a company that apparently lacked commitment to extending some expression of moral guidance to a generation, and instead was willing to prostitute a generation to make a dollar, or in this case, a pound. Why, instead, could they not search for a way to demonstrate some kind of moral corporate responsibility to a culture of young people in search of their identity?

Once she recovered from her shock and gathered her composure, she replied, "Well, sir, I'm sure you are aware we have complete freedom of speech to call our products whatever we like." I agreed and replied that I, too, had freedom of speech and would exercise that right by telling everyone I teach about their products.

AS EACH NEW PIECE OF THE PUZZLE IS ADDED, IT CREATES A TOXIC ATMOSPHERE THAT ENCOURAGES YOUNG PEOPLE TO PARTICIPATE IN THEIR OWN SELF-DESTRUCTION THROUGH UNRESTRAINED EXPRESSIONS OF SEXUALITY.

I was one tired preacher in an exhausted and unrestrained
state, unleashing my fury against a demonic stronghold that, at that
moment, was rearing its ugly head in a cosmetics store. Wearing *Hot
Pants* lip gloss won't singularly cause the destruction of a daughter's
life. However, if you add *Hot Pants* lip gloss to the sex lyrics on the
radio, the latest television show full of young people having sex, the
most recent raunchy music video, and Abercrombie and Fitch's thong
underwear for 11-year-olds with the words "eye-candy" on them, an
eclectic puzzle picture begins to emerge with clarity. As each new piece
of the puzzle is added, it reveals a toxic atmosphere that encourages
young people to participate in their own self-destruction through
unrestrained expressions of sexuality.

We are constantly inundated with sexual images. A sexy, sultry
look is the image of the age. Our appearances are evaluated on the
basis of sex appeal. Sexuality is used to sell everything from cars to
sports to food. You name the product, and we have used sex to sell
it. Little girls are being trained by the fashion industry, years before
they even have an inkling of what they are being sold into, to dress
in a way that emphasizes sexuality. If you feel you are not attractive
enough, you can go to a surgeon who will pump up, cut out, paste in,
or erase whatever you feel is holding you back from feeling confident
about yourself. Our language has even changed. Looking sharp is
now called "getting pimped out." Dirty Girl, another cosmetics line,
encourages the wearer to, "release the dirty girl within you," and "think
dirty-girl thoughts." Ten years ago, Hard Candy offered nail products
called *Trailer Trash, Pimp,* and *Porn.* I cannot imagine buying such
products for my daughter. "Put this on, honey. I bought it especially
for you. *Trailer Trash* — that suits you. That's what you are, right,
honey?" Unfortunately, those product names now seem tame with
new companies such as Orgasm Cosmetics sporting product names
such as *Climax, Easy But Not Cheap,* and *What Happened Under the
Covers?* NARS Cosmetics' contribution to the formation of morality
in a generation of young women includes product names such as *Sin,
Multiple Orgasm,* and *Deep Throat.* What began as a groundbreaking,
barrier-shattering porn movie in the early 1970s with *Deep Throat,*
returns nearly 40 years later as the product name for a blush targeted to
young teens. Shame on us!

THERE IN THE GROCERY STORE, I ENCOUNTERED THE NEW PORNOGRAPHY — NOT THE OLD PORNOGRAPHY OF PLAYBOY AND PENTHOUSE, BUT WHAT I CALL THE NEW, IDEOLOGICAL PORNOGRAPHY — IN A SLEW OF WOMEN'S MAGAZINES.

This cultural sexual assault was apparent to me some years back as I started looking at the magazine rack at our neighborhood grocery store. We ran out of milk one Saturday morning — a frequent occurrence when we still had eight children at home. In the grocery store, I encountered the new pornography — not the old pornography of *Playboy* and *Penthouse,* but what I call the new, ideological pornography — in a slew of women's magazines. In the lead, was the flagship promoter of sexuality, *Cosmopolitan.* Whereas the old pornography primarily used images to define women as sexual beings, the new pornography often uses words and ideas to achieve the same goal, to establish sexuality as our primary identity. As I stood in line to pay that Saturday morning, the lead article prominently displayed on one magazine cover offered, "Ninety-nine ways to keep your man happy in bed." The title of another article exclaimed, "Twenty-six new hot spots found on the human body never known to man before this week — just discovered in France!" I went running home with my milk, burst into the kitchen, and said to my wife, "Honey! Something terrible! I can't believe it!"

Sensing my alarm, my wife inquired. "Honey, what is it? What's wrong?"

I blurted out, "I can't believe it! They just discovered twenty-six hot spots on the human body never known to man before this week. We have been married to each other for all these years, and we have missed out on everything!" (No, we didn't actually have that conversation. But you get my point.) Publishing is another avenue whereby this generation is being inundated with not just sexual images, but with a sexual philosophy of life.

I often see young women in airports and on planes reading the most recent editions of such magazines. In almost every case, the lead articles are about sex responses or sex tricks. The articles promise to enlighten them and lead them to personal fulfillment through sexuality. I find it interesting that these young women don't usually hold the magazine up for everyone to see, but have it carefully tucked away in their carry-on bag. They discreetly take it out and keep it rolled up as they work through the pages. I sense they feel some shame that causes them to be secretive as they partake of this ideological pornography. I know that as they read, the innocence of their hearts is stolen away paragraph by paragraph, page by page.

Sexuality dominates movie screens with increasing boldness. Thirteen years ago, my daughters wanted to watch a popular new movie. "Everyone" was watching the PG-13 movie, and we had been eagerly awaiting its release. "It's a movie about history," we were told, "about fashion, ballroom gowns, chandeliers, and true love." I watched the show on my own to check it out before the girls watched it. I was assaulted as the young actress posed nude in one of the scenes for a photographer. The image seared itself into my spirit. Another scene showed two young people having sex in the backseat of a car, but because they were in love and beautiful music was soaring in the background, it was portrayed as romantic, beautiful, and acceptable. Our girls agreed not to see that movie.

I LOOK AT ADVERTISEMENTS, THE CLOTHING, THE MOVIES, AND THE MAGAZINES, AND I ASK MYSELF, "IS THIS THE HEART OF A WOMAN?"

I stand back and try to take it all in. I look at advertisements, the clothing, the movies, and the magazines, and I ask myself, "Is *this* the heart of a woman? Is *this* what each of my six daughters really aspires to?" I watch the women in metro stations, on street corners, in malls, in restaurants, and when I preach in church meetings. I strain to find the same look I have seen in the faces of my daughters, faces full of trust and purity. Instead, I am confronted by sad, non-smiling looks on the faces of far too many of the women. I see femininity and even beauty, but all too often those are accompanied by a tremendous hardness and a haunting sorrow. Where do those come from? What is going on? Why aren't the girls or the women smiling?

FROSTING

Let me give a simple analogy. When I was a little boy, my family used to spend summers at my grandparents' cabin at Hayden Lake in Northern Idaho. One summer, Mom and Dad went to town and left my three brothers and me at the cabin, alone, with three boxes of brownie mix in the cupboard. As they drove away, we opened, mixed, and baked all the packages at once. When we pulled them out of the oven, we immediately dove in, rolled the hot dough into little balls in our fists, and ate and ate and ate. It was not too long before I began to feel sick. To be honest, I don't know if I like the taste of brownies to this day.

IF SEX IS LIKE FROSTING, OUR CULTURE SAYS YOU NEED TO FIND THE BIGGEST BOWL AVAILABLE, FILL IT WITH FROSTING, GET THE BIGGEST SPOON POSSIBLE, AND EAT AS MUCH FROSTING AS YOU CAN, AS OFTEN AS YOU CAN, WITH AS MANY PEOPLE AS YOU CAN.

Culture views sex as I viewed the brownies. If sex is like frosting, our culture says you need to find the biggest bowl available, fill it with frosting, get the biggest spoon possible, and eat as much frosting as you can, as often as you can, with as many people as you can. In fact, our culture tells us frosting is what life is all about; it gives meaning to life and is the greatest human experience known to man. Furthermore, if you have already eaten frosting the traditional way, you need to try it while standing on one foot because that will add a whole new dimension to the experience. Then you might want to try hopping on one foot, then spinning around and eating frosting all at the same time. Now, there is an experience you won't want to miss! And finally, and I have reserved the best for last, the most exhilarating frosting experience of all — *stolen* frosting! Have you ever eaten stolen frosting? It is equal only to *secret* frosting.

Obviously, I am being sarcastic, but it appears as if the quest for the ultimate "frosting experience" never ends. Our culture is hanging over the edge of the frosting bowl and gorging itself with little thought about the long-term, let alone short-term, consequences.

With such a strong, collective cultural endorsement in media, film, advertisement, and music, in which it appears as though everyone else is participating in sexuality without any thought for God and His intentions, many people have obtained their frosting any way possible. However, people are forgetting something in the midst of all of this: if what the culture says about frosting is true, then everyone who is engaged in the pursuit of the "frosting world" should be skipping down the street laughing. If frosting in any form is fulfilling, in and of itself, then prostitutes should be the happiest people on earth, right next to the mafia guy with a hooker on each arm. Similarly, the young woman who has just given herself away to a young man should be skipping down the street, her head thrown back, eyes sparkling, and laughter coming out of the deepest part of her spirit — in spite of the fact that he left her the next morning. Across the continents, we should hear the same story over and over again from women, "I don't need permanence and security. I can be as unattached as the young men in this culture are. I don't need promises and commitment. I gave myself to him, and he left . . . ha, ha ha. I don't care if men leave me. I gave myself away to another man, and he left, too. It's no big deal. I'm getting frosting. That's all that really matters to me."

GOD DID NOT DESIGN MEN AND WOMEN TO LIMP FROM ONE DISAPPOINTING RELATIONSHIP OR SEXUAL ENCOUNTER TO ANOTHER, TRYING TO FIND THE MAGICAL FORMULA OR PERSON WHO WILL FULFILL THE CULTURAL PROMISE THAT SEX IS THE CENTRAL EXPERIENCE OF LIFE.

In reality, the young woman is not laughing or skipping, nor are her eyes sparkling. Instead, she, along with the rest of her generation, is on hold waiting for an appointment at the offices of psychologists, counselors, and psychiatrists. She is making appointments with her pastor and picking up anti-depressant prescriptions at pharmacies as she struggles to recover the broken pieces of her life. She is not laughing because God did not design women to market sexuality in order to be loved. He did not design men and women to limp from one disappointing relationship or sexual encounter to another, trying to find the magical formula or person who will fulfill the cultural promise that sex is the central experience of life. As a result, fulfillment is never found, and all that remains in the wake of those sexual experiences is pain, confusion, and devastation. I teach at churches, men's and women's retreats, conferences, and discipleship schools, and time after time I hear the same story told in countless different ways: "I bought the lie; I chased my fantasy; I slept with my boyfriend; I had an affair; I used sex to get love; I was abused; I manipulated love to get sex." The end result is always the same: "It has just about destroyed my whole life."

WHAT ABOUT US, THE CHURCH?

Despite the obvious human devastation that has resulted from all of this, the church has been primarily reactive in its attitude about what is happening in the culture. We still aren't being proactive and talking about sexuality in the church. Not really. We do ask our kids to make a pledge for purity, to wait until marriage to have sex, and to say, "No!" to drugs and alcohol, but we do not go much further than that. When was the last time you heard a sermon from the pulpit that covered sexuality and included more than a list of prohibitions? It is very rare to even talk about sexuality in the church. Often our method of training a generation to deal with sexuality has been the equivalent of challenging them "not to think about monkeys" at the count of three. "Ready? One, two, three!" Images of monkeys peeling bananas and swinging from branch to branch are the typical response in our young people. That demonstrates how ineffective many of our current methods are.

NOW, MORE THAN EVER, WE NEED TO TAKE SEX OFF THE "NO" LIST AND PUT IT ON THE "HOLY" LIST.

Young people *do* think about sex. They wonder whom they will marry and what a Christian girl is supposed to do with her heart, and how a single, Christian young man should act sexuality. They wrestle with their needs and desires. It is naïve of us to think our children are not affected by the culture. Parents can no longer afford to look at their children and imagine it is possible for them to navigate through the moral depravity in our culture and emerge completely unscathed. These are not young people trying to find an escape hatch in order to satisfy their own desires. Many are the next generation of leaders who have been handed a list of standards and prohibitions without the reasons behind them. They do not need another list of prohibitions in the area of sexuality. If the sum of our sex-education training is to tell young people that sex before marriage is bad, we just add to their confusion. They ask, "How does walking down a wedding aisle make something that has been bad all my life suddenly good?" What they desperately need from us is a revelation of God's special gift of sexuality, the context He has provided for it to be expressed in, and a revelation of the goodness of the God who created it and put boundaries around it. Now, more than ever, we need to take sex off the "no" list and put it on the "holy" list.

For the past fifteen years, I've traveled the globe preaching a message about sexuality and the culture. I have visited countless discipleship schools and Bible schools filled with young people who want to serve God with their whole lives. They are, for the most part, kids who grew up in church, who were supposedly protected from moral corruption. Many are second, and some, even third-generation believers. However, time and time again, despite their youth, their stories are filled with desperation — with abortion, same-sex encounters, incest, molestation, premarital sex, relationships with older, married men, and group sex — even sex with animals. The list goes on and on. I am not surprised by anything anymore. In a way, I am encouraged and discouraged all at the same time. I am discouraged because of the incredible depths of the devastation I am seeing in the lives of young people; I am encouraged because I know God is the One who can bring truth, healing, and restoration to a hurting and lost generation. I know because I have witnessed, first hand, the restoring work of God in young people's lives.

Unfortunately, the comment I hear most often after speaking is, "We have never heard a message like this before. No one talks about this kind of stuff." Our church youth and college/career ministries sometimes confess that their gatherings more closely resemble a "meat-market" or a bar without alcohol than a gathering of young believers, or said in another way, the "singles match-making club where everyone is looking for Mr. Right or Miss Right." In the midst of this, the question we need to ask is, "How *can* we talk about sexuality in a way that is accurate, proper, and helpful?"

RE-DEFINING PURITY

How we choose to define purity is extremely important. A technical definition allows a Christian boy and Christian girl to go on a Christian date, go to the Christian coffee shop, get a Christian latte, listen to Christian music, and watch a Christian movie. After that, they get in a Christian car complete with a Christian bumper sticker, wearing their new Christian bracelets they bought for each other, and attend a Christian concert with a Christian mosh-pit. They complete the evening by going to a quiet Christian place, doing some Christian necking, drawing some Christian lines, and are, technically, still virgins. Technically, they may be virgins, but they have missed the whole point of purity.

THE REAL QUESTION WE NEED TO ASK IS, "HOW MAY I PLEASE THE LORD WITH MY LIFE AND MY SEXUALITY?"

They live just as do their non-Christian friends. There are many Christian young men and women who are, technically, virgins but who walk in a high level of seduction and impurity. On the other hand, I have met redeemed prostitutes who walk in a level of purity that far outshines technical virginity because of God's restoration in their lives. God is not impressed with technical virginity. Purity is a matter of the heart and the direction in which it is pointed. The question is not, "How much can I do?" or "How far can I go and still be considered a virgin?" The real question we need to ask is, "How may I please the Lord with my life and my sexuality?"

God's Ideas about Purity

If talking about sexuality is important, it would follow that God would make that evident in His Word. I assumed if I looked closely enough, I would discover a blueprint from which we could learn to properly deal with sexuality in the church. I decided to start with the Ten Commandments. Of the Ten Commandments God gave His people, four refer to our relationship with God and six to our relationships with one another. Of those six, two are directly sexual in nature: *You shall not commit adultery,* and *You shall not covet your neighbor's wife* (Exodus 20:14, 17). In other words, one-third of the commandments that outline how we ought to treat one another, and one-fifth of the total commandments deal directly with sexuality, our sexual nature, and God's loving boundaries for His sons and daughters. Twenty percent of His commandments deal with our sexuality. In other words, our sexuality is important to God — extremely important.

Next, I thought about Paul, who helped birth the church in the sex-saturated Greek and Roman world. Paul, when exhorting Timothy, his son in the faith, on how to conduct himself in the cosmopolitan and highly eroticized atmosphere of Ephesus, stated, *Let no one look down on your youthfulness, but rather in speech, conduct, love, faith, and purity, show yourself an example of those who believe* (1 Timothy 4:12). Speech, conduct, love, faith, and purity — these things will mark a generation for God. Purity makes the top five. Is this God's blueprint? Does He mandate leaders to emphasize the importance of purity a full 20 percent of the time? If that were the case, 10 out of 52 sermons a year would be dedicated to this important topic.

Proverbs is filled with warnings about the "strange woman" and the "seductress." I was confident the emerging pattern I had seen in the Ten Commandments and in Paul's exhortation to Timothy would be repeated in this body of wisdom literature. To my dismay, of the 875 verses in Proverbs, only 78 dealt with sexuality or closely related topics, not even 10 percent. At this point, I realized that the first nine chapters have a different flavor than the rest of the book. Over and over in the first nine chapters, we read, "My son, if you will receive my sayings . . ." and "My son, do not forget my teachings . . ." I recounted the verses and found that of the 216 verses in chapters one through nine, 69 verses, or about

30 percent, are directly related to sexuality, much of it detailed warnings about the woman of seduction. Then it dawned on me — the first nine chapters capture the first conversations of a father with his son, in which the father is training his son and preparing him for life. Do you see that a tremendous amount of that father's conversation with his son is directed to a proper understanding of sexuality, including strong warnings about compromising purity? What a mandate for fathers as they train their sons! What a blueprint for the church!

Life in an atmosphere of sexual preoccupation and saturation is not a new phenomenon. If it doesn't manifest in daughters wearing belly-button-revealing tops or "freak dancing" in the middle schools, it will be some other manifestation. There is always a new interpretation of the old trends, but it is always the same spirit behind the trends. Our responsibility as believers is to get a revelation from God regarding the issue, to go beyond teaching our children only sexual prohibitions, and to teach them God's ways and boundaries which are set in place for our protection and our greatest blessing.

CHAPTER FOUR

NAKED AND NOT ASHAMED

"Firsts" are significant. When we look at the first time something occurs in Scripture, we find precedent-setting principles that establish a foundation of understanding which remains consistent throughout the rest of the Bible. The book of Genesis is bursting with "firsts": first man, first woman, first marriage, first sin, first moment of sexual awareness, first time shame entered the human race, first time man hid from God, first time God came looking for man, first time humans hid from each other, first time the effects of sin were evident, first time powers of darkness talked to a human, and first lie told in the human race. I believe that with those "firsts," principles were established and precedents were set that we can refer to for guidance and aid in our understanding of what God wants for us in the area of sexuality.

THE MAN AND HIS "GIRLFRIEND"?

God has talked about marriage since the very beginning. In setting a precedent for marriage, Genesis 2:25 states: *The man and his girlfriend were both naked and not ashamed.* Isn't that what God said? As long as they really love each other, that's OK isn't it? Isn't that what we believe? Let's try again. I've got another version, the *Modern Liberated North American Version* which says: The *man and the gal he was shacking up with were both naked and not ashamed.* Unfortunately, that version doesn't seem to be any better than the last one. Wait! I've got the latest *New College Revised Version: The guy and the gal he was hooking up with were both naked and not ashamed.*

THE MAN AND HIS GIRLFRIEND WERE BOTH NAKED AND NOT ASHAMED. ISN'T THAT WHAT GOD SAID?

Unfortunately, that is what too many people have come to believe.

What Scripture actually says is this: *The man and his wife were both naked and not ashamed.* The man and his *wife*. This is God's simple, but exceedingly clear blueprint for His gift of sexuality. It has to do with marriage, public commitment, and promises of safety, security, and permanence — the very things a daughter's heart was designed to have. God put this protective boundary around His gift of sexuality because He knows us better than we know ourselves and does not want us to be destroyed. His is the perfect blueprint. However, our culture desperately wants to circumvent this simple, but straightforward, protective law of God surrounding sexuality; our culture wants to change the standard. The problem is, many in our culture have adopted the modified standard, and, as a result, their lives are being destroyed.

THE FIRST ASSAULT

Now the serpent was more crafty than any beast of the field which the Lord God had made, and he said to the woman, "Indeed, has God said, 'You shall not eat from any tree of the garden'?" And the woman said to the serpent, "From the fruit of the trees of the garden we may eat, but from the fruit of the tree which is in the middle of the garden, God has said, 'You shall not eat from it or touch it, lest you die.'" The serpent said to the woman, "You surely shall not die!" (Genesis 3: 1-4)

Picture, if you will, the serpent knocking on the door of Adam and Eve's home. Satan, that slippery snake, put on his kindest face and asked in a gentle and inquiring voice, "Is the man of the house at home?" He peaked inside and saw there was no one else around. "No? Well, Eve, I'd like to talk to you for a few minutes if you don't mind." Eve can't imagine closing the door on such a nice man. He is so friendly and polite that she opens the door a little more and waits for him to continue.

Did you notice the first person the serpent ever talked to on the face of the earth was a woman? He didn't come for a visit, he came with an agenda, a scheme; he set Eve up. Adam should have answered the door and said, "Excuse me. Who are you? Sorry. We're not interested. Take a hike." But Adam was nowhere to be found. Maybe he was downstairs in the den with the sports channel blaring and the remote control nearby, or maybe he was out practicing his latest hobby. Or possibly he was present but silent, afraid to take his position of authority to confront the devil. Regardless of the reason for his absence or silence, because of Adam's abdication of responsibility, the serpent got an opportunity to talk to Eve.

Remember who the serpent is. He is Satan. He is the *father of lies* (John 8:44), *the thief* who *comes only to steal, kill and destroy* (John 10:10). The DNA of hell is to destroy. Any word Satan speaks, any scheme he creates, any activity in which he is involved is intended to destroy, steal from, and break the heart of humanity. He is our *adversary, the devil, who prowls about like a roaring lion seeking someone to devour* (1 Peter 5:8). His intent is to consume and "take out." He is not walking casually in the desert savannah; he is not passing time; he has a target and a plan, and he is actively seeking destruction.

"I want to ask you a question," Satan said to Eve. "Did God *actually* say you couldn't eat from any of the trees in the garden? He didn't really *say* that, did He?" Eve hesitated. She questioned. Do you see the *modus operandi* of the enemy? The enemy always takes our nature and design into consideration in setting his schemes against us. He was sweet and compelling to Eve, almost helpful. Slyly, he sowed a seed of doubt into the heart of a daughter who was designed by God to trust. Doubt is one of his favorite assaults against a daughter's heart. If he can plant a seed of doubt, she will not be able to fully trust the character of her Father and will not be able to fully embrace His protective boundaries. And so Eve wondered, *Did God really say that?* I frequently see young women with that same look of doubt on their faces. A young man whispers in her ear, and she wonders, *He's telling me he cares about me, and we love each other. Did God really **say** not to cross this line? If there's love, it's going to be okay, isn't it?*

HE TEMPTS DAUGHTERS, TODAY, TO GIVE UP THEIR SEXUAL PURITY FOR THE "SAKE OF A RELATIONSHIP."

Satan tempted Eve with the fruit of the tree. He tempts daughters, today, to give up their sexual purity for the "sake of a relationship." A daughter was designed for safety and security. Possibly, the greatest need in her life is to be able to trust. The enemy comes in with a question just suggestive enough that she begins to wonder if God's boundaries are really that important, especially in the face of her great need and desires. That scenario plays out every day in every nation on earth. Just a little seed of doubt is sown so that God's loving boundary around His gift of sexuality is questioned.

"He didn't *really* say that, did He?" continued the serpent.

"Oh no," Eve responded. "God didn't say that. He just said we couldn't eat from *that* tree." She pointed to the Tree of the Knowledge of Good and Evil. "God said we can't touch it or eat from it because if we do, we will die."

> EITHER WE BELIEVE GOD IS A LOVING FATHER WHO SET A LOVING BOUNDARY AROUND THE GIFT OF SEXUALITY ... OR HE IS A COSMIC KILLJOY WHO LOVES TO WITHHOLD GOOD THINGS FROM PEOPLE.

The serpent said to the woman, 'You will not die!" I can imagine Satan's tone of voice being careful, almost hesitant and full of feigned surprise. "What? You're not going to die. Come on! That tree? It's beautiful. How would you die just from eating that fruit? No! You're not gonna die. In fact, if you eat from it, you'll become like God. That's why He's keeping it to Himself." He progressed from planting a little seed of doubt in the daughter's heart to directly contradicting God's promised consequences and questioning God's character and motives. His simple, challenging question progressed to a full-blown lie. Bit by bit, Satan contradicted the consequences God laid out for violating His standard as he subtly put God's character in question. You cannot assault God's standard without assaulting His character; the two always go hand-in-hand. We have a choice to make. Either we believe God is a loving Father who set a loving boundary around the gift of sexuality because He knows us better than we know ourselves and doesn't want us to be destroyed, or He is a cosmic killjoy who loves to withhold good things from people. The choice we make will determine how we live.

The same voice that spoke to Eve speaks today. How many daughters hear that voice? I am not saying every young man is the serpent incarnate, but many young men are broken and confused. They believe physical intimacy is the source of life. We have to admit that the general tendency of a young man's heart, apart from the saving and transforming work of Christ, tends toward predatory sexual activity. As a result, daughters are subjected to that same voice, "Come on. You're not gonna die!" Of course the verbiage is more modern. It sounds more like, "It's natural. If you loved me, you'd let me. It's beautiful. We're going to get married someday, so it's fine." Those same words were spoken in the back seats of cars in the free-love generation of the 1960s, and those same words are being spoken into the ears of today's young girls, the latch-key generation, as they meet for sexual encounters in their parents' bedrooms after school. That voice whispers into the ears of daughters in every sorority, workplace, dorm, dance club, bar, school, and any place young people gather. Without the armor of truth, many young women have nothing with which to protect themselves against those words of doubt and contradiction.

SEXUAL SATISFACTION

God is not against sexual intimacy. God speaks about married sexuality in Genesis 4:1. Scripture tells us Adam "had relations with" or "knew" his wife Eve. This implies true intimacy involving body, soul, and spirit oneness. In Scripture, there is a marked contrast between intimacy in the context of marriage and sexual experience outside of God's boundaries. When God talks about sex outside of His boundaries, such as sex with animals, sexual assault, immorality, sexual violation, sex with a prostitute, and molestation, He uses this word: he "lay" with her — the physical act of sex, void of intimacy. Two different words — an eye-opening teaching all by themselves. Unfortunately, today's bankrupt culture has reduced sexuality to an act that is simply physical.

SEX WITHIN HIS DESIGNED CONTEXT IS A BLESSING TO BE ENJOYED AND NEVER RESULTS IN GUILT, REGRET, SHAME, OR EMBARRASSMENT.

The world and the culture say sex is the highest human experience; they say human worth, experience, and fulfillment are all centered on each individual's unrestrained discovery of, and participation in, their sexuality. Therefore, they lament, "That God of the Christians! He gave them a sex drive and then told them not to use it. If church people would just talk to us, we could really help them. We understand sex. We've got it all figured out, and everyone is thrilled!"

I find it extremely interesting that sexual satisfaction surveys reveal that married Christian couples report the highest level of sexual satisfaction of any group. What conclusion should we come to? Perhaps God's gift of sex, exercised within His boundaries, results in His greatest blessing. Sex within

SEXUALITY WAS HIS IDEA. HE MADE THE MAN. HE MADE THE WOMAN. HE DESIGNED OUR EMOTIONS. HE CREATED OUR BODY PARTS. HE KNOWS HOW IT ALL WORKS TOGETHER BEST.

His designed context is a blessing to be enjoyed and never results in guilt, regret, shame, or embarrassment. It also never results in sexually-transmitted infections — only unmarried or homosexual sex results in sexually-transmitted infections or STIs (previously referred to as STDs, sexually-transmitted diseases). Instead, within the confines of marriage, sex becomes an experience of true intimacy. Since God is the Creator and Designer, His blueprint is perfect. Sexuality was His idea. He made the man. He made the woman. He designed our emotions. He created our body parts. He knows how it all works together best. Those who receive the gift of sexuality and employ the "user's manual" without experimenting on their own, have the highest level of satisfaction. The commands, *You shall not commit adultery,* and *You shall not covet your neighbor's wife,* were not given to limit our pleasure but to protect us and allow us to experience His greatest blessing.

SHAME

Finally, Satan led Eve closer to the tree and pointed out how beautiful the fruit was. All her reasons for resistance now gone, Eve picked and ate

some of it. Discovering how delicious it was and realizing it didn't kill
her just as the serpent had promised, she then shared some of the fruit
with her husband Adam, and he ate it as well. Their eyes were suddenly
opened, and they realized they were naked. Embarrassed and afraid,
Adam and Eve hid themselves from God. In a single moment, their
ability to have intimacy and communicate honestly decreased. As soon as
sin entered the world, shame, and guilt became their closest companions.

SHAME PUTS PEOPLE ON A TREADMILL OF OBLIGATION AS THEY ATTEMPT TO WORK OFF THE WRONGS THEY HAVE DONE.

They hid themselves. When sin is involved, especially sexual sin,
the result is shame. That is how God protects His gift of sexuality. It is
similar to the warning light in our car that alerts us to the fact something
is wrong, and that we need to take heed. When people cross God's sexual
boundary, shame is the result. I see it in the eyes of those who sit in the
church services in which I minister. I see it in the eyes of waitresses in
restaurants and girls on the street. Shame is like a huge wall between us
and God, blocking our intimacy with Him. It alters all of our primary
relationships. It changes how we think God feels about us. It colors every
interaction we have with people because we are afraid they might know
the truth about us. It even changes how we see ourselves. Shame takes a
son or daughter of God and turns them into a slave. Shame puts people
on a treadmill of obligation as they attempt to work off the wrongs they
have done. As humans, we tend to build scales on which we measure
the good and the bad in our lives. We are forever hoping to put more on
the good side of the scale to balance out the bad — the history we are
ashamed of. God wants to smash those scales and gently put His cross in
front of us and say, "You can't do it. There's nothing you can do to earn
your way back to Me. That is why My Son Jesus came." God's design for
us is that we would live with no shame. He wants to break it off of our
lives.

I believe this is one of the reasons our culture has created the "right
to privacy." In other words, whatever two consenting adults decide to do
behind closed doors is their own business. Under the twin umbrellas of

the Declaration of Independence and the Bill of Rights, ensuring us life, liberty, and the pursuit of happiness, we have twisted our forefathers' words to justify and make provision to do things that lead to shame, things usually done in the darkness, things for which we must concoct some "right to privacy" in order to continue in those behaviors. We have said that two consenting adults can do whatever they want in the privacy of their own bedroom. However, God likes to walk right past the "two consenting adults in the privacy of their own bedroom door," bang the door open, and say, "You shall not commit adultery; you shall not covet your neighbor's wife because I love you and have a special design for you that will protect you and ensure your greatest joy."

TWO QUESTIONS

Not long after they ate the apple, God went looking for Adam and Eve. *Then the Lord God called to the man, and said to him, Where are you?* (Genesis 3:9). After they emerged from their hiding place, He looked at Eve and asked, *What is this you have done?* (Genesis 3:13). Two people, two entirely different questions.

> ### TO THE MAN HE ASKED THE "POSITION" QUESTION: "WHERE ARE YOU?" THIS WAS A LEADERSHIP QUESTION.

To the man He asked the "position" question: "Where are you?" This was a leadership question. Unfortunately, Adam answered as would the average unredeemed man of America. He said, *Lord, the **woman** whom **You** gavest to be with me, **she** gave me from the tree, and I ate* (Genesis 3:12, emphasis mine). His answer is full of excuses; he takes zero responsibility for his actions. He is slow to repent because he wants to hold on to his sense of honor. He places blame on Eve and on God — God, for giving Eve to him, and Eve, for giving the fruit to him. We often do that as men. We are slow to admit guilt, and we are slow to repent. Why can't we say, "Honey, I was wrong. Please forgive me," or in this case, "God, You are right. I was wrong. I need your forgiveness"? The world is full of men who want to be right, when actually the secret of a man's strength and his pathway to true honor is his ability to admit fault when he has failed. God wants to fill the church with men who can say they are wrong when they are wrong. A man who is willing to humble himself before God and his family and say, "I was wrong," will find that his family has all the confidence in the world in him and will much more readily follow him. If he stubbornly refuses to repent or admit he was wrong, their confidence in him and in his leadership erodes.

To the woman, God asked the relational question, "What is this you have done?"

As these questions are being asked, Adam and Eve are both hiding from God's presence. In essence, God is asking, "Daughter, what happened to our relationship? What is this distance between you and Me?" His question to her reveals that she was designed for intimacy and relationship. Relationships are an extension of who women are; women are designed to be in a relationship and to be loved. Eve, in response to God's question about their relationship, says plainly, *The serpent deceived me, and I ate* (Genesis 3:13). She admits she was deceived and believed the lie. There is a propensity for deception in the heart of a woman that is not resident in a man. This further explains God's inquiry of Adam and His demand to know where he was and why he was not in his place of leadership protecting his wife. It is an issue of "covering."

Covering has nothing to do with who is the boss; it has everything to do with protection over the spirit of a daughter. Women carry with them an extra sensitivity to spiritual things, and men were designed to be a protective covering for that sensitivity.

WOMEN ARE OFTEN WILLING TO BELIEVE A LIE IN HOPES OF HAVING THEIR DEEPEST NEEDS MET.

Eve was deceived by the serpent and believed a lie. Women are often willing to believe a lie in hopes of having their deepest needs met. That is precisely where the enemy will meet them and take advantage of them. God intends for young women's hearts to be filled by the words and attention of their fathers. If that is not the case, they will be needy, and, as a result, much more vulnerable to the lies and propositions of young men. When a young woman has an unfilled heart, and some guy says, "Hey baby, you're beautiful!" she thinks, "He likes me. He likes me!" His attention carries with it the potential of delight and fulfillment for her. She believes if she gives him what he wants, he'll stay with her. Soon she discovers he wants the most precious thing she can give, and she must gamble with her very soul to give that to him. That happens once, and "Mr. Right" becomes "Mr. Goodbye." Then another potential "Mr. Right" comes along and says, "Hey, you're something else!" She catches her breath and thinks, "Maybe, this time!" and this time, with a little less hesitancy, she takes the gamble again. Some young women end up having 40, 50, or 100 sexual partners as a result of that kind of deception.

She uses her sexual beauty and "power to attract" to secure what she hopes will be permanence and commitment. If she is not protected, she will be deceived time and time again in her search for those things.

Deception and lies are ubiquitous. They are in movies, in magazines, on billboards, and on the Internet. Their message is that a woman's primary value is sexual. And, because her value is sexual, she better cultivate it and train herself to walk a certain way, talk a certain way, stand a certain way, look a certain way, and dress a certain way or she is going to be rejected, alone and forgotten. It is our job as fathers and leaders to fill the hearts of our daughters with the love and attention they need and to proclaim God's true identity over them, thereby protecting them from giving way to the assault of lies and deception that constantly bombards them.

CHAPTER 5

THE HARLOT BRIDE

Everyone loves a bride. That is what weddings are all about. When the bride enters the room, everyone stands, craning their necks to "ooh" and "awe" at how beautiful she is. I can still feel the hand of my eldest daughter Allison on my arm as I was about to walk her down the aisle on her wedding day. As we walked into the church everyone stood and did their best to catch a glimpse, not of me, but of my daughter the bride. Most onlookers smiled. Some cried. When a woman has been honored and loved, there is something about the look on her face on her wedding day that is nearly impossible to describe. It is a unique expression of deep trust, beauty, and joy.

With six daughters, we have had lots of "bride" and "wedding" activity at our house over the years. The girls all dressed up as brides when they were little. Later, they bought bridal magazines every time we took a vacation and poured over them together, choosing their favorite gowns and floral arrangements. It is still hard for me, though, to reconcile myself to the reality of my daughters, my little girls, leaving home and getting married. I remember when their hands were barely big enough to wrap around one of my fingers as they toddled along learning how to walk. Their hearts belonged entirely to me as their dad and, of course, to their wonderful mom. I remember how their births revolutionized my life and how completely and immediately I loved them. I remember how they needed me and how they asked the cutest questions. "Moments later," my daughters' hearts were won over by young men, and they have walked out of our home and established their own homes with their husbands.

Brides are God's idea. Since human history began, one of the main messages God has been trying to communicate to us is that He is seeking a relationship with us, just as a groom seeks to find his bride. God is so intent on helping us understand His intentions toward us, that He constantly draws on metaphors to help us understand the relationship He intends to have with us. In Scripture, when God talks about Israel, His people, He likens her to a young woman responding to Him in the context of covenant and marriage. If Israel is faithful to Him, she is His bride. *For this cause a man shall leave his father and mother, and shall cleave to his wife; and the two shall become one flesh. This mystery is great; but I am speaking with reference to Christ and the church* (Ephesians 5:31-32). But if Israel, His wife, is unfaithful, she is likened to a harlot. *For a spirit of harlotry has led them astray, and they have played the harlot, departing from their God* (Hosea 4:12). In Ezekiel, He says, *you spread your legs to every passer-by to multiply your harlotry* (Ezekiel 16:25). To the casual reader, it may seem as if God is using incredibly graphic terminology and perhaps being overly dramatic about unfaithfulness. However, that is His way of expressing the seriousness of our relationship with Him and underlining how necessary and valuable our purity of devotion is to Him.

WE ARE CAUGHT IN THE MIDST OF A WAR BETWEEN THE POWERFUL TRUTH OF GOD'S DESIRE TO HAVE A RELATIONSHIP WITH US AND SATAN'S HATRED FOR EVERYTHING THAT COMES FROM THE HEART OF GOD.

If a bride symbolizes God's desired relationship with His people, imagine how the devil feels about a bride. Because Satan understands the value of this reality and the corresponding images God is using to perpetuate relationship with His people, he seeks to violate every visual and symbolic depiction of God's redemptive purposes on the earth. Therefore, Satan is opposed to a spotless bride. He goes to war against the bride, who is the face of devotion and fidelity, designed to be pursued and loved. He attempts to alter, pervert or erase every concept of purity, faithfulness, or fidelity so that our understanding of who we are and what kind of relationship God longs to have with us is obscured. We are caught in the midst of a war between the powerful truth of God's desire to have a relationship with us and Satan's hatred for everything that comes from the heart of God. We can either walk in relationship with God and impact the culture with His truth, or we will fall prey to the lies of the enemy and become increasingly confused about who we are, who God is, and what He wants to do in our lives and on this earth.

TWO MANDATES

When God gave His commandments to the people of Israel, He included two mandates to help His people understand how they were to interact with Him and with the world at large. First, there was what I call the "temple mandate." The temple mandate represented requirements connected to temple worship, including the offering of sacrifices and incense as well as observing festivals and attending gatherings. Everything that took place in the temple was intended to keep the people in relationship with God and produce the life of God in the people. Secondly, there was the "marketplace mandate," which put a demand on the life of God within His people to go into the marketplace and make a difference in the culture. The life of God birthed in His people was supposed to propel them to demonstrate that life in the marketplace in order that people outside the temple could see the reality of God.

IDENTIFY, CONFRONT, TEAR DOWN, AND DESTROY.

When Israel was departing from Egypt en route for the Promised Land, God warned them against making covenants with the inhabitants still living in the land or with their gods. God was using Israel as an instrument of judgment upon the Canaanites who were living in the land because they were worshipping false gods whose worship involved acts diametrically opposed to everything God had in His heart for humanity. God clearly states, *I will deliver the inhabitants of the land into your hand, and you will drive them out before you. You shall make no covenant with them or with their gods. They shall not live in your land, lest they make you sin against Me; for if you serve their gods, it will surely be a snare to you* (Exodus 23:31-33). Furthermore, He stated, *You shall drive out all the inhabitants of the land from before you, and destroy all their figured stones, and destroy all their molten images and demolish all their high places* (Numbers 33:52). Again God demands, *You shall utterly destroy them, the Hittite and the Amorite, the Canaanite and the Perizzite, the Hivite and the Jebusite, as the Lord your God has commanded you, in order that they may not teach you to do according to all their detestable things which they have done for their gods, so that you would sin against the Lord your God* (Deuteronomy 20:17-18). They were told to drive out and destroy the false-god worship. The prophet Jeremiah was given a similar charge. *I have appointed you this day over the nations and over the kingdoms, to pluck up and to break down, to destroy and to overthrow, to build and to plant* (Jeremiah 1:10). Later in the book of Jeremiah, it is apparent that Jeremiah lived in the midst of God's people who were steeped in false-god worship. As was Jeremiah, the people were commanded to destroy everything that led to reliance on, or devotion to another god. In other words, God continually called them to single-hearted devotion to Him.

However, the people did not obey God.

SEQUENCE OF APOSTASY

No one progresses from worshiping God one day to worshiping false gods the next day. Or, to use our analogy, no one progresses from being a beloved bride to a harlot overnight. Keith Tucci, former director of Life Coalition International, presents this important insight in his study, *Abortion is a Gospel Issue*. Israel's transition into harlotry began by merely mingling with other nations in a state of peaceful co-existence. *They did not destroy the peoples, as the Lord commanded them, but they mingled with the nations, and learned their practices, and served their idols, which became a snare to them* (Psalm 106:34-36). They mingled . . . and learned . . . and served. Their seemingly innocent mingling with the nations led

> UNCONFRONTED IDOLS EXERT INFLUENCE. THEY NOT ONLY LED GOD'S PEOPLE INTO HARLOTRY, BUT THEIR WORSHIP INVOLVED HIDEOUS DISOBEDIENCE TO THE ONE TRUE GOD.

them to learn their practices and serve their gods. Instead of fulfilling the marketplace mandate to take God into the marketplace and *influence* culture, it appears they were being influenced *by* culture. They were not willing to identify, confront, and tear down the false-god worship in the culture. Initially, it may have seemed like an inconsequential act.

No big deal. However, unconfronted idols exert influence. They not only led God's people into harlotry, but their worship involved hideous disobedience to the One True God.

WORSHIP OF FALSE GODS

Among the gods mentioned in the Old Testament were Baal and Molech (or Milcom) and their female counterparts, Asherah and Ashtoreth. They were gods of fertility, fire, and war. Since the people at the time lived in an agrarian culture, their livelihoods depended on the abundance or fertility of their crops and herds. Worship of Baal and Asherah, therefore, was part of the equation to secure their economic prosperity and welfare. The children of Israel were no strangers to those gods, and Scriptural references to them abound. King Ahab *erected an altar for Baal in the house of Baal . . . and also made the Asherah* (I Kings 16:32-3). As recorded in I Kings 18, Elijah challenged 450 prophets of Baal and 400 prophets of Asherah to a confrontation in the presence of the people on Mount Carmel. The altar of Baal and the Asherah idol were the two items God told Gideon to destroy before he could lead the people into battle, a story told in Judges 6. King Manasseh . . . *erected altars for Baal and made an Asherah . . . he built altars for all the host of heaven in the two courts of the house of the Lord* (II Kings 21:3, 5). Even King Solomon's heart was seduced away from the worship of God when he married foreign wives with foreign gods. *For it came about when Solomon was old, his wives turned his heart away after other gods; and his heart was not wholly devoted to the Lord his God, as the heart of David his father had been. For Solomon went after Ashtoreth the goddess of the Sidonians and after Milcom the detestable idol of the Ammonites* (I Kings 11: 4-5).

> THE THREE PRIMARY WAYS THOSE FALSE GODS WERE WORSHIPPED WERE THROUGH SEXUAL IMMORALITY, TEMPLE PROSTITUTION, AND CHILD SACRIFICE.

What did the worship of these false gods entail? Were they harmless statues? Why was God so adamant His people not get caught up in their worship? It was because they were not harmless statues. The three primary ways those false gods were worshipped were through sexual immorality, temple prostitution, and child sacrifice — all abominations to God in direct contradiction to His ways and His heart! (Winkey Pratney offers a more in-depth look at the worship of those false gods in his book, *Devil Take the Youngest.*)

SEXUAL IMMORALITY

In an effort to appease the gods of fertility and entreat them to release blessing on their crops and herds, the people activated and exercised their own sexuality in hope that their sexual experience would allow them to become one with the god or goddess of fertility. The people believed that in response to their offerings of human sexuality, the gods would cause their crops to be abundant, enable their herds to multiply, and generally bring economic blessing to their lives through the fertility of the land, plants, and animals.

Baal and Asherah were worshipped in groves of trees on the high places, and their worship involved gluttony, drunkenness, and sexual sin. Worshippers engaged in sexual relationships with each other and with both the male and female temple prostitutes. Asherah poles were usually placed near the altars to Baal. These poles, trees with the branches and tops cut off and then fashioned into the male sexual organ, were giant, visual, and erotic carved images that sexualized the entire environment. Scripture calls the Asherah a "horrid image" in I Kings 15:13. Over and over again, *The Message Bible* calls the false gods the "sex-and-religion gods," because the main element of their worship entailed sexual immorality. *He* (Manasseh) *rebuilt all the sex-and-religion shrines that his father Hezekiah had torn down, and he built altars and phallic images for the sex god Baal and sex goddess Asherah . . .* (II Kings 21:3 TMB).

Experiments have been conducted on people who are observing a sexual encounter through film or who are present while others engage in sexual relations. By using sensors that measure heart rate and reactions in skin, researchers recorded physical response in the observers' bodies similar to responses in those actually involved in the encounter. That explains why high places had such a powerful influence. These sex shrines were not hidden in out-of-the-way places. They permeated the culture. *For they also built for themselves high places and sacred pillars and Asherim on every high hill and beneath every luxuriant tree* (I Kings 14:23). The high places proliferated at an accelerated rate as Israel's apostasy increased. Soon high places were found not only on the hills or in the shade of tree groves, but on every street corner and in every square. *You built for yourself a shrine and made yourself a high place in every square. You built yourself a high place at the top of every street* (Ezek. 16:24-25). The fact that they were public and their worship was very observable meant that they saturated, sexualized, and eroticized the atmosphere of the culture, unrelentingly pushing sexuality to the forefront of the people's minds.

TEMPLE PROSTITUTION

The gods were also worshipped with some form of cultural invitation and expectation to participate in sexual experience. James Frazer, in his book, *The Golden Bough* (© 1922, Macmillan Co.), confirms that many females had to prostitute themselves in the temple of the most popular female gods (such as Aphrodite) before they could marry. He states the motive for the women prostituting themselves was "not as an orgy of lust, but as a solemn religious duty performed in the service of the great Mother Goddess." Frazer lists a number of cities and nations that had this custom (p. 384):

- In Cyprus, all women had to prostitute themselves to strangers in the sanctuary of Aphrodite and Astarte before they married.

- In Babylon, every woman, rich and poor, had to prostitute herself in the temples of Mylitta, Ishtar, and Astarte for money that was donated as wages to the goddess.

- In Phoenician temples, women prostituted themselves, believing that their services would appease the goddess and win her favor.

- In the ancient city of Heliopolis in Syria, there was a law that required every maiden to prostitute herself to strangers at the temple of Astarte.

THE GODS WERE ALSO WORSHIPPED WITH SOME FORM OF CULTURAL INVITATION AND EXPECTATION TO PARTICIPATE IN SEXUAL EXPERIENCE.

In a culture that worshipped these false sex-and-religion gods, there was an expectation, anticipation, and cultivation of the young women in the culture to take their turn in the temple and invite the young men of the culture to worship these gods with them. Anyone simply walking past the high places could see people, in plain view, engaged in sexual activity. Generations of sons and daughters grew up under the deliberate creation of an atmosphere of sexual promiscuity. All of this spoke a message of expectation and cultivation, "Come on. You're going to get involved in this. This is our culture and way of life. This is your life, your future!" God warned His people and commanded, *None of the daughters of Israel shall be a cult prostitute, nor shall any of the sons of Israel be a cult prostitute* (Deuteronomy 23:17). Despite the warnings and prohibitions from God through the prophets, the people disobeyed.

CHILD SACRIFICE

The gods were also worshipped with child sacrifice. The altar of Molech represented the female womb. The sacrificed child was placed in the cavity of the idol, which had been heated up with fire, and pounding drums drowned out the child's screams as the young child burned on the altar. It was a practice abhorrent to God. *And they built the high places of Baal that are in the valley of Ben-hinnom to cause their sons and their daughters to pass through the fire to Molech, which I had not commanded*

> INSTEAD OF CONFRONTING, TEARING DOWN, AND DESTROYING THE HORRENDOUSLY EVIL WORSHIP OF THESE FALSE GODS AS GOD COMMANDED, ISRAEL CHOSE TO PEACEFULLY CO-EXIST — THEIR ANCIENT VERSION OF OUR MODERN-DAY SPIRIT OF TOLERANCE.

them nor had it entered My mind that they should do this abomination, to cause Judah to sin (Jeremiah 32:35). Instead of confronting, tearing down, and destroying the horrendously evil worship of these false gods as God commanded, Israel chose to peacefully co-exist — their ancient version of our modern-day spirit of tolerance. As a result, Israel learned the foreign

practices, worshipped their false gods, and even sacrificed their own
children to the idols. The horrific practice demonstrated how far God's
people had gone in apostasy and harlotry. Their ancestors were the ones
whom God miraculously delivered from slavery in Egypt, who saw the
parting of the Red Sea, who received the manna in the wilderness, whose
sandals lasted throughout their 40-year journey, and who experienced
the presence of the Living God with them daily in the pillar of fire by
night and the cloud by day. It is shocking to see that *only one generation
later* they had abandoned the One True God and were sacrificing their
own children to false gods! Their immorality and child sacrifice were such
an abomination to God, that, as we will see later, they provoked God's
judgment on their nation.

THE INFLUENCE PRINCIPLE

Unexposed, unaddressed demonic strongholds exert tremendous power. If
you don't proactively influence the culture, the culture will influence you.
Ephesians says, *Do not participate in the unfruitful deeds of darkness, but
instead even expose them* (Ephesians 5:11). The worship of other gods was
diametrically opposed to the worship of God. The way those nations served
their gods was by *every abominable act which the Lord hates* (Deuteronomy

IF YOU DON'T PROACTIVELY
INFLUENCE THE CULTURE, THE
CULTURE WILL INFLUENCE YOU.

12:31). That is why God made His command so clear. *You shall utterly
destroy all the places where the nations whom you shall dispossess serve their
gods, on the high mountains and on the hills and under every green tree. And
you shall tear down their altars, and smash their sacred pillars, and burn their
Asherim with fire, and you shall cut down the engraved images of their gods,
and you shall obliterate their name from that place* (Deuteronomy 12:2-3).
The posture God wanted His bride to take was that of actively identifying,
confronting, tearing down, and destroying the false-god system. He used
vivid action words to describe what they were to do: Utterly destroy!
Dispossess! Tear down! Smash! Burn! Cut down! Obliterate! No allowance
was made for passive co-existence with those gods.

THE SEXUALIZED CULTURES
OF THE NEW TESTAMENT

High places, sacrifices, and the worship of false gods weren't simply primitive, barbaric practices that faded quietly into the pages of the Old Testament never to resurface in more modern, sophisticated societies. In the book of Acts, we read about the sex-saturated, sensual, body-conscious Greek and Roman world with which the early church had to contend. Once again, we find the same elements of sexual immorality, temple prostitution, and child sacrifice committed as acts of worship to false gods. Prostitution flourished in Rome, and celebrations of the male and female sexual organs were common. Corinth had such a reputation

> HIGH PLACES, SACRIFICES, AND
> THE WORSHIP OF FALSE GODS
> WEREN'T SIMPLY PRIMITIVE, BARBARIC
> PRACTICES THAT FADED QUIETLY INTO
> THE PAGES OF THE OLD TESTAMENT,
> NEVER TO RESURFACE IN MORE
> MODERN, SOPHISTICATED SOCIETIES.

for homosexuality that references linking the two continue to be used in literature today. Corinth was given to drunkenness and orgies, and temple prostitutes serviced the sailors as they arrived in port. There were 1000 temple prostitutes in Corinth and 1000 in Ephesus. The most overtly sexual Greek god was Dionysus, the god of passion and sensuality. His Roman counterpart was Bacchus, and his worshippers participated in wild orgies in his honor. The decorations on Greek pottery have left us with what amounts to a visual history of what life was like. Much of it is highly sexual in content. Satyrs and nymphs prance naked under the olive trees, while young men and women engage in bathing, dancing, and sexual activity. John Clarke, in his book, *Roman Sex: 100 BC-AD 250*, gives us insight into the highly sexualized atmosphere in which the New Testament church lived.

> In the town of Pompeii, thoughtfully left to
> us damaged but intact by the fury of a nearby
> volcano, we find visual evidence of Roman

sexuality everywhere. Upper class Roman houses
are filled with frescos and artwork depicting people
unabashedly engaged in sexual theatrics. Gardens
are filled with statues of fertility gods with giant
phalluses. Lower-class taverns and bordellos possess
their own distinct and frank explorations of Romans
sexuality. Everywhere in town, talismans and
amulets of phalluses are erected to ward off evil
spirits. The ubiquitous nature of sexuality shocked
the archaeologists who first discovered it. How could
Romans be so frank about sex, leaving these obscene
items around where even children could see them?
How could Roman women be so forthright about
enjoying sex? And most disturbing of all, how could
Romans engage in same-sex or group-sex activities?

As the Romans were a religious people, many came
to see sexual ecstasy as a gift from Venus and Cupid,
or cultic deities like Dionysus. Who could begrudge
the gods their influence? The idea that phalluses
and displays of fertility gods could ward off evil
spirits also reached its height. Every street corner
and doorway seems to have had a representation of a
[male sexual organ.]

Child sacrifice was practiced in the New Testament era through child
abandonment. Especially in cases where children were conceived through
temple prostitution or were simply unwanted, the practice was to leave
them abandoned outside the city walls. Left exposed to the elements, the
babies died, and often, animals fed on them. The early church, however,
because of their ethic to protect and honor life, rescued, adopted, and raised
the children as their own.

Challenge to New Testament Believers

The New Testament believers had to be confronted and reminded about
what their attitudes and posture should be toward the false gods and the

resultant rampant sexuality. The book of Acts says that when Paul, one of the fathers of the New Testament church, visited Athens, *his spirit was provoked within him because the city was full of idols* (Acts 17:16). Archeological digs have unearthed little idols of the goddess Artemis (also called Diana). She appears as a mother figure, and between her neck and her waist are hundreds of breasts, embodying the blending of the maternal spirit of nurture with the sexual, sensual nature of the female. She was worshipped by prostitution, as were many of the ancient gods.

The New Testament records a confrontation between Paul and the worshippers of Artemis:

> *About that time there arose no small disturbance concerning the Way. For a man named Demetrius, a silversmith, who made silver shrines of Artemis, was bringing no little business to the craftsmen; these he gathered together with the workmen of similar trades, and said, "Men, you know that our prosperity depends upon this business. And you see and hear that not only in Ephesus, but in almost all of Asia, this Paul has persuaded and turned away a considerable number of people, saying that gods made with hands are no gods at all. Not only is there danger that this trade of ours fall into disrepute, but also that the temple of the great goddess Artemis be regarded as worthless and that she whom all of Asia and the world worship should even be dethroned from her magnificence* (Acts 19:23-27).

Paul's posture toward those gods was to identify, confront, tear down, and destroy them and their influence. As Paul worked to establish the early Christian church, his message was *not*, "Come to Jesus. We won't talk about the false gods you're involved with or the consequences of worshiping those false gods. Above all, we are committed to making sure you feel comfortable."

However, that so often *is* the message and posture of the 21st-century church. When someone enters the Kingdom of God and begins to worship the One True God, we need to address what the worship and practices of the false gods meant in their life. The blood of Christ needs to be allowed to reach into the very depths of where

IN ORDER TO BRING HEALING AND RESTORATION TO A GENERATION, WE NEED TO LOVE BELIEVERS ENOUGH TO TALK ABOUT SEXUAL SELF-IDENTITY AND THE IMPACT THAT WORSHIPING THOSE FALSE GODS HAS HAD ON THEIR LIVES.

their sin has taken them. In order to bring healing and restoration to a generation, we need to love believers enough to talk about sexual self-identity and the impact that worshiping those false gods has had on their lives.

At the same time Paul lifted up Jesus, he confronted those false gods and addressed their influence. I love to imagine Paul preaching to the early church, to daughters who used to be temple prostitutes and to young men who visited those daughters and exploited them. As Paul preached, they heard about godly sexuality for the first time in their lives. Look at the New Testament and read what Paul wrote to the churches. To Timothy, he said, *Now flee from youthful lusts, and pursue righteousness, faith, love, and peace, with those who call on the Lord from a pure heart* (II Timothy 2:22). He preached that if you sin sexually, you sin against your own body. *Do you not know that your bodies are members of Christ? Shall I then take away the members of Christ and make them members of a harlot? May it never be! Or do you not know that the one who joins himself to a harlot is one body with her? For He says, "The two will become one flesh." But the one who joins himself to the Lord is one spirit with Him. Flee immorality. Every other sin that a man commits is outside the body, but the immoral man sins against his own body. Or do you not know that your body is a temple of the Holy Spirit who is in you, whom you have from God, and that you are not your own? For you have been bought with a price: therefore glorify God in your body* (I Corinthians 6:15-20). Talk about sexuality was an integral part of instruction to new believers.

PAUL TALKED ABOUT ISSUES THAT NEEDED TO BE ADDRESSED IN ORDER TO DISCIPLE THE CHURCH INTO MATURITY.

Paul talked about issues that needed to be addressed in order to disciple the church into maturity. He didn't ignore where they had come from but aggressively postured himself against false gods, tearing down what was false and lifting up what was true regardless of what it might cost him. When Paul dealt with the darkness and spoke against Artemis, people in the community became enraged and in the ensuing riot, they yelled and shouted in defense of their god for two whole hours. And we think *we* have long worship services!

SIGNS OF A NEW TESTAMENT BELIEVER

The New Testament book of Acts records a council of early church leaders which was convened to determine what was required of non-Jews when they came to faith in Jesus. More and more people were becoming believers every day, and they did not all come out of Judaism. In fact, many came straight out of the culture of Artemis-worship. Some had been temple prostitutes. Others were young men who visited the temple prostitutes to worship Artemis. Some leaders wanted to make the new converts adhere to Jewish traditions so they would look and act like the Jewish Christians. Others disagreed. The debate raged. "What," they argued, "should Christianity look like for these people?" The council came to an agreement; the message the council circulated to the churches concerning the non-negotiable essentials involved in conversion to Christ was, *Abstain from things sacrificed to idols and from blood and from things strangled and from fornication; if you keep yourselves free from such things, you will do well* (Acts 15:29). Here is how Bob Deffinbaugh explains these prohibitions. ". . . they lifted the obligation of non-Jewish converts to keep the Jewish laws, and imposed on them only the universal laws that God had established from the beginning in Genesis" (The Great Debates: Acts 15: 1-41, www.bible.org). In other words, they freed them from keeping the Jewish law but told them to keep four prohibitions because they were universally binding on all men since the time of creation.

What were the four prohibitions?

- Abstain from things dedicated to idols. In other words, step back from things associated with this spirit of idolatry. Whatever is associated with it, discern it, and step back from it. Withdraw. Don't be involved in things that are dedicated to that spirit. In order to separate yourself from the false-god system of worship, you have to identify it. You have to be able to say, "Here is what I was involved in. Here are the consequences. Here is the damage done, and here are the lies perpetrated by the system."

- Abstain from blood . . . for *the life of the flesh is in the blood* (Leviticus 17:11).

- Abstain from things strangled. This is similar to the prior prohibition because strangled meat is un-bled.

- Abstain from sexual immorality. In other words, walk and live in moral purity.

IT AMAZES ME THAT THE CHURCH FATHERS DECIDED THE SIGNATURE OF THE NEW TESTAMENT SAINTS WAS SEXUAL PURITY AND WITHDRAWAL FROM ANYTHING ASSOCIATED WITH THE DEMONIC SYSTEM OF WORSHIP.

That's what Christianity looks like. Welcome to the Kingdom of God! How's that for a paradigm of salvation? It amazes me that the church fathers decided the signature of the New Testament saints was sexual purity and withdrawal from anything associated with the demonic system of worship. That's it. There isn't any other list of "do's" and "don'ts."

CONCLUSION

When Old Testament Israel failed to confront and destroy the false-god systems of worship, they forsook their treasured status as God's bride and became like harlots, living lives of immorality and sacrificing their children to the demons. New Testament believers were also called to contend with the worship of the sex-and-religion gods. The Apostle Paul was not afraid to confront false-god worship—identifying the false gods and lifting up the One True God — thereby fulfilling both the temple mandate and the marketplace mandate of the church. Worship of the True God is evidenced by a departure from anything to do with the worship of the false gods and is marked by a lifestyle of moral purity. As we look further, we will see that all of these elements — true devotion to God, moral purity, and confrontation of idol worship — are necessary for national revival to be realized.

Chapter Six

We're not Guilty, Are We?

I can already hear voices of protest saying, "Thank you for that interesting history lesson, Jim, but things have changed. We do not have altars of Baal or Asherah poles in our cities. We do not have temple prostitutes, and most assuredly there is no way such a tragedy as child sacrifice could go on in this day and age without a massive public outcry. Things have changed. What does any of this have to do with us, especially in the church?"

True, things have changed, but not as much as we would like to imagine. I picture the older generation looking at the younger generation with a sense of consternation, pacing back and forth, both hands on their heads, pushing their hair back and moaning, "I can't believe it. There are so many belly buttons everywhere we look! So many belly buttons and so much sexuality with the young people! It's gotten so bad. It's never been like this before. What are we going to do?"

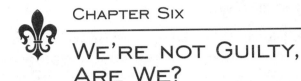

IN EVERY AGE, GOD'S PEOPLE HAVE FACED A FALSE-GOD SPIRIT THAT WAS WORSHIPPED WITH SEXUAL IMMORALITY, A FORM OF TEMPLE PROSTITUTION, AND CHILD SACRIFICE.

The truth is, it has always been so. In fact, I propose to you that the same spirits that demanded worship by sexual promiscuity, prostitution, and child sacrifice during the Old and New Testament eras are still at work today in the cultures of the earth. Yes, even in our enlightened, educated, refined, and highly evolved North American society, the worship of the false gods of sexuality continues to thrive. In every age, God's people have faced a false-god spirit that was worshipped with sexual immorality, a form of temple prostitution, and child sacrifice.

Pastor Jeffrey Johnson, in his study on The Song of Solomon, tells a similar version of the following story to drive this point home: Imagine being on vacation, and as you come out of your hotel, a man walks past you, limping. His left leg is gone below the knee. You don't want to be rude. You do not stare and do not ask what happened to him. Then you notice that the bellhop pushing the luggage cart is missing an arm. *Strange*, you think to yourself, but you carry on. As you go throughout your day, you cannot help but notice that everyone you encounter has an injury of some sort. It could be something as small as a scar on the guy who skated past you or as horrible as the poor man on a cart with no arms and legs. You find you can no longer contain yourself, so you begin to ask, "What happened to your arm?" or "Where did you get that scar?" but people look away and still do not answer. The man on the cart with no arms or legs looks at you like you are crazy, as if there is nothing abnormal about his condition whatsoever.

Finally, in a coffee shop, you encounter someone who is willing to talk. "There's been an epidemic of alligator attacks," they say. "We do not know how to stop it. We are just happy we have survived and that our injuries are minimal."

"Why don't you post warning signs, or say something about it?" you ask. "This is dangerous! Almost everyone is maimed or injured!"

Your informant looks away nervously, "It is embarrassing to us. We do not want to scare tourists away. Besides, in our culture, it isn't socially acceptable to discuss alligator attacks."

That is largely how we have reacted in our culture, even in the church culture, to the worship of the sex-and-religion gods, as *The Message Bible* calls them. People are being ravaged by pain, shame, confusion, guilt, disease, fear, and regret because of sexual immorality, but there is no place to talk about it, and few are willing to discuss the matter. I have faced this attitude many times in my travels. A couple of years ago, on an overseas ministry trip, I was invited to speak at a church. I arrived with very little time to spare before the service, and the moment I walked through the door, the pastor and his leadership team ushered me into a room off of the church sanctuary. I was told I should consider it a privilege to be preaching in one of the greatest churches in that entire country. Then they asked if I would tell them the topic of my message. Since they had invited me, I was a little surprised they did not already know, but, through the interpreter, I explained I would be preaching from Genesis about Adam and Eve and dealing with sexuality, purity, fathers, and the heart of a daughter. The ministers began to shake their heads. "No, no, no. This is not good. You cannot talk about that. You need to preach on something more encouraging like . . . evangelism." I shook my head in disbelief. Hadn't they seen the things I had just seen in their city? I had just come from the mall where the young women were seductively dressed and were hanging all over the young men. We had just driven through the city where, in the central square, we had seen multiple posters of nearly-naked women hanging the length of ten-and-fifteen-story apartment buildings to advertise a clothing line.

It was as if the pastors and leaders believed their congregation members and young people were immune to the rampant sexuality in the culture, along with the prevalent, blatant invitation to worship the false gods of sexuality. Or, possibly, the pastors and leaders had been so influenced by the culture themselves that they didn't even *see* the problem.

Unfortunately, that is the posture of much of the church worldwide.

SAME OLD STORY ALL OVER AGAIN

There is a measure of pride that tends to overtake us as we examine the mistakes of our predecessors. We imagine we could never fall prey to the same delusions. For some reason, it is really easy to distance ourselves from events that have happened in the past. On the other hand, it often becomes difficult to accurately identify and deal with major present-day issues simply because we are profoundly caught up in them ourselves.

IT APPEARS THE ONLY SOCIAL
GUIDELINES SURROUNDING SEXUALITY
AND RELATIONSHIPS TODAY ARE
THAT THERE SHOULD BE NO LAWS,
LIMITS, OR JUDGMENTS PLACED ON
SEXUALITY AND SEXUAL EXPRESSION.

I propose that the same elements of sexual immorality that existed
in the Old and New Testament worship of false gods exist today. Look
around. They are prevalent everywhere. It would take several chapters
to describe how far our culture has wandered from God's original
command stating, *You shall not commit adultery* (Exodus 20:14) and from
the New Testament warning where Jesus upped the ante and informed
His followers that not only was the act of adultery wrong, but that . . .
*every*one *who looks on a woman to lust for her has committed adultery
with her already in his heart* (Matthew 5:28). Sometimes, I scan tabloid
headlines or channel surf through daytime television talk shows to get a
pulse on the culture. I am shocked at how shameless people have become.
They brag about how many sex partners they have had; they boast about
sexual encounters. The more bizarre the encounter, the prouder they
seem. Certain groups of people consensually switch spouses for sexual
entertainment. "Hooking up" no longer means "making sure we meet
up later." It now means a casual sexual encounter void of any promise of
future relational connection or expectation. Blatant violations of God's
standards of sexuality are happening everywhere — in bars, junior-high
and high-school campuses, college campuses, and workplaces. It appears
the only social guidelines surrounding sexuality and relationships today
are that there should be no laws, limits, or judgments placed on sexuality
and sexual expression. It reminds me of Paul's letter to the Corinthians in
which he states, *It is actually reported that there is immorality among you,
and immorality of such a kind as does not exist even among the Gentiles, that
someone has his father's wife. And you have become arrogant and have not
mourned . . .*

(I Corinthians 5:1-2). That same statement could be spoken today!
Our culture has wandered far from God's intentions for sexuality and far
from mourning. We are often as guilty as the culture.

WHETHER WE REALIZE IT OR NOT, WE HAVE BECOME ACCUSTOMED TO IMAGES OF PEOPLE ENGAGED IN SEXUALLY PROVOCATIVE BEHAVIOR.

What if I were to assert that temple prostitution continues to exist? I realize there do not appear to be any temples set aside for Baal, Asherah, or Diana worship, but what is a "temple?" Aren't temples simply places dedicated to the worship of a person or an idea? Think. Are there institutions, realms of influence, sites or organizations dedicated to promoting a god of sexuality? Yes, there are. Besides the obvious example of Planned Parenthood, take a look at what is being shown in the movie theatres, on the Internet, on television, and in magazines. Observe the sports and entertainment world, the publishing industry, the cosmetic and fashion industry, and popular literature. Listen to what is being taught in sex-education classes in the public schools. Listen to the lyrics of songs and the accompanying music videos marketed to young teens. All are "temples" of thought and ideology, and we have been sucked into their alluring traps. In the same way the Old Testament temple prostitutes invited young men to worship with them, and in the same way the high places publicly displayed sexual activity for all to see, modern-day temples reinforce a cultivation, expectation, and invitation for others to join in, sexualizing and eroticizing the entire atmosphere of our culture. Everywhere we look, we are faced with images of sexuality and the ideology of immorality. Whether we realize it or not, we have become accustomed to images of people engaged in sexually provocative behavior. It is all around us, whether we are driving down the highway past a billboard, checking our email, watching a sports program, or reading a magazine. The invitation to worship the god of sexuality is constantly extended to us. It is an unavoidable reality; the temple worship of the sex-gods is prevalent here and now.

ABORTION IS THE NECESSARY END OF THE CONVEYOR BELT IN A SOCIETY THAT WORSHIPS SEX.

It is obvious that abortion clinics are the modern-day places in which we sacrifice the lives of our children to the gods of sexuality.

Abortion is the necessary end of the conveyor belt in a society that worships sex. There has to be some way to get rid of the unwanted result of sexual activity. Scripture states . . . *children are a gift of the Lord, the fruit of the womb is a reward* (Psalm 127:3). Yet the primary message in the culture is that children are a major financial consideration, a burden or a liability, or a conditional blessing provided you only have very few. Our culture is not a child-friendly atmosphere when you consider that 95-98 percent of the reasons young couples list for having an abortion are comfort, ease, convenience, material security, and reputation. When a woman becomes pregnant, whether she is a 15-year-old who risks losing her boyfriend or popularity amongst her peers; a 35-year-old office manager who is carrying the child of a co-worker rather than that of her own husband; or a young woman in a happy marriage who has plans, a degree to earn, a house to buy, trips to take, or a lifestyle she wants to maintain, the advent of a child can be a major threat to the uninterrupted maintenance of her comfort, ease, convenience, material security, and reputation. The gods of sexual immorality are worshipped when the acceptable and reasonable solution offered to the difficulties of an ill-timed child is termination of that child's life.

As a father of eight children, I have encountered this spirit many times, sometimes in the form of stares or snide remarks, and other times in the face of startling opposition. One summer, Lisa and I packed our kids and all our suitcases into our 15-passenger van and headed out on the highway to spend some time on the Oregon coast for our vacation. We were having a great time talking and driving when suddenly I heard yelling and saw a commotion in the lane beside me. A young man drove up beside us while the woman he was with hung her hand out the window waving a used condom and yelling at us. I guess we offended them with our numbers, and they were insinuating that our children were the result of our irresponsibility.

We can't escape the fact that we live in a society that wants every limit and boundary around sexuality removed, that spends its time and energy promoting and pushing its sexual license on others, and then attempts to remove any long-term consequences by sacrificing children conceived in the worship of the false god of sexuality. Sound familiar? Little has changed. The same spirit of sexual immorality, the same collective cultivation and expectation to participate in temple worship, and the same child-sacrifice thrive in our modern North American

THE VERY SAME GODS WHO DESTROYED THE ISRAELITES ARE WORSHIPPED IN OUR CULTURE AND THE CULTURES OF THE EARTH TODAY.

society (and in the societies of the earth) as they did in ancient times. The very same gods who destroyed the Israelites are worshipped in our culture and the cultures of the earth today.

BACK TO THE UNCOMFORTABLE CALL TO IDENTIFY AND CONFRONT

Unfortunately, all too often we have the same mentality Israel did. We do not want to do that uncomfortable "identify-and-confront-thing." Remember that Israel mingled with the nations and chose peaceful co-existence with them by their choice not to confront the false gods of the day. In doing so, they worshipped the god of tolerance in the name of peace. Perhaps we reason (as they might have), "Lord, we

IF YOU MINGLE WITH THE NATIONS, YOU LEARN THEIR PRACTICES AND EVENTUALLY SERVE THEIR IDOLS.

have a plan. If we worship You extra hard, maybe it will make up for our unwillingness to identify, confront, tear down, and destroy false gods. If we sing louder, dance a hole in the rug, etc. . . . then God, You will be so pleased, You will forget what we have *not* done and just pay attention to what we *have* done." However, just as Israel and the New Testament believers discovered, co-existence with false gods never remains neutral. It did not then, and it will not now. Eventually, one side or the other is influenced. If you mingle with the nations, you learn their practices, and eventually serve their idols. You worship the very gods you are supposed to identify, confront, tear down, and destroy.

Was it a coincidence that Gideon's first assignment, before he was given specific strategies to rout the Midianites, was to tear down Baal's altar in front of his father's house? Before victory over any enemy army, God's people had to deal with the adversary within. Just after taking the city of Jericho, a major victory, the army of Israel lost men in a minor skirmish because Achan disobeyed the command of God and took spoils for himself and hid them under his tent. God told Israel, *There are things under the ban in your midst, O Israel. You cannot stand before your enemies until you have removed the things under the ban from your midst* (Joshua 7:13). There has to be purity within before we can do battle without.

God expressed his frustration through the prophet Isaiah when He saw worship being performed by rote and without follow-through. If we are not in the marketplace doing what God has asked us to do as part of His church, all the dancing and sacrifices we make in worship do not impress God. *I have had enough of burnt offerings of rams and the fat of fed cattle. And I take no pleasure in the blood of bulls, lambs, or goats . . . Bring your worthless offerings no longer, their incense is an abomination to me . . . I cannot endure iniquity and the solemn assembly. I hate your new moon festivals and your appointed feasts. They have become a burden to me* (Isaiah 1:11, 13-14). Essentially, God is saying, "Every time you fulfill the church (temple) mandate, even though I told you to do it, I want to vomit because it never translates into reality in your personal life or in the marketplace. You never deal with your own impurity. You never deal with the widow and the orphan. You never deal with the issue of innocent blood and other justice issues." In the book of Isaiah, He says judgment will come . . . *Because this people draw near with their words and honor Me with their lip service, but they remove their hearts far from Me, and their reverence for Me consists of tradition learned by rote . . .* (Isaiah 29:13). God saw that while the Israelites went through the motions of worship in the temple, they omitted true devotion and failed to aggressively identify, confront, and destroy the false religious systems which threatened to permeate their own beliefs and practices.

Therefore, just as God gave the temple and marketplace mandates to the people of Israel in the Old Testament and the early Church in the New Testament to help guard and guide them in the culture, we, too, have been given the same mandates to guard and guide us. The temple mandate is our life in the church. We pray. We worship. We read the Scripture. We go to Bible studies, Bible school, Sunday school, small groups, conferences, and seminars. We read books. We are filled with the Holy Spirit, knowledge, and wisdom. We are given spiritual gifts. Our minds are renewed, and we are changed from glory to glory. However, God does not want us to stop there. After all that, the marketplace mandate comes into play. We offer our bodies as living sacrifices to God so His life in us can be extended into the culture. We enter into the marketplace and learn what it means to be the church outside of the four walls of the church building, confronting structures of evil that oppress and destroy people. Our job is to seek justice, find out what is breaking the heart of God, find the fingerprints of hell in the culture, and do something about those things.

COMPROMISE, THE CHRISTIAN, AND THE CULTURE

God was not interested in compromise then, and He is not now. The mandate to worship God in the temple and the marketplace are of equal importance. Together they characterize the true worship of God. God has mandated us to identify, confront, tear down, and destroy the false gods. In order to do this we need to identify the systems of false-god worship that have worked destruction in our lives and the lives of so many others, and then distance ourselves from whatever contributes to them and propagates them. Either we are changing and pushing out darkness through the enabling power of the Holy Spirit, or the darkness is exerting influence on us.

IT IS SHOCKING TO ME THAT THERE ARE SO FEW PEOPLE WHO ARE WILLING TO HONESTLY ADDRESS THIS ISSUE.

I have prayed with former Russian prostitutes. I sat in a room in Nepal and listened as young girls told stories of how they had been tricked and sold into lives of sexual slavery. I regularly teach in discipleship schools and pray with young women scarred by negative sexual experiences. Meeting after meeting, I talk with people, young and old, who are completely broken because of sexual sin. I have seen and heard firsthand, in country after country, how twisted and broken God's gift of sexuality can become. It is shocking to me that there are so few people who are willing to honestly address this issue. As with the alligator analogy at the beginning of this chapter, it appears we prefer to act as though the enemy is not wreaking havoc in the lives of so many people.

NO ONE BRINGS UP THE FACT THAT WE HAVE ALL BEEN TRAPPED IN A CULTURE-WIDE SNARE ROOTED IN WORSHIP TO FALSE GODS.

If it were possible for the church to maintain its integrity inside its four walls without confronting what is going on outside in the culture, our problems might not appear too great. However, that is not reality. Idol worship is not only affecting those outside the church, it is significantly affecting those inside as well. Men in the church are hooked on pornography. New couples coming through the doors of the church are living together. Girls in youth group are sleeping with their boyfriends. Young couples are sexually involved before marriage. When people come through the doors of the church, they drag their idols with them. But so often, instead of helping the new believers identify and confront the false-god worship in their lives, we say nothing. Maybe we don't recognize it. Maybe those idols are active in our lives, also. The church world is full of singles groups that have become a place to find potential dates. Many of the women dress seductively and have seductive spirits. Many of the men are predators, not protectors. The truth is, oftentimes the church does not look much different than the rest of the culture. No one brings up the fact that we have all been trapped in a culture-wide snare rooted in worship to false gods.

The repetition of such behavior from the Old Testament through today clearly demonstrates an intrinsic tendency for God's people to prefer to obey His temple mandate while ignoring the marketplace mandate. This is not what Jesus died for. Jesus is after a bride who has a revelation of pure fidelity to Him. He is calling for a bride who boldly declares, "I don't want to see how long I can be exposed to darkness without being completely saturated. I don't care what the culture is doing. I want to be free from the effects of this idol worship in my own life. I choose to flee youthful lusts and run in the opposite direction." Think about Joseph. He ran from that broken-hearted daughter, Potiphar's wife. *She said, "Lie with me"* (Genesis 39:7). She came to him every day repeating her invitation. It got to the point where Joseph couldn't . . . *listen to her . . . or be with her* (Genesis 39:10). He refused to even associate with her. He rejected her advances and was unjustly accused of sexual assault in the process, but he was willing to pay a price for walking in moral purity. The declaration he makes to the seductress calls to us today to do the same. *How then could I do this great evil, and sin against God?* (Genesis 39:9)

SHAME MANAGEMENT RELOCATION PROGRAM

We need to start talking to a generation about sexuality instead of dancing around the issue and pretending nobody in the church has been affected by it. When we do that, hope comes and things change. When we deal with the issue in the church, we then have a message for the culture. We are called to have powerful, honest, life-changing stories of redemption and restoration proclaimed from a restored generation to their lost and broken peers. However, all too often, shame tends to silence our testimonies and nullify the work of the cross and the blood of Jesus

> **WE NEED TO START TALKING TO A GENERATION ABOUT SEXUALITY INSTEAD OF DANCING AROUND THE ISSUE AND PRETENDING NOBODY IN THE CHURCH HAS BEEN AFFECTED BY IT.**

in our lives. Instead of sharing testimonies of what God has done in our lives, we tend to offer shame-filled attempts to reach a lost generation in the form of an invitation to a church meeting. To coin a phrase, I call this the "Shame Management Relocation Program." I am not discounting the practice of inviting people to church or a special meeting where they will possibly experience a divine encounter with the One who created them.

However, shame often causes us to substitute an invitation to church for our testimony. Let me give you an example of this. When we encounter daughters of a broken generation, we often invite them to change the location of their shame management practices instead of offering them release from their shame. Our dialogue might sound like this, "Hi! God has changed my life, and I invite you to come to church and join me in managing your shame. We can give you a closet just like mine. You can paint the door white, put ribbons and flowers on the front, and put everything you don't want anyone else to know about inside of it. We even have pink padlocks with which you can secure the door. We can also give you special scales on which you can balance the shame of your past with the good deeds you will now do. That will make up for the things of your past that never seem to go away. Come to church with me and manage your shame like I do. No one will ever have to know anything about your sordid past."

FREED ONES CAN RELEASE THEIR TESTIMONY BY DECLARING, "I KNOW THE WAY OUT OF HELL."

I don't believe young women in bars, raves, sororities, dorms, high schools, or junior highs want or need an invitation to manage their shame elsewhere. They are already working hard to manage and deal with their shame outside of the church. What they need is someone who can give them hope to be released from their sin and shame. That hope comes from those who have been set free themselves. Freed ones can release their testimony by declaring, "I know the way out of hell. Let me tell you how I felt when I realized I was being used and lied to by the young man I gave myself to. Let me tell you my story about what it is like to have your dreams stolen away. Let me tell you about my guilt and loneliness, about the torment of losing my purity and feeling as though I can never get back what I lost, and about tormenting memories from negative, unfulfilling sexual experiences. Let me tell you how it felt to stay in a sex-centered relationship with someone I knew didn't care about me just because I was afraid to be alone. Oh, let me also tell you about the God of Restoration who forgave all my sins and broke the power of my shame. He is the one who gave me the chance to be restored." That kind of testimony has the potential to profoundly alter our attempts to reach a generation for God. The key to those types of testimonies is the breaking of shame off those currently bound by it, for a daughter will never reveal her past brokenness to someone else if shame is not broken off of her own life first. She will not want to reveal her past to anyone, especially to young men who are potential husbands.

The good news is that I am seeing God bring restoration to a generation trapped in shame. God is setting young people free from the shame of their sexual pasts. Instead of feeling marked forever by their sinful, sexual history, young men and women are now being freed to talk about their former lives in a redemptive manner. It is as if they are speaking about another person. In fact, it *is* the "old man" they are speaking about. *Therefore, if any man is in Christ, he is a new creature; the old things have passed away; behold, new things have come* (I Corinthians 5:17).

Freed and restored young men can declare to their generation, "Let me tell you what it feels like to have self respect for the first time in my life. God has shown me what true manhood is all about. I've learned how to honor the women in my life instead of take advantage of them. I'm not trapped by pornography anymore. Let me tell you how I've been changed."

Freed and restored daughters can stand up and say, "I know the way out of hell. Let me show you. Immorality was destroying my life. I have now found a place of healing and restoration. Let me tell you how I've been changed." When the church is willing to deal with the reality and consequences of the worship of the sex-gods in its own midst, it will then be positioned to be a voice and an influence in the culture.

CHAPTER SEVEN

LESSONS FROM THE OBITUARIES

Reading the obituary section of the newspaper can be interesting. It is amazing how much you can learn about a person's life from only a few sentences. First and last names give clues to ethnicity. Notes about how they died, how long they lived, lifetime achievements, hobbies and interests, surviving relatives, the tone or absence of attached messages from family members — every aspect of the obituary is an indication of the nature of the life lived by that individual. I find such brief encapsulations strange, even anticlimactic ends to someone's existence and one's life experience. I know people who regularly read the obituaries. To some it might sound like a morbid fascination, but to others it is a way of reconciling themselves to life and death and a way of participating in, and honoring every piece of human history. It can also be a way to learn about what matters most in life.

The Bible also contains what you might call obituaries. For example, after the reign of Solomon, the books of Kings and Chronicles in the Old Testament chronicle the kings of Israel and Judah. Entire chapters are dedicated to describing one king after another through their obituaries. The lists and accounts read much like a report card. After the king's name and the country he ruled, they usually list the name of his father and/or mother. They report how many years that king reigned and if he was a good king or a bad king. Included might be significant accomplishments or things in which he participated. Records usually conclude with his manner of death and indicate if he was buried with his fathers. It is a pretty simple, repetitive, and formulaic way of presenting information that does not result in a gripping literary experience. In fact, most people are likely to glance over these lists rather than read through them and process the information they contain. However, if you read closely you will notice that each biographical record contains commendation or criticism about the life of each ruler. If we take the time to pay closer attention to the accounts, taking bits of revelation and piecing them together, perhaps we will discover a God's-eye view on what matters to Him in our lives. Since among God's people, it was the king's responsibility to lead the people in the ways of the Lord, whatever happened in the nation during that king's reign was a direct reflection of the king's relationship with and obedience to God. Of the 20 kings of Judah chronicled, 14 were reported as evil, and six were reported as good. It would behoove us to take a closer look at what constituted a good or bad king.

The following is an example of one king's obituary: *In the seventeenth year of Pekah the son of Remaliah, Ahaz the son of Jotham, king of Judah, became king. Ahaz was 20-years old when he became king, and he reigned 16 years in Jerusalem; and he did not do what was right in the eyes of the Lord his God, as his father David had done. But he walked in the ways of the kings of Israel, and even made his son pass through the fire, according to the abominations of the nations whom the Lord had driven out from before the sons of Israel. And he sacrificed and burned incense on the high places and on the hills and under every green tree* (II Kings 16:1-4). Not a very good report card. Ahaz was obviously one of the bad kings.

Azariah, on the other hand, is an example of one of the six good kings. His record reads, *In the twenty-seventh year of Jeroboam king of Israel, Azariah son of Amaziah king of Judah became king. He was sixteen years old when he became king, and he reigned fifty-two years in Jerusalem; and his mother's name was Jecholiah of Jerusalem. And he did right in the sight of the Lord, according to all that his father Amaziah had done* (II Kings 15:1-3). His obituary continues, and although it states he did right in the sight of the Lord, it also says, *Only the high places were not taken away; the people still sacrificed and burned incense on the high places. And the Lord struck the king, so that he was a leper to the day of his death* (II Kings 15:4-5). Based on these two obituaries, what does God seem to care about? Ahaz is clearly criticized for failing to follow God and for engaging in foreign practices such as sacrificing to false gods and passing his son through the fire. Azariah, after 52 years of being a good ruler, has seven verses recorded about his entire life, one of which focuses solely on what he did *not* do — he did not take away the high places.

EVERY TIME A GOOD KING DID NOT TEAR DOWN THE HIGH PLACES WHERE OTHER GODS WERE WORSHIPPED, DESPITE ALL THE OTHER GOOD THINGS THEY MAY HAVE DONE IN THEIR LIFETIME, EACH OF THEIR OBITUARIES CONCLUDED WITH THE SAME PHRASE, *ONLY THE HIGH PLACES WERE NOT TAKEN DOWN.*

Could this be God's way of saying, "Pay attention! This is important to me."?

I believe it is. Every time a good king did not tear down the high places where other gods were worshipped, despite all the other good things they may have done in their lifetime, each of their obituaries concluded with the same phrase, *Only the high places were not taken down.* This holds true for Kings Jehoash, Amaziah, Azariah, and Jotham. Is God indicating that kings are entrusted with a governmental mandate from God to tear down the high places of their day? God does not waste words or need to keep records for Himself, so those verses are more than a mere exercise in record keeping. Since kings are an example of leadership in the Old Testament, their obituaries can also be read as a commentary on leadership. Kings had the dual roles of leaders of God's people and leaders of a nation. When we read the comments God leaves about those men who were leaders, we need to ask ourselves why He placed so much importance on tearing down the high places. What wisdom can we gain from all of this to apply to leadership in the church today?

GOOD KINGS AND REVIVAL

We have yet to exhaust the insights hidden in the Old Testament kings' obituaries. If you survey the 20 kings of Judah, you will notice that only six encouraged the people to follow God. Of the six good kings, records state that four were good and followed in the ways of the Lord themselves. The remaining two, however, were the only ones mentioned as having torn down the high places. Interestingly enough, only those two kings brought revival to Israel. Could it be coincidence that Josiah and Hezekiah, the only two kings who tore down the high places, were also the only two kings to usher revival into Israel? I think not. Instead of just a few short verses in their obituaries, I and II Kings include chapters describing the accomplishments and reforms of Josiah and Hezekiah. After they tore down the high places, they discovered the lost book of the law, repaired the temple door, reinstituted the Passover and the covenants, and reformed worship.

> ## COULD IT BE COINCIDENCE THAT JOSIAH AND HEZEKIAH, THE ONLY TWO KINGS WHO TORE DOWN THE HIGH PLACES, WERE ALSO THE ONLY TWO KINGS TO USHER REVIVAL INTO ISRAEL?

The remaining four good kings did not confront and tear down the altars of the false gods, and, as a result, failed to usher revival and reformation into their nation. They never took up that still-relevant mandate, the original directive Israel received when they first entered the Promised Land, *Watch yourself that you make no covenant with the inhabitants of the land into which you are going, lest it become a snare in your midst. But rather, you are to tear down their altars and smash their sacred pillars and cut down their Asherim — for you shall not worship any other god, for the Lord, whose name is Jealous, is a jealous God — lest you make a covenant with the inhabitants of the land and they play the harlot with their god, and sacrifice to their gods, and someone invite you to eat of his sacrifice; and you take some of his daughters for your sons, and his daughters play the harlot with their gods, and cause your sons also to play the harlot with their god* (Exodus 14:12-16). Refusal to deal with the high places aggressively condemned the future generations to apostasy. Without this foresight and understanding, the four status-quo kings were relegated to mere seven-line biographies/obituaries that decried . . . *only the high places were not taken away.*

REFUSAL TO DEAL WITH THE HIGH PLACES AGGRESSIVELY CONDEMNED THE FUTURE GENERATIONS TO APOSTASY.

Only two kings had the foresight and understanding to take them down. Josiah was one of those kings. His obituary states: *Josiah was eight years old when he became king, and he reigned thirty-one years in Jerusalem. And he did right in the sight of the Lord, and walked in the ways of his father David and did not turn aside to the right or to the left. For in the eighth year of his reign while he was still a youth, he began to seek the God of his father David; and in the twelfth year he began to purge Judah and Jerusalem of the high places, the Asherim, the carved images, and the molten images. And they tore down the altars of the Baals in his presence, and the incense altars that were high above them he chopped down; also the Asherim, the carved images, and the molten images he broke in pieces and ground to powder and scattered it on the graves of those who had sacrificed to them. Then he burned the bones of the priests on their altars, and purged Judah and Jerusalem. And in the cities of Manasseh, Ephraim, Simeon, even as far as Naphtali, in their surrounding ruins, he also tore down the altars and beat the Asherim and the carved images into powder, and chopped down all the incense altars throughout the land of Israel. Then he returned to Jerusalem* (II Chronicles 34:1-7).

HE SPENT SIX FULL YEARS DEMOLISHING THE SYSTEM OF FALSE-GOD WORSHIP.

Josiah became king when he was eight years old. The young king did right in the sight of God, for in the eighth year of his reign, when he was 16 years old, he began to seek God. In the 12th year of his reign, when he was 20, he began to tear down the high places. By his 18th year, the land had been purged. He spent six full years demolishing the system of false-god worship. He aggressively went after the demonic powers sown into his nation and didn't stop or slow down until the job was completed.

Hezekiah was the other revivalist king. His obituary is recorded as follows: *Now it came about in the third year of Hoshea, the son of Elah king of Israel, that Hezekiah the son of Ahaz king of Judah became king. He was twenty-five years old when he became king, and he reigned twenty-nine years in Jerusalem; His mother's name also was Abi the daughter of Zachariah. And he did right in the sight of the Lord, according to all that David his father had done. He removed the high places, and broke down the sacred pillars and cut down the Asherah. He also broke in pieces the bronze serpent that Moses had made, for until those days the children of Israel burned incense to it; and it was called Nehushtan. He trusted in the Lord, the God of Israel; so that after him there was none like him among all the kings of Judah, nor among those who were before him* (II Kings 18:1-5). Like Josiah, Hezekiah was a reformer. He destroyed everything to do with the false gods and even broke the bronze serpent, which in Moses' time had brought healing to God's people. It, too, had become an idol, and the people had begun to worship it. Hezekiah . . . *clung to the Lord; he did not depart from following Him, but kept His commandments* (II Kings 18:6). Verse five said that because of his trust in the Lord, no other king surpassed him. That is a high commendation given to a man in a very difficult and demanding position of leadership. But, that evaluation was appropriate because Hezekiah thoroughly tore down the high places in his faithfulness and service to God.

A brief examination of Hezekiah's genealogy, one generation previous, reveals a vital puzzle piece to this story. Hezekiah's father's name was Ahaz. Ahaz's obituary reads . . . *but (Ahaz) walked in the way of the kings of Israel, and even made his son pass through the fire, according to the abominations of the nations whom the Lord had driven out from before the sons of Israel. He sacrificed and burned incense on the high places and on the hills and under every green tree* (II Kings 16:3-4). Hezekiah grew up surrounded by worship to these false gods. He saw the sexual immorality and the child sacrifices on a regular basis. In fact, he was a survivor; at least one of his brothers was sacrificed to the gods by his father. What impact might this experience have had on a young Hezekiah? Oftentimes, we need to read between the lines as Scripture often relates only a summarized version of stories. Imagine young Hezekiah as he discovered his mother was pregnant. Each day, he watched as his mother's belly grew, and at some point he could lay his hand on her stomach and feel the baby move. He was excited about being a big brother. Then the big day arrived — his brother was finally born. Every morning he awakened to the baby crying or cooing and would run to see his new little brother, sticking his finger in the crib to touch him. He was already imagining how much fun they would have playing together in the future. One morning, he heard no crying at all, only silence. He ran to the nursery, and the baby was gone. Quickly he raced to his mother's room, and seeing her face blotched from weeping, asked, "Mama, what's wrong. Where is the baby?"

"HEZEKIAH, WHEN IT'S YOUR TURN, WHEN YOU BECOME KING, DO NOT FORGET YOU HAD A BROTHER WHO WAS SACRIFICED TO THE GODS... USE YOUR INFLUENCE TO BREAK THIS EVIL OFF OF OUR LAND."

Abi responded, "Your father took him to the high place today to be sacrificed to Baal. He will never come home." Imagine the impact of those words upon his young heart. From a young age, he understood very well what the worship of the false gods meant. That day and repeatedly during his life, Abi must have whispered in his ear, "Hezekiah, when it's your turn, when you become king, do not forget you had a brother who was sacrificed to the gods. You are a survivor. Don't forget it, and don't forget them. When you are placed in authority, remember your brother and speak out. Your day will come. Use your influence to break this evil off of our land." He didn't forget. When he became king, he eradicated the evil practice along with everything else involved in false-god worship, and as a result God brought revival and reformation to His people.

REVIVAL AND THE HIGH PLACES

When a nation or leader does not identify, confront, and tear down the false gods, unconfronted demonic strongholds exert a tremendous amount of influence and power. Remember, we are not talking about innate, harmless statues or altars. These altars are places of demonic connection, and the worship offered there results in demonic empowerment in an individual, generation or nation. The spiritual principle is that we are either influencing these strongholds or we are being influenced by them. Left untouched, the high places stand ready, a monument to the past and a current reminder of other gods and other practices. That is why God wanted the high places eradicated. If all the structures remained — the groves, the altars to Baal, and the Ashera poles — it was easy to resume the idol worship involving sexual immorality, temple prostitution, and child sacrifice. If it took Josiah six years to simply tear all the structures down, it would certainly take a lot of time, effort, and deliberate planning to re-establish idol worship. That is why God was always telling them, "Tear them down. We want to make it as difficult as possible for you to fall back into the sin that was destroying your life and nation." Part of tearing down the high places meant there would be no visible reminder of their past idolatry. Every altar, site, and obscene symbol would be destroyed and removed from the gaze of the people, helping to purify and make holy once again the eroticized atmosphere that had saturated their culture.

As we mentioned earlier, it is not enough to simply supercharge our temple experience. The temple mandate is incomplete without the marketplace mandate. If there is great evil in the land and God's people are absent, evil will continue unabated. However, if God's people show up, speak up, and act in the midst of a great evil, God promises victory. In order for us to experience revival, we must understand and fearlessly address what is happening in our culture. If we are going to be reformers and revivalists in our nation, we must demolish the high places. True leadership looks at the forces causing devastation in people's lives and the culture and says, "We are going to address them and eradicate them." I believe this is precisely what God is asking of the church today. Then, and only then, will our obituaries read like those of Hezekiah and Josiah.

CHAPTER EIGHT

CURSES AND CONFUSION

Conversation is animated in the room during the few moments before the meeting begins. The sound of the banging gavel results in a lessening of the noise. "Will the meeting come to order?" Once again the sound of the gavel can be heard. "All rise for the chair of the meeting." A strategy meeting in the boardroom of hell has convened. Satan himself will be leading the discussion. Today's topic? The development of a strategy to destroy one of the nations of the earth.

"Suggestions for the accomplishment of our goal?" Satan inquires.

One of the older demons offers a suggestion. "Targeting infrastructures that affect the quality of life would surely accelerate the demise of a nation. I suggest polluting the water supply and disrupting the transportation system by adding a significant number of potholes to the roads."

The younger demons are disgusted. *These old-timers are completely out of touch. Don't they understand we are in a technological revolution?* "I suggest we concentrate on disruption of the entire cell-phone system, along with the breakdown of the Internet. No texting. No calls. No surfing. No social sites. Complete communication breakdown and resultant isolation." This comment has come from one of the younger demons, offered with a sense of self-satisfied superiority especially in light of the previous suggestion.

Satan, watching this unfold, finds himself frustrated at the lack of progress he has made in bringing the older demons up to speed and in helping the new ones understand the critical nature of targeting. Impatiently he explains, "We need to stay focused on the long-term strategies that have worked to bring former civilizations to their knees. Broken systems are evidence of the breakdown of a nation but they

are not our primary target. First, we hit our target hard! We focus
on the time-tested weaknesses of the human and their most primary
relationships. Whether they are riding a horse or in a jet plane, we need
to assault their identity, their sexuality, their marriages, and their families
— the things their money can't buy. The wealthy could easily replace
infrastructure in a nation; they can't buy a good marriage, moral purity,
familial love, and unity. Those are our time-tested targets — the means of
destroying nations."

> WHETHER THEY ARE RIDING A
> HORSE OR IN A JET PLANE, WE
> NEED TO ASSAULT THEIR IDENTITY,
> THEIR SEXUALITY, THEIR MARRIAGES,
> AND THEIR FAMILIES — THE THINGS
> THEIR MONEY CAN'T BUY.

If the boardroom of hell was having a meeting and the whole
point of the discussion was to devise a plan to destroy our nation, what
strategies do you think they would consider? Would the conversation
center on schemes to disrupt communication or transportation systems?
What about clean water? If they targeted the water, they could create
massive amounts of disease. Would that be enough to destroy us? What
about an assault on sexuality? Or the family? What if the enemy could
bring confusion to the sexual, emotional, and governmental definition
of a man — the definition of true Biblical manhood? What if there
was a cloud of confusion around the true definition of what it means
to be a daughter and what is in the deepest part of her heart? What
about children and family? A bride? What about an assault on purity?
Redefining marriage would be a plausible strategy. What if the enemy
could change all such definitions and what they represent to us? What
would happen then? What if hell could alter those essentials and assault
them as many times as possible? Would we then watch a nation unravel?

> THERE IS A FRONTAL ASSAULT
> AGAINST GOD'S GIFT OF SEXUALITY
> THAT ORIGINATED IN THE
> BOARDROOM OF HELL.

There *is* a frontal assault against God's gift of sexuality that originated in the boardroom of hell. Without much effort, you can observe it in the culture. It affects everything. Things once clearly defined have now become clouded and are under fire.

Who thought up the idea of sex? Did God design it? What does God's gift of sexuality entail? Does His plan work best? Why is there so much pain associated with sexuality? Is sex the highest human experience? What is a woman? What is her role? What is a man? What is his true role? Is it permissible for men to be with men and women to be with women? Can't Johnny be raised equally well with two mommies or two daddies as with a mommy and daddy? What difference does it make if two people live together before marriage? We *have* fallen into a state of confusion, and people are asking questions they have never asked before. There *is* debate about the sexual identity of men and women. If we stripped away all the messages in the culture and looked at the heart of a woman, what would we find there? If we stripped away the current messages and practices of the culture, what would we discover about the God-ordained role of a man?

NO WONDER THE DEVIL HATES THE WHOLE CONCEPT OF A BRIDE. HER SUBMISSION TO HER HUSBAND IS A SYMBOL OF THE CHURCH AND ITS RELATIONSHIP TO GOD, AND HER PURITY IS A PICTURE OF OUR SINGLE-HEARTED DEVOTION TO HIM.

Marriage is currently touted as an arrangement whereby Mr. Right comes to rescue Miss Right from her sad, lonely, single life, providing them both with eternal sexual ecstasy and fulfillment. However, when those expectations are not met, marriage becomes a whole lot of work, and people want out. As a result, the whole institution has come under ridicule because it cannot deliver what was promised. We have lost the true definition of marriage. Is there no longer the possibility that marriage might be God joining two people together for His Kingdom, purposes, and glory? Purity, a picture of obedience and integrity before God, has become a thing of the past. A bride dressed in pure white has been reduced to a color dictated by tradition rather than a current and living testimony, a symbol of chastity and fidelity. Brides are the target of demonic hatred because of what they represent — Jesus' church. No wonder the devil hates the whole concept of a bride. Her submission to her husband is a symbol of the church and its relationship to God, and her purity is a picture of our single-hearted devotion to Him. Our modern culture shows little evidence of this type of understanding. How did hell convince a nation to submit to such a cloud of confusion on every one of those levels?

NEW ORLEANS

In the early 1990s, I traveled to New Orleans to join fellow believers from across the nation for a week of pro-life prayer rallies. At that time, New Orleans was the murder capital of the country with 13-17 murders weekly. As pro-life people began pouring in from all over the country for the scheduled event, the abortion clinics shut down for the week in order to avoid having to deal with us. Despite those closures, we obtained the appropriate permits and gathered in front of the clinics. Generators for sound systems were set up, and worship teams led us as we gathered to pray and worship God. Where days before there had been altars of death in the city, we established altars of life in their place. In a place of despair, we spoke hope.

Something very strange happened. Not only were no abortions being performed, but the first day we prayed, worshipped, and stood in open opposition to abortion, not a single murder was committed in the entire city of New Orleans. We continued to worship on day two, again building altars to God in our hearts in the places where the enemy had been having his way with a generation. Again, the entire second day passed, and not a single murder was committed. The same thing happened on the third day. This phenomenon of consecutive homicide-free days was so significant and noticeable that on the fourth day the police called a press conference to announce that as a result of the superior training and vigilance of the New Orleans police force, the murder rate was plummeting. While that sort of logic is similar to saying incidences of fires decreased as a result of superior fire and rescue training, that was their only plausible explanation.

We continued to worship and pray for days five, six, and seven. On the eighth day, it was rumored that a murder had taken place outside of the city limits, yet New Orleans itself continued to remain murder-free. Police reports announced that 30 percent of every category of crime had also dropped. Some of the police officers joked with us, asking us to stay longer, "It is like having a paid vacation. We love having you here." Pro-life activists were having their pictures taken with the police commanders. Police began giving us escorts, surrounding us on the highway with their lights flashing as we drove to yet another clinic in the city to pray and worship God.

We began to ask ourselves if there could be a link between our activities and the crime-free atmosphere of the city. In that week — when all the abortion clinics were shut down, altars of worship to God were erected in their place, and prayers for His mercy had been offered — the atmosphere in the entire city of New Orleans was tangibly altered. I wonder if, in that little window of eight days, heaven opened over a city because innocent blood had, for the moment, ceased being shed. It was as if sanity broke through the fog and began to settle over the minds of the people in the city. After we left, the abortion clinics resumed their practices, and the crime statistics rose back to their normal rates. Was God trying to teach us something, or was it a gigantic coincidence?

IT MATTERS IF THE BLOOD IS INNOCENT

Genesis 4 recounts a story of jealousy and the shedding of innocent blood. In that story, Cain goes to his brother Abel while he is out in the field, strikes him, and kills him. No one sees the murder, but the Lord goes to Cain and says, *The voice of your brother's blood is crying to me from the ground. And now you are cursed from the ground which has opened its mouth to receive your brother's blood from your hand* (Genesis 4:10-11).

For me, this is, without a doubt, some of the most haunting imagery in Scripture: the land opens its mouth and receives blood that has fallen from an innocent man. Then, when the ground, a literal geographic location, has swallowed the blood, God hears a haunting chorus crying out to Him. What a powerful and strange connection! It is as if the ground receives the blood as a historic marker, a memory of the event that took place in that spot.

When God says to Cain, "You are now cursed from the ground," I believe it means that when the innocent blood of his brother went into the ground, it was as if Cain planted a seed of death in the ground. That seed produced a curse over his life.

IF THOSE TERRIBLE SEEDS OF INNOCENT BLOOD ARE PLANTED, A GREAT DEMONIC FOG RISES, AND A CURSE EMERGES OVER THAT GEOGRAPHICAL AREA, ALTERING THE PHYSICAL AND SPIRITUAL ENVIRONMENT.

Now think back to New Orleans. An atmospheric alteration was present there as a direct result of the shedding of innocent blood. God gave man dominion over the earth, and God holds delegated authorities responsible for whatever good or evil occurs in their geographical area. If those in charge of the land forfeit their responsibility to govern justly in that region and innocent blood is shed, the land is marked. If those terrible seeds of innocent blood are planted, a great demonic fog rises, and a curse emerges over that geographical area altering the physical and spiritual environment.

The concept of innocent blood was clear in the minds of the Hebrews. In fact, God instituted regulations which addressed this very issue. God had His people set aside cities of refuge so that innocent blood would not be shed in the land of Israel. Anyone accused of murder unjustly could flee to a refuge city for protection and spare the nation the shedding of innocent blood (which could have come through revenge killing). For example, Hebrew law stated that if a man . . . *pushed* [someone] *suddenly without enmity, or threw something at him without lying in wait, or with any deadly object of stone, and without seeing it dropped on him so that he died, while he was not his enemy nor seeking his injury, then the congregation shall judge between the slayer and the blood avenger, according to these ordinances. The congregation shall deliver the manslayer from the hand of the blood avenger, and the congregation shall restore him to his city of refuge to which he fled* (Numbers 35:22-5). For example, *When a man goes into the forest with his friend to cut wood, and his hand swings the axe to cut down the tree, and the iron head slips off the handle and strikes his friend so that he dies — he may flee to one of these cities and live* (Deuteronomy 19:5).

It is similar to our manslaughter laws which differentiate between premeditated murder and accidental death. In the case of the man chopping wood, since there was no premeditation, any further blood (shed on the part of the blood avengers) would have been innocent blood. Six cities were designated as places of refuge in order to allow that particular man and any others like him to go there and say, "I'm seeking asylum. A man died. It was my fault; it was an accident, and now his brothers want to avenge his death by killing me." He would then be allowed refuge in that city until the current high priest died. It was God's way of ensuring no more innocent blood would be shed.

The significance of the shedding of innocent blood and the resulting judgment on the one responsible is also illustrated in another scenario. If a man was found lying dead in the open country, Hebrew law demanded that the residents of the closest city sacrifice a heifer to the Lord, and the elders of that city needed to testify, *Our hands have not shed this blood, nor did our eyes see it* (Deuteronomy 21:7). Regardless of the fact that they had nothing to do with this man's death, they had to deal with it appropriately and absolve themselves of the innocent blood. The act of sacrificing a heifer ensured that they would be purged from the guilt of innocent blood in their midst. God made provisions for such situations because He knew if innocent blood was shed, the whole atmosphere of the nation would begin to change and people would find themselves under a curse. They would be caught in a spiritual fog, separated from God and the blessings of His love laws. Such laws helped God's people become aware of the curses resulting from the shedding of innocent blood and taught them to take great pains to avoid having any innocent blood held against them.

There are more examples in Scripture that teach us about innocent blood than you might imagine. The book of Jonah illustrates people's reticence to implicate themselves with innocent blood. Jonah went on a "disobedience detour," refused to warn Nineveh about God's coming

WHETHER OR NOT THEY WERE FOLLOWERS OF YAHWEH, THEY TREMBLED WITH FEAR AT THE THOUGHT OF SHEDDING INNOCENT BLOOD.

judgment, and found himself on a ship sailing to Tarshish in the midst of a great storm. He soon realized the tempest was sent because of his disobedience and asked the men to throw him overboard believing that would save the lives of the rest of the men. The sailors, faced with the decision to save their own lives or throw Jonah overboard at his own request were still reluctant to have any part in his death. Whether or not they were followers of Yahweh, they trembled with fear at the thought of shedding innocent blood and prayed, *O Lord, do not let us perish on account of this man's life and do not put innocent blood on us* (Jonah 1:14).

IT IS REMARKABLE THAT THE SIMPLE MENTION OF INNOCENT BLOOD CHANGED THE TENOR OF JEREMIAH'S ACCUSERS, AND IMMEDIATELY THE CROWD DECLARED, *NO DEATH SENTENCE FOR THIS MAN!*

Another example occurred when Joseph's brothers approached the official of Egypt, who, unbeknownst to them, was Joseph, the brother they thought had died at their hands. While Joseph questioned and challenged them, they said to one another . . . *now comes the reckoning for his blood* (Genesis 42:22). They were referring to the evil they had done to Joseph, thinking that the acts they had committed in abandoning and selling him had resulted in his death. They immediately assumed they were rightfully reaping punishment for innocent blood. Later in the Old Testament, the prophet Jeremiah had just finished prophesying the word of the Lord to the people of Judah during the reign of Jehoiakim. The priests and prophets became angry with Jeremiah and seized him to kill him. Jeremiah, knowing their culture and understanding their regard for innocent blood, quickly reminded them, *Do with me as is good and right in your sight. Only know for certain that if you put me to death, you will bring innocent blood on yourselves, and on this city, and on its inhabitants*

(Jeremiah 26:14-15). It is remarkable that the simple mention of innocent blood changed the tenor of Jeremiah's accusers. Immediately, the crowd declared, *No death sentence for this man!* (Jeremiah 26:16). He was released at once. Their collective conscience and their immediate response to the charge of innocent blood were so strong, they saved Jeremiah's life.

In the New Testament, when Pilate's attempts to free Jesus were thwarted by the Pharisees and the people, and he was trying to figure out what to do with Jesus in response to their demands to crucify Him, Pilate said, *Why? What evil has He done?* (Matthew 27:23). Pilate recognized Christ's innocence and that no valid charges had been laid against him. When the crowds continued to shout at him, Pilate washed his hands saying, *I am innocent of this Man's blood; see to that yourselves* (Matthew 27:24). Again, in the New Testament, when Judas felt remorse for his part in turning Jesus over to the officials and tried to return the 30 pieces of silver the Pharisees had paid him, he said, *I have sinned by betraying innocent blood* (Matthew 27:4). The Pharisees, despite their complicity in the death of Jesus, refused to take the money. They said, *It is not lawful to put them into the temple treasury, since it is the price of blood* (Matthew 27:6). They understood that innocent blood came with a curse and did not want the curse attached to that money to become attached to them.

INNOCENT BLOOD TODAY

I once read a story about a man called General Naked. He was a rebel in the Liberian civil war in the mid 1990s. The headline read, "Hired Killer Now Bares Only His Soul." Here are excerpts of the story:

> The macabre annals of Liberia's civil war include gunmen in drag, human skulls used as soccer balls, and the videotaped torture of the ousted president. But nothing compares to the tale of Gen. Naked. Nude except for lace-up leather shoes and a gun, the general led his fierce Naked Battalion into battle on behalf of the warlord Roosevelt Johnson, who hired the unclothed warrior for his fearlessness and fighting skills.

"I was just an ordinary man, but I was also very spiritual. I was deep into occult," Blahyi, 25, said as he explained how he became a ruthless general. His fighters were among the most notorious in the seven-year conflict that wracked the West African nation, founded 150 years ago by freed American slaves.

BLAHYI SAID HE WAS REQUIRED TO MAKE A HUMAN SACRIFICE BEFORE BATTLE. USUALLY IT WAS A SMALL CHILD, SOMEONE WHOSE FRESH BLOOD WOULD SATISFY THE DEVIL.

Civilians rarely seemed fazed. But the Naked Battalion stood out, not just for its nudity but for its brutality and its apparent fearlessness. Blahyi says this was a result of a contract with the devil, sealed at the age of 11, when he was initiated into a satanic society that demanded regular human sacrifices and nudity on the battlefield to ensure protection from his enemies. Blahyi said he was required to make a human sacrifice before battle. Usually it was a small child, someone whose fresh blood would satisfy the devil. "Sometimes I would enter under the water where children were playing. I would dive under the water, grab one, carry him under, and break his neck. Sometimes I'd cause accidents. Sometimes I'd just slaughter them," he said in a matter-of-fact manner.

It was during one of these battles, on the New Bridge linking central Monrovia to the outskirts, that Blahyi's conversion (to Jesus Christ) began. He was naked on the frontline when, he says, God appeared and told him he was a slave to Satan, not the hero he considered himself to be. Blahyi admits it took awhile to accept his new calling, but in November he finally turned full-time to preaching and even attended theology school in Nigeria. When he goes out to preach now, he says he sometimes encounters relatives of his victims. "I feel very bad, so bad," he said, but he insists it was satanic powers that possessed him in the past and he cannot be held responsible.

To try to make up for his past, Blahyi is now selling cassettes of his sermons for $20 each to raise money for a school for ex-fighters such as himself. "Even now I'm fighting. I'm fighting a spiritual war," Blahyi said, before heading outside into the rain for another day of preaching. (Associated Press, 1997)

This did not occur in the Old Testament or early-church era. This is a current event. This demonstrates the reality of demonic spiritual empowerment connected to the shedding of innocent blood.

THE CONSEQUENCES OF SHEDDING INNOCENT BLOOD

God's judgment on nations that shed innocent blood is very pronounced in Scripture. God promised, *Behold, I am bringing such calamity on Jerusalem and Judah, that whoever hears of it, both his ears shall tingle* (II Kings 21:12). The reason for this promised calamity is found further on, *Surely at the command of the Lord it* (judgment) *came upon Judah, to remove them from His sight because of the sins of Manasseh, according to*

WHAT ENVIRONMENTALIST TODAY WOULD ACKNOWLEDGE THAT OUR PHYSICAL LAND SUFFERS BECAUSE OF MORAL SIN AND OFFENSE AGAINST GOD?

all that he had done, and also for the innocent blood which he shed, for he filled Jerusalem with innocent blood; and the Lord would not forgive (II Kings 24:3-4). Read the word of the Lord through Hosea, *For the Lord has a case against the inhabitants of the land because there is no faithfulness or kindness or knowledge of God in the land. There is swearing, deception,*

*murder, stealing, and adultery. They employ violence, so that bloodshed
follows bloodshed. Therefore the land mourns, and everyone who lives in
it languishes along with the beasts of the field and the birds of the sky; and
also the fish of the sea disappear* (Hosea 4:1-3). Talk about caring for our
environment! What environmentalist today would acknowledge that our
physical land suffers because of *moral* sin and offense against God? When
mankind does not commit to protect the life of God's highest creation,
man, the life and quality of God's lesser but still very valuable creation is
also put at risk. When humans fail to govern responsibly and guard life,
not only does the land receive the blood, but it mourns and languishes,
along with the beasts, birds, fish, and people in the midst of it. Hosea's
words described the atmosphere of a nation under such judgment;
everything changed because of the people's sin and the innocent blood
they shed.

BISHOP MUTHEE

Years ago, my church invited Bishop Thomas Muthee from Kenya, a
man who had been featured in the *Transformation* videos, to come and
speak. His testimony told of ridding his area of oppressive demonic
forces. Through aggressive intercession and spiritual warfare, believers in
his region pushed forces of darkness out of their region and cleared the
spiritual atmosphere from the effects of the spirit of death and human
sacrifice. One of our interns picked him up from the airport, and as they
were driving down into the city, Bishop Muthee turned to the intern
and said, "I feel the spirit of human sacrifice here." Usually you expect
to hear comments such as, "My, it sure is beautiful in your country!" or,
"How long have you lived in Spokane?" or even, "Are you enjoying your
internship program?" It is quite a challenge to respond appropriately to,
"I feel the spirit of human sacrifice here." It was not a strange comment
for Bishop Muthee. He was very aware of what it was like to live under a
cloud of oppression caused by human sacrifice, and when God gave him
the strategy and power to break that demonic force over his region and
it lifted, he was equally aware of its absence. He could feel and see the
difference.

What could he have been sensing? It could have been the black-
magic witch-covens where daughters are sexually abused and impregnated

in satanic rituals, after which those babies are sacrificed to Satan. It is all in secret; they are pregnant at home and give birth at home. I prayed with a woman who had been ritually, satanically, sexually abused, and had held a human heart in her hand. These events are real. They occur over much of America. Maybe that is part of what Bishop Muthee sensed. Or possibly, he was sensing the 2000 abortions that are performed at our local Planned Parenthood clinic every year, 500 of which are performed on teenagers. Whatever the cause, he could feel the atmosphere of human sacrifice in our city. It was tangible to him.

THE MORE WE MINGLE WITH AND ARE AFFECTED BY THE WORSHIP OF THE FALSE GODS, THE THICKER THAT DEMONIC FOG BECOMES IN OUR NATION.

I have talked to many people who, when traveling from one part of the state to another or from one part of the nation to another, can sense differences in the spiritual atmosphere of different regions or cities. The cause could be anything from abortion, to demonic powers, to economic powers that impact the "feel" of a locale. When there is innocent blood going into the ground, a curse rises up over that area, and the spiritual fog is tangible. The fog over our nation has diminished our ability to understand God's created order. In Hosea it is called a moth judgment, *Therefore I am like a moth to Ephraim, and like rottenness to the house of Judah* (Hosea 5:12). This judgment acts as an imperceptible erosion in a nation. It is similar to finding that moths have riddled our favorite wool sweater with holes over the summer. Sometime during the spring, summer, or fall, although you were completely unaware of them, moths were working away at your sweater. Slowly, secretly, and insidiously, they gnawed at its fibers and destroyed it.

The more we mingle with and are affected by the worship of the false gods, the thicker that demonic fog becomes in our nation. It also occurs slowly, secretly, and insidiously so that we hardly recognize its effect. As more innocent blood is shed, the fog increases in thickness, and our ability to see clearly the truths of God decreases.

We are living in the midst of judgment and destruction and don't even perceive it.

The enemy understands the laws of sowing and reaping. He lures us across a line with lies and empty promises, and once we cross that line, only then do we see the horrible consequences of our decisions. In 1973, the Supreme Court decision in Roe versus Wade opened the door to abortion in our nation. We were hardly aware of the innocent blood that was regularly and openly shed in our nation. We now have the blood of more than 50 million innocent children in the ground. The resultant fog is so thick and impenetrable that we do not even realize what has happened to us. We are living in the midst of judgment and destruction, and we don't even perceive it. If we were talking about a small amount of blood and a correspondingly thin fog, we could possibly see through it and still identify God's blueprint for life and culture. The fog is so thick, however, we have almost completely lost our understanding of God's ways. We don't know that we don't know. And we don't see that we don't see. We no longer know what is the true definition of a man. We do not understand anymore what a woman is created to be. We do not know what the true essence of a man or woman's sexual identity is. How is a Christian woman supposed to behave? How is a Christian man supposed to think? How are young people supposed to navigate their relationships? Our thinking has changed. Confusion abounds. The enemy's assault against us has been extremely successful.

Cultural Indicators

If we observed social and cultural indicators—murder, rape, sexual assault, child molestation, teen pregnancy, drug addiction, crime, abortion, the divorce rate, alcoholism, suicide rate, sexually-transmitted diseases — from 1900 through the present day, would we see these elements on the rise or decreasing? Many argue that the cultural indicators were fairly flat-lined from the early 1900s until 1962 when prayer was taken out of public schools. At that point, we could see a small spike in the indicators. However, if we observed what happened after 1973, the year the Supreme Court ruled in favor of abortion, we would see that an explosion took place on the scale. Crime, murder, rape, suicide, and other social indicators jumped 200 to 500 percent. In the 1960s, there were only two significant sexually-transmitted diseases. Today there are over 25, some of which are incurable. With the Roe vs. Wade ruling, we made a governmental decree stating that it is permissible to break God's laws in order to solve man's problems. We took the seeds of death and violence, sowed them into the soil of our nation, and now reap a harvest of increasing confusion, death, and violence.

This discussion of innocent blood has ramifications for the multitudes of mass shootings occurring in our country. When the shootings happened at Columbine High School, where two alienated young men shot 12 students and one teacher to death, I was incredibly saddened. Some years later, we experienced the mass shooting at Virginia Tech, which left 33 dead and 20 wounded. Again, I was saddened.

WE TOOK THE SEEDS OF DEATH AND VIOLENCE, SOWED THEM INTO THE SOIL OF OUR NATION, AND NOW REAP A HARVEST OF INCREASING CONFUSION, DEATH, AND VIOLENCE.

However, I was not shocked. What *is* surprising to me is that this sort of thing isn't occurring more frequently. An entire generation has grown up watching its elders sow seeds of violence and death into the soil of our nation. *We* have modeled a lifestyle of condoning violence to achieve our desired ends. I once read a story about a gang member on death row for murder who stated in his defense, "You kill them in the womb, we kill them outside the womb. What's the difference?" While this devastating kind of logic doesn't provide a reasonable justification for murder, the fact that young people are living out an ethic that has been modeled and handed down to them by us should not come as a shock to us. They are simply living out a morality consistent with the morality we have given them. We, the older generation, are largely responsible for the eroding morality of our nation. We are the "Haight-Ashbury Generation" that introduced free love, free sex, and the philosophies of living for one's self and hating everything that represents authority. The young people inherited those philosophies from us, and yet, we wonder why their lives are so broken.

BEFORE AND AFTER BY CONTRAST

There were times in the Old Testament when clear thinking was prevalent, when God's blueprints for life were still being honored. Before the land was stained with blood and a demonic force was exerting power over the nation, a moral sanity still reigned. Abraham, while traveling through the land of Gerar, lied to King Abimelech about his wife Sarah, saying she was Abraham's sister. The king took Sarah into his palace, but

ABIMELECH UNDERSTOOD THAT MORAL SIN HAS CONSEQUENCES.

then had a dream in which God said to him, *Behold, you are a dead man because of the woman you have taken, for she is married* (Genesis 20:3). Abimelech immediately released Sarah and rebuked Abraham saying, *What have you done to us? And how have I sinned against you, that you have brought on me and on my kingdom a great sin? You have done to me things that ought not to be done* (Genesis 20:9). The king realized that if he had violated another man's wife, he would have incurred God's awful judgment on his kingdom. Abimelech understood that moral sin has consequences. He got it; nothing obscured his vision. When he realized his sin, he became passionate about rectifying the situation.

When . . . *they sacrificed their sons and their daughters to the demons, and shed innocent blood . . . the land was polluted with the blood* (Psalm 106:37-38), and the atmosphere of the nation changed. People changed. Observe the sequence in Hosea when the people turned from God: *Harlotry, wine, and new wine take away the understanding. My people consult their wooden idol, and their diviner's wand informs them; for a spirit of harlotry has led them astray, and they have played the harlot, departing from their God. They offer sacrifices on the tops of the mountains and burn incense on the hills, under oak, poplar, and terebinth because their shade is pleasant. Therefore your daughters play the harlot, and your brides commit adultery. I will not punish your daughters when they play the harlot, or your brides when they commit adultery, for the men themselves go apart with harlots and offer sacrifices with temple prostitutes; so the people without understanding are ruined* (Hosea 4:11-14). Notice the progression: the people played the harlot with other gods and forsook the Lord their God. They then lost understanding, which in turn led to their ruin in that nation, and that led to their demise.

Some Hebrew scholars have said the . . . *voice of your brother's blood* (Genesis 4:10) in the story of Cain and Abel can be translated the *voice of your brother's bloods,* referring not just to the voice of Abel, but the voice of the children he would have had and their children's children down through history. In other words, all the voices of Abel's descendants cried out because they had been cut off. When God looked at Abraham, he saw his descendants as numerous as the stars in the sky. God cannot look at us without seeing the future generations that will come forth from us; He cannot look at me without seeing my seed extend into the future. How can we grasp what God — who views all things and all times simultaneously — sees and hears when Abel and all his children, whose lives were cut off, cry out to Him? How many children would Abel have had? And what about their children? And those children's children? Now take that and apply it to the 50 million children who have been aborted in our country alone, not to mention the other countries of the earth, and try calculate how many millions of innocent human beings, precious in God's heart, have been cut off from life and their posterity. How many millions, or possibly billions, of voices cry to Him from the ground of the nations of the earth?

REVELATION

Innocent blood is not the only thing that brings a curse on the land. The whole chapter of Leviticus 18 exhorts us: *Don't live like the people of Egypt where you used to live, and don't live like the people of Canaan where I'm bringing you. Don't do what they do. Obey My laws and live by My decrees* (Leviticus 18:1-4 — *The Message Bible*). This exhortation is then followed by 17 verses outlining, in specific detail, prohibitions on our sexual lives. These include prohibitions against incest, sex with any relative, adultery, and sex with animals. These prohibitions are so exhaustive, they clearly exclude sex with anyone but one's spouse. What are the consequences for violating these prohibitions? They are pollution and expulsion from the land. *Don't pollute yourselves in any of these ways. This is how the nations became polluted, the ones that I am going to drive out of the land before you. Even the land itself became polluted, and I punished it for its iniquities — the land vomited up its inhabitants. The people who lived in this land before you arrived did all these things and polluted the land. And if you pollute, it, the land will vomit you up just as it vomited up the nations that preceded you* (Leviticus 18:24-28 — *The Message Bible*). What a revelation! Not only does abortion pollute the land and invite God's judgment, so does sexual immorality. The horrendous extent to which we practice both abortion and sexual immorality portends terrible consequences for us as a nation.

In November, 1989, Lech Walesa, then President of Poland, made a statement regarding our nation. "America has advanced technologically, economically, scientifically," he said, "but America has not kept pace morally. I fear for you." God hates the shedding of innocent blood. God hates sexual immorality. God says to His people through Hosea: *So you will stumble by day, and the prophet also will stumble with you by night; and*

WHAT A REVELATION! NOT ONLY DOES ABORTION POLLUTE THE LAND AND INVITE GOD'S JUDGMENT, SO DOES SEXUAL IMMORALITY.

I will destroy your mother. My people are destroyed for lack of knowledge. Because you have rejected knowledge, I also will reject you from being My priest. Since you have forgotten the law of your God, I also will forget your children (Hosea 4:4-6).

I, too, fear for my nation.

CHAPTER NINE

KEYS TO REVIVAL

When I travel from church to church, I constantly encounter young men who ask, "May I help you with anything, Pastor Jim?" Then there are usually a couple of follow-up questions, "May I carry anything for you, or get you something to drink?"

I smile. They have no idea what they are in for. They know I am the "Daughter, Flower, Princess" preacher, the guy who talks about sexuality, the man who makes girls cry and intimidates the guys. Honestly, these are fairly brave young men to come up to talk to me. I almost feel bad for what I put them through, but somehow, I can't resist. I turn to them and say, "Absolutely. In fact, there is something you can do for me." Their eyes light up, their backs immediately straighten, and they are ready to move into action. "Could you get out there and end pornography? That would really help. And when you are done with that, go out and end abortion, too. I would really appreciate that. Thank you." You should see their faces. Sometimes their mouths hang open and their faces turn white. Here stands the poor young man, who braved intimidation in order to assist me, gulping, not sure if I am joking or deadly serious. When I do that, although it serves as a shocking reality check for these young men, it really isn't fair. In all honesty, only God can heal our land. However, we can play a significant part in that healing. Let's take a closer look at the part He has called us to play.

THE REAL CULPRIT

A sad phenomenon occurs in the church. After getting saved and living in the Christian culture long enough, we begin to see ourselves as having less and less in common with the world and its needs. Our mentality changes from awareness that we are all sinners who need a

Savior to disgust with "all those bad people out there." We begin to believe that it is Hollywood's pornography producers who are wrecking our country. We say to one another, "If those abortionists, drug dealers, and prostitutes would just stop it, our country would be a much better place." That seems like a logical statement, yet I would argue from a Biblical perspective, that drug dealers, abortionists, and prostitutes are not responsible for the decline of morality in our country. Nor are they responsible for its recovery. God's Word states, *If . . . My people who are called by My name humble themselves and pray, and seek My face and turn from their wicked ways, then I will hear from heaven, will forgive their sin, and will heal their land* (2 Chronicles 7:14). Did you notice He did not say anything about drug dealers or Hollywood being the answer? He said *My people* must humble *themselves.* God is not holding the corrupt politicians, bank robbers, drug dealers, or homosexuals responsible. He is holding us, His church, responsible for the current state of affairs.

> ## THE STATE OF A NATION IS A REFLECTION OF THE PEOPLE UNDER GOD'S AUTHORITY, WHO ARE CALLED BY HIS NAME, NOT "THOSE SINNERS OUT THERE."

The state of a nation is a reflection of the people under God's authority, who are called by His name, not "those sinners out there." He is waiting for us to align ourselves with His will, turn our hearts to Him and say, "Whatever You want, Lord, I want it too." I call II Chronicles 7:14 the revival Scripture, because it says if we, individually and corporately, are willing to do four things we *can* do — humble ourselves, pray, seek His face, and turn from our wicked ways — then God promises to do three things we *cannot* do — hear from heaven, forgive our sin, and heal our land. If we do the things we can do, God will do the things we cannot do.

> ## IF WE DO THE THINGS WE CAN DO, GOD WILL DO THE THINGS WE CANNOT DO.

Humble Ourselves

When my son Luke was a little guy, he was often spanked multiple times a day. He was one of those strong-willed children who are a challenge to raise but have great leadership potential. We would hear his sisters screaming, and we would ask, "Luke, what are you doing? Are you poking your sisters again?" He would nod his head. "Luke, you are not supposed to do that. What happens when you do that?" I asked.

"I get a spank," he replied.

"That is right," I said. Then I spanked him and watched his face to see if any enlightenment came to him. He cried and repented, after which I forgave him, told him he was a good boy, and we hugged and prayed together. It happened over and over again, often multiple times in a day. It was exhausting but necessary. Each time we disciplined him, we watched his face and his behavior to see if anything was getting through to him.

Sometimes the Lord "spanks" a nation and looks to see what kind of response is on the face and in the heart of that nation. He wants to know: Are you turning towards Me during this difficulty, or are you continuing to turn away? What is in your heart?

America was shaken on 9/11 when the Twin Towers in New York City fell in a moment of time during a terrorist attack. Immediately America got "religion." We could pray openly anywhere—at baseball games, schools, in the workplace. Church attendance skyrocketed. Abercrombie and Fitch cancelled their fall catalog, rife with images of unclothed young men and women intertwined in suggestive poses, because they realized that publication at that particular time would have been an affront to the people of America. People in the middle of divorce proceedings experienced a sudden and stark realization of what was important in life, and some halted the process. In a moment, our proud independence was stripped away and people said, "Wait a minute, I need God." We were humbled and shaken. Unfortunately, our repentance and turning to God were short-lived.

The revival promise in II Chronicles 7 was given when Solomon dedicated the temple to the Lord. God responded to Solomon's dedication prayer by saying, *I have heard your prayer and have chosen this place for Myself as a house of sacrifice* (II Chronicles 7:12). Strangely, however, God follows this affirmation with an abrupt change in tone. The verse immediately following the commendation continues, *If I shut up the heavens so that there is no rain, or if I command the locust to devour the land, or if I send pestilence among My people* (II Chronicles 7:13) . . . followed by the promise of II Chronicles 7:14. In essence, God was saying, "If you backslide or fall into disobedience, I am willing to shut the heavens or send the locust or send pestilence in order to get your attention — in other words, to discipline you. However, if, at that point, you humble yourselves, become desperate, and begin to pray and cry out to Me, I will answer you, forgive you, and heal your land." People tend to turn to the One True God in the midst of difficult circumstances. Society during Solomon's reign was largely agrarian, so when God talked about sending droughts or natural disasters, there was an impending economic disaster attached to this promise. God knew that He often needed to "hit the people in their pocketbooks" in order to get their attention and draw their hearts back to Him. The people needed to be reminded that God was the source of their provision and prosperity.

MERCY ALLOWS US TO ENDURE A SHAKING THAT ERODES THE STRENGTH OF OUR FALSE GODS, SHOWS US THEY ARE FALSE, AND CAUSES US TO TURN BACK TO GOD.

God's willingness to discipline us is a demonstration of His mercy. Harsh judgment would be to leave us in our sin and apostasy, thinking we are right. Mercy allows us to endure a shaking that erodes the strength of our false gods, shows us they are false, and causes us to turn back to God. God shakes us and gets our attention to apprehend our hearts completely for Him. *He humbled you and let you be hungry, and fed you with manna which you did not know, nor did your fathers know, that He might make you understand that man does not live by bread alone, but man lives by everything that proceeds out of the mouth of the Lord* (Deuteronomy 8:3). He does this with individuals, He does it with nations, and He does it with the church, His bride, because humility is born out of an acknowledgement of our own desperation and need of Him.

ICE CREAM, PAPA

Some think revival is a thing of the past, something we read about in history books. We read about George Whitefield, John and Charles Wesley, Charles Finney, or Jeremiah Lanphier and tend to think the revival and reformation that occurred through their lives was a random intervention of God and there is nothing we can do to make revival happen once again. With that mindset, we come to God trying to twist His arm with our prayer, believing that we are attempting to get Him to do something He doesn't want to do. We cry, "Oh Lord, save my generation," as if it's something He has never considered or does not care about.

> HE WANTS US TO ASK HIM
> FOR REVIVAL, FOR GOD HAS
> LIMITED HIMSELF TO WORK
> THROUGH HUMAN AGENCY IN HIS
> ENDEAVORS UPON THE EARTH.

I have a revelation for you that will change your prayer life: God wants revival more than you do. He has more of a burden for what is going on in our culture than we do. He would love to break the darkness that threatens to envelop entire generations in confusion and destruction. When we pray and seek His face, we discover revival is already in His heart. He wants us to ask Him for revival, for God has limited Himself to work through human agency in His endeavors upon the earth.

I love the revival promises found in Scripture. One is especially interesting to me, because it contains the phrase, "You who remind the Lord." It reads: *On your walls, O Jerusalem, I have appointed watchmen: All day and all night they will never keep silent; You who remind the Lord, take no rest for yourselves; and give Him no rest until He establishes and makes Jerusalem a praise in the earth* (Isaiah 62:6-7). This describes the role of those who intercede, who are asking God to make His people a blessing in all the earth. After reading that, you might ask yourself, "Does God need reminding about anything?" Let me tell you how I came to understand this verse and how it helps my understanding of revival.

My kids love ice cream. There have been times when they have begged, and I have promised that later in the day we would all walk to the ice cream shop and I would buy them each a cone. Often, as the day progressed, I became distracted with work and phone calls and forgot my promise to them. One (or all) of my kids inevitably came to remind me, "Dad, you said you would take us out for ice cream."

Immediately, I remembered my promise and said, "Yes, ice cream! Let's go." And out we went.

My kids were not twisting my arm. They were only asking for what was already in my heart to do for them. I had promised it; I intended to do it; I wanted to give it to them. Their reminder simply activated the intention of my heart.

> ## WHEN WE GO TO HIM AND REMIND HIM OF HIS PROMISES, WE CAN BE CONFIDENT HE WILL DO WHAT HE SAID HE WOULD DO.

God loves His children even more than I love mine, and He, unlike me, does not forget His promises. When we go to Him and remind Him of His promises, we can be confident He will do what He said He would do. When I get up in the morning to pray and walk, I think about our nation and how much we need God's intervention and healing in our land. Sometimes I simply say, "Ice cream, Papa," knowing that what I am asking is already in His heart. I let my heart cry out to God, and my prayers are gathered together with the prayers of all the other saints as incense into the bowls of heaven. As we read His Word and discover His heart and intentions, we can then go to Him confidently with our requests. He is waiting for each of us to align our hearts with His will and say, "Lord, what You want is what I want. Do it, Lord. Ice cream, Papa."

TWO KINDS OF BOWLS AND A
STRANGE RACE

As Dutch Sheets exhorts us in his book, *Intercessory Prayer*, **our prayers do make a difference**. *And another angel came and stood at the altar, holding a golden censer; and much incense was given to him, that he might add it to the prayers of all the saints upon the golden altar which was before the throne. And the smoke of the incense, with the prayers of the saints, went up before God out of the angel's hand. And the angel took the censer; and he filled it with the fire of the altar and threw it to the earth; and there followed peals of thunder and sounds and flashes of lightning and an earthquake* (Revelation 8:3-5). This Scripture says the elders around God's throne hold censers/bowls that fill up with our prayers,

PRAYERS ASCEND THEN ARE RELEASED TO THE EARTH TO SHAKE GOVERNMENTS AND NATIONS AND BREAK DEMONIC STRONGHOLDS.

and when the bowls are filled, they are thrown back down to the earth to cause thunder, lightning, and an earthquake. Prayers ascend and are then released to the earth to shake governments and nations and break demonic strongholds. What do you think caused the Iron Curtain, that demonic wall of communism in the former Soviet Union, to fall? Could it have been the brokenhearted cries of an oppressed people? We do not know how many dear saints spent years in the prison camps there. We cannot pretend to understand or empathize with the suffering and depths of sorrow they experienced as a people. But out of that suffering, the prayers of the saints ascended, the bowls in heaven were filled, and they were then thrown down to earth. The shakings came and the liberation of God was released. Millions of people were loosed from that atheistic, communist stronghold, and according to Scripture, the release came through prayer.

In contrast, Revelation paints a picture of another type of bowl being filled in heaven and poured out on earth. *And one of the four living creatures gave to the seven angels seven golden bowls full of the wrath of God,*

who lives forever and ever . . . And I heard a loud voice from the temple,
saying to the seven angels, "Go and pour out the seven bowls of the wrath of
God into the earth" (Revelation 15:7, 16:1). Two types of bowls are being
filled in heaven—one with the prayers of the saints and one with the
wrath of God. Our prayers help determine which bowl is poured out on
the earth.

UNLESS WE FILL UP THE BOWLS OF PRAYER AND INTERCESSION, THE BOWLS OF WRATH WILL BE POURED OUT ON OUR NATION.

To use another analogy, I believe there is a strange kind of race
occurring in heaven. On the one hand God says, if . . . *My people who*
are called by My name humble themselves and pray, and seek My face and
turn from their wicked ways, then I will hear from heaven, will forgive their
sin, and will heal their land (II Chronicles 7:14). On the other hand God
also says that innocent blood cries out to Him from the ground. Is the
collective voice of humility and repentance from the saints louder than
the voice of the shed blood of the innocent? Which is getting more of
God's attention? Or, to use our other analogy, is the bowl of God's wrath
filling up more quickly than the bowl of the prayers of the saints? Our
only hope of revival is that God's people will awaken and cry out louder
than the voice of the blood. Our only hope is to turn from our wicked
ways — our individual sin and our corporate national sin—and begin
to pray, "Lord, we plead a greater blood, the blood of Christ, to cover
the innocent blood that has been shed in our nation." Unless the church
awakens and cries out to God, a sure judgment is coming. Unless we
fill up the bowls of prayer and intercession, the bowls of wrath will be
poured out on our nation. No nation, individual, court, or institution
can ever break God's law and succeed. Eventually, God's law will break
them. When the United States Supreme Court ruled that abortion was
legal, they declared, "We are going to break God's law to solve human
problems." It might appear to many that we, as a nation, have gotten
away with it. However, when any institution condones that seeds of
violence and death be sown into the soil of a nation, harvests of death and
violence will spring up and bring that nation to its knees.

More is Needed.

The solution, unfortunately, is not as easy as simply uttering a prayer. God declares plainly . . . *when you spread out your hands in prayer, I will hide My eyes from you; Yes, even though you multiply prayers, I will not listen. Your hands are full of bloodshed* (Isaiah 1:15). Isaiah delivered the message that God was not going to listen to the prayers of the people as they were being offered since we cannot win God's heart while there is blood on our hands. However, he followed it with some hopeful instructions. He said, *Wash yourselves, make yourselves clean; remove the evil of your deeds from My sight. Cease to do evil, learn to do good* (Isaiah

God's ears become unplugged when we turn from our wicked ways and come back into alignment with Him again.

1:16-17). When we have forsaken God and His ways, we are as a faithless harlot to Him. God's ears become unplugged when we turn from our wicked ways and come back into alignment with Him again. This true repentance is described thus: *Is this not the fast which I chose, to loosen the bonds of wickedness, to undo the bands of the yoke, and to let the oppressed go free, and break every yoke? Is it not to divide your bread with the hungry, and bring the homeless poor into the house; when you see the naked, to cover him; and not to hide yourself from your own flesh?* (Isaiah 58:6-7). That is true repentance. We need to take a further look at what this repentance means.

Turn From our Wicked Ways

During the Finney revival in the 1840s, 1.5 to 2 million people came to know the Lord at a time when the entire population of the United States was estimated to be between 16 and 20 million. That means that 10 percent of the entire population of America was converted under Finney's ministry, all without microphones, recordings, radio, television, or other means of modern technology! Wow! Eighty-five percent of those converts stayed true to the Lord.

Today it is reported that only 5-10 percent of those saved at Billy Graham meetings stay true to their faith and are part of a church one year later. I'm sure Billy Graham's ministry grieves over that fact. Part of the problem is that our modern American Gospel is full of compromised truth and morality. We hate to make people feel awkward in our 21st-century churches, so we water down the message. Instead of allowing God's truth to convict people of sin, to press them to turn from godless living and to accept God's mercy and saving grace in their lives, we often circumvent God's moving and offer them a more palatable Gospel. However, God is more concerned about the true salvation of our souls than He is about the levels of comfort or discomfort we endure in the process.

Not only does God want to bring salvation to individuals that results in a cleansing from sin, God also wants to pour out His healing on nations through revival that changes the moral climates of our communities. Moral climate change means that we turn from our wicked ways; that is the mark of true revival. A simple increase in religious activity is not the mark of true revival.

GOD IS NOT INTERESTED IN INCREASING CHURCH ATTENDANCE UNLESS THOSE WHO ATTEND AMEND THEIR WAYS AND BEGIN TO LIVE HOLY LIVES.

A.W. Tozer wrote the following in his book, *Keys to the Deeper Life*, regarding true revival:

> Revival must make of necessity an impact on the community, and this is one means by which we may distinguish it. Revival will always vitalize God's people. But revival is not welcome. For many the price is too high. There's no cheap grace in revival. It entails repudiation of self-satisfied complacency. Revival turns careless living into vital concern and exchanges self-indulgence for self-denial. We must have a reformation within

the church. To beg for a flood of blessing to come
upon a backslidden and disobedient church is to
waste time and effort. A new wave of religious
interest will do no more than add numbers to
the churches that have no intention to own the
Lordship of Jesus and come under obedience to His
commandments. God is not interested in increasing
church attendance unless those who attend amend
their ways and begin to live holy lives. Prayer for
revival will prevail when it is accompanied by
radical amendment of life, not before. All-night
prayer meetings that are not preceded by practical
repentance may actually be displeasing to God . . .
We must return to New Testament Christianity, not
in creed only but in complete manner of life as well.
Separation, obedience, humility, simplicity, gravity,
self-control, modesty, cross-bearing: these all must
again be made a living part of the total Christian
concept and be carried out in everyday conduct. We
must cleanse the Temple of the hucksters and the
money-changers and come fully under the authority
of our risen Lord once more . . . Then we can pray
with confidence and expect true revival to follow.
As a church we need to take an honest look at what
is going on and say, "Lord all this stuff that we have
been doing hasn't accomplished what we would like.
After doing all the things we have done, we haven't
seen the change in our nation, in our generation.
The burden hasn't lifted.

Most Christian historians believe the 600,000 lives lost in the
Civil War were a judgment on our nation as a result of the barbaric
system that made slaves of 2.5 million African men, women, and
children. If that was indeed the case, then we need to ask, "God, should
Your sowing and reaping go forth in our nation, what kind of judgment
will the lives of more than 50 million aborted babies require?" Now
more than ever, we need to turn from our wicked ways (individually
and corporately), repent, and plead the blood of Jesus over our sins and

the sins of our nation.

REVIVAL'S LINK TO INJUSTICE

There are many examples in history of social transformation resulting
from revival. Before the Wesleyan revival in the 1700s, England was
in a state of serious moral decline. J. Wesley Bready, in his history of
pre-revival English conditions entitled *England Before and After Wesley*,
describes the dismal atmosphere: "The penal code included 160 different
laws, which if violated, incurred the death penalty. Infractions such as
picking someone's pocket for more than a shilling, shoplifting any item,
stealing a horse or sheep, breaking a young tree, snatching gathered
fruit, snaring a rabbit on a gentleman's estate, or appearing on a high
road with a blackened face all warranted execution. Thousands of
people would congregate every six weeks in London to be entertained
by what they called *Hanging Shows*. Charles Wesley once preached
at a prison where 52 people were waiting to be hung, among them a
10-year-old child." After the hangings, corpses were often left hanging
in city squares as a warning to the local populace. Incurring debt did
not result in hanging, but it was an infraction that resulted in a prison
sentence. People in debtors' prison were not released until their original
debt and additional interest were paid in full. Often, the only hope for
men in debt was for their wives and daughters to sell themselves into
prostitution until they had earned enough money to pay the money
they owed. England's economic industry boasted that one of every three
businesses sold alcohol. Factories employed children who worked six
days each week, 12 to 14 hours per day, in dismal working conditions.
Children employed at match factories were so polluted with chemicals
that their eyes glowed in the dark at night, foretelling their imminent
death due to systemic chemical poisoning. Mothers sold their preteen,
virgin daughters to rich passersby in a perverted version of *My Fair Lady*
in order to have more money for gin. Parliament, the nation's governing
body, was filled with men who profited from the slave trade. Such was
the condition of England before revival. The ways of that England were
definitely wicked ways.

In the midst of that darkness, men of God began to preach God's
truth. George Whitefield's sermons were deemed too upsetting for the

people, so he was expelled from preaching in the church. Undaunted, he began to preach in fields and the open air. He preached at five o'clock in the morning as the coal miners went to work. He stood on a stone fence so they could gather around to hear him. Then, after 12 to 14 hours of work, the coal miners returned to find men like Wesley and Whitefield preaching there again. White lines slowly appeared on the coal-blackened faces of the men as tears of contrition fell, and the men gave their hearts to God. Prayer meetings, Bible studies, and cell groups sprang up. People confessed their sins and repented. Not even the mobs hired by churches to cause disturbances could break up their meetings.

AS THE REVIVALISTS PREACHED RIGHTEOUSNESS, THE PEOPLE BEGAN TO ADDRESS INJUSTICE.

As the revivalists preached righteousness, the people began to address injustice. Robert Raikes, a newspaper editor in England, noticed that children from poor families labored six days a week in miserable working conditions. Even if they did not work, their families could not afford to send them to school, which existed only for the upper classes. Raikes knew if these children did not learn to read, they would be doomed to spend the rest of their lives in slave labor. With God's burden, he took it upon himself to elevate their status and give them an opportunity to change their lives. He decided the best solution would be to invite children to a school held on Sundays, the only day they didn't have to work. Sunday school was not just a class held the hour prior to a church service, but the beginning effort to educate the masses of the poor. It was born out of a revival spirit dealing with injustice.

William Wilberforce, a British politician who was converted during the First Great Awakening, was disturbed when he discovered the wicked realities of the slave trade. He committed his life to the eradication of slavery in his nation and used a variety of strategies to bring to light that evil upon the public conscience. He stood in Parliament rattling the slave chains which hung around his neck, crying, "The blood of the slaves fuels our entire economy. Our money is tainted with the blood of slaves. It is on our hands." In spite of many failed attempts, he worked tirelessly

for nearly 20 years before a vote finally passed through Parliament
prohibiting England's ships from being used to transport slaves.

THE REVIVAL AFFECTED SEXUAL MORALITY AS WELL. ILLEGITIMATE BIRTHS DROPPED BY 44 PERCENT DURING THE FIRST YEAR AFTER THE REVIVAL.

In the early 20th century, conditions in Wales were equally as
dismal as those in England. Miners spent paydays in the pubs drinking
away their paychecks — until revival came. J. Edwin Orr, a revival
historian, reported that the Welsh revival produced some interesting
results — an increase in music, an increase in bankruptcy, and a
decrease in coal production. When revival came, coal miners got saved.
Crime dropped, and people lined up at police stations to confess their
trespasses and make amends. With decreasing crime, the police sat
idle, so they formed quartets, wrote music, and sang songs — thus an
increase in music. The miners who typically used their paycheck to
get drunk and subsequently went home to beat their wives and break
the furniture now walked past the pubs, went home, and gave their
paychecks to their wives to buy food for their families. One woman,
when asked if she had seen any miracles in the revival replied, "Well, I've
seen God turn beer into furniture." To explain this strange phenomenon,
she said, "My husband used to come home drunk, beat me and the kids,
and break every stick of furniture that we owned. But he doesn't do that
anymore. So, I guess God turned beer into furniture." Pubs went broke
and shut down, resulting in increased bankruptcies. Finally, the miners,
who cursed and beat the donkeys to coerce them to pull cartfuls of coal
out of the mines, got saved. The men's natures changed so drastically
that they stopped cursing and beating the animals. The donkeys, not
used to such kind behavior, would not move without the provocation of
a beating. The result? A decrease in coal production. The revival affected
sexual morality as well. Illegitimate births dropped by 44 percent during
the first year after the revival.

Amy Carmichael was a frail, young British girl in the late 1800s when she traveled as a missionary to India and saw little girls being sold into temple slavery and prostitution. Girls as young as eight were married to the gods and subjected to many kinds of sexual perversion in the name of Hindu worship. Thus married, they spent the rest of their lives as property of the priests in that temple, never to have their own husbands or families. However, because Amy responded to that injustice by speaking, writing, and talking about it, laws changed, and temple slavery in India was outlawed. She identified and confronted injustice, and, as a result, it was torn down.

Revival has always linked itself to action against injustice, exemplifying two revival principles.

1) A great evil, without the intervention of God's people, guarantees the evil will continue and grow greater. This is the unfortunate equation of the history of many nations.

2) If God's people are present and respond with His heart to societal evils that are destroying people's lives, the result is societal transformation and God's promised victory. This, too, is the history of nations that we are praying will become a 21st-century reality for our nation.

REVIVAL AND SEXUALITY

How does worship of the sex-gods relate to revival and God's judgment on nations? In my readings, I have discovered that among the civilizations that have vanished into the ash heaps of history, there are common elements that have led to their demise. Jim Nelson Black, in his book, *When Nations Die,* lists 10 common elements that contribute to the extinction of nations. Gibbon, in *The Rise and Fall of the Roman Empire,* lists six factors that led to the fall of the Roman Empire. In every similar study, two elements were consistently present among these now-extinct societies.

• Increase in the loss of respect for life.

• Increase in sexual perversion and immorality.

In other words, sex and death. Sex outside of God's boundaries and death are always linked: homosexual sex and AIDS; sex outside of marriage and sexually-transmitted diseases; sex outside of marriage and abortion. Sex and death always run together.

AS LONG AS THE CHURCH REFUSES TO CONFRONT THE FALSE GOD OF SEXUALITY, WE WILL NOT SEE REVIVAL.

We will not have revival if the church is silent about these issues. As long as the church refuses to confront the false god of sexuality, we will not see revival. The god of sexual immorality not only destroys life by its culminating with child sacrifice, it also destroys the hearts of the women in a nation. We must address the damage being done to our daughters, wives, sisters, and mothers. We must identify and confront the false images being perpetrated by the media, which tell our women their highest value is sexual. We must call men to be protectors of the women in their lives, not predators who use women to satisfy their own lusts. We must challenge the dating system that causes so many to lose their virginity, and we must offer another way by which young people can find their mate and maintain their purity. We must talk about pornography, sexual immorality, and abortion in the church so people can confess their sins, receive forgiveness, and forsake their wicked ways.

WHAT BOTHERS YOU?

God desires that out of our relationship with Him,—,the "seeking His face" part of the revival formula,—,we will begin to love the things He loves and hate the things He hates. As you walk with God, what do you see in culture that bothers you? If you don't see anything that breaks your heart, ask God to soften your heart; ask Him to break your heart for the things that break His heart. God broke Robert Raikes's heart over the unreached, impoverished children. He broke Amy Carmichael's heart over the children caught in the worship of the sex-gods. He broke William Wilberforce's heart over the slave trade. Let God fasten your heart onto something so much so that you break inside and become willing to be part of the answer. That is where revival starts.

ABORTION IS THE END RESULT OF THE WORSHIP OF THE SEX-GODS.

God has given me His hatred for some things. God first began to break my heart over the killing of the unborn in 1989. He moved me to action, and I did something about it. I traveled all over the nation to participate in national pro-life events where we attempted to rescue babies from death and close abortion clinics. At those events, we also gathered, prayed, and repented over the sins of our nation. God moved me to begin to work locally to mobilize the church to respond to the issue of abortion. As I spoke and began to address the issue, He began to broaden my message and open doors to speak in other places. The more I spoke and the more I saw, the more He began to show me that abortion was not a stand-alone issue. It is the end of the conveyor belt in a nation that worships sex; abortion is the end result of the worship of the sex-gods. In order to see abortion end, we first need to go to the root of the problem and expose the cultural sexual assault the enemy has perpetrated in the nations of the earth.

Not only do I hate abortion, I now also hate the resultant damage that the worship of the sex-gods has done to the women of the earth. I long to see men become protectors, not predators, of the women in their lives. I long to see authentic manhood restored. I long to see intact, whole families be the norm again so that every little boy and girl can grow up with both their mother and father in their home. I want fathers to speak on a daily basis to their sons and daughters, saying, "Son, I'm proud of you." and "Honey, you are beautiful. You are precious to me." I want the dance clubs and bars emptied. Instead, I would like to see basketball and football stadiums filled with thousands of young people worshipping God. That's what I dream about.

Others have different burdens from God. Some have a burden over sexual slavery issues. Others have a burden for single moms, or the poor, or the homeless, or for adoption. The burdens of God's heart are vast. I believe God has given us the key. If we do what we can do, God will do what we cannot do. Allow God to give you a piece of His heart.

Allow Him to share one of His burdens with you. Then ask Him what He wants you to do about it. As with Robert Raikes, Amy Carmichael, and William Wilberforce, God, through us, can make a difference. We, through our repentance, prayers, and righteous actions, can help usher in revival.

CHAPTER TEN

DATE RAPE B.C.

Protection. That is a word I use to describe one of the primary things every daughter needs from her father. Often, though, when I use it in that context, I'm confronted with blazing eyes and angry protestations. Female backs straighten, and formerly friendly faces turn an indignant red. It is one of the battlefields in which the demonic war against our language has been concentrated. Certain words have been targeted until the original meanings are so obscured that the word now carries a negative connotation. Protection has been so altered by the feminist movement that an entire generation of young women screams, "We don't need or want any protection!" Protection has become anathema to them, synonymous with a lack of intelligence and wisdom. In today's lexicon, it describes someone who is incapable, cannot fend for himself or herself, and has nothing significant to contribute to society.

WHEN I USE THE WORD PROTECTION, IT HAS NOTHING TO DO WITH A LACK OF INTELLIGENCE, TALENT, CAPABILITY, OR GIFTEDNESS.

However, when I use the word protection, it has nothing to do with a lack of intelligence, talent, capability, or giftedness. My daughters are capable, intelligent, wise, talented, and resourceful, and they have much to contribute to both the Kingdom of God and society. They are anointed preachers, intercessors, worship leaders, fashion designers, leaders, and business entrepreneurs. Some of them are also wonderful mothers and wives. They are going to be history makers and world changers. They are not helpless wimps. But I must tell you, as long as they are under my care, I protect them. The enemy wants to make it "either/or." I say it is "both/and."

AMNON AND TAMAR

Allow me to use the story of Amnon and Tamar in II Samuel 13 as
a stepping stone to further explain the concept of protection. Here's
a condensed version of the story: Absalom, the son of David, had a
beautiful sister named Tamar. Amnon, his stepbrother, loved her. Tamar
was a virgin, and Amnon became so frustrated over his inability to seduce
her that he actually made himself physically sick. He had a shrewd friend
named Jonadab, and, in a scene typical of a modern-day locker room,
Jonadab concocted a scheme by which Amnon could get Tamar alone
and violate her.

He told Amnon to pretend to be sick and then to ask the king to
send Tamar to prepare a meal for him in private. King David believed
Amnon's story and sent Tamar to tend to her sick brother. Once she
arrived, Amnon sent all the servants away and raped her. Having satisfied
his physical lust, he then sent her away.

As we look at different aspects of this story, we can learn some
things that will help us.

THE PROBLEM WITH LUST

Amnon noticed Tamar. He wasn't thinking, "Oh, that Tamar! Her mind
is exquisite. I just love the way she thinks and the way she is able to
convey her ideas so clearly. You should hear how she discusses political
science! I really like that."

YOU CAN'T KEEP THE BIRDS FROM FLYING OVER YOUR HEAD, BUT YOU CERTAINLY CAN KEEP THEM FROM BUILDING A NEST IN YOUR HAIR.

Simply put, he lusted after her. He noticed her beauty, and then he
allowed those thoughts to turn to lust. His original attraction toward
her might not have been sin; it was what he did with that attraction that
determined if it became sin or not. We all notice the opposite sex, and we
all face sexual temptation. *No temptation has overtaken you but such as is*

common to man; and God is faithful, who will not allow you to be tempted beyond what you are able, but with the temptation will provide the way of escape also, so that you will be able to endure it (I Corinthians 10:13). Thoughts of sexual temptation are not reason for condemnation. However, what we do with those thoughts is the determining factor. I often use Martin Luther's analogy of birds in discussing this with young men, since young men especially tend to feel condemned when they are sexually tempted in their thoughts. Luther said, "You can't keep the birds from flying over your head, but you certainly can keep them from building a nest in your hair." The point is that thoughts for which we are not responsible will come to us from the powers of darkness. We didn't invite them, nor did we generate them. They are the "birds flying over our head." If they knock on our door looking for a convenient landing strip and we simply open the door, see what is there, and shut the door in the face of those unwanted visitors, then we are absolved of guilt. However, if we allow them in, it is as though we are allowing them to build a nest in our hair. Instead of exercising self control, Amnon allowed his attraction to Tamar to turn into lustful thoughts, which led him to lustful action and sexual violation, as is spoken of in James 1:15: *Then when lust has conceived, it gives birth to sin.* His lust definitely gave birth to sin.

MANY MEN LOSE ANY PRETENSE OF BEING PROTECTORS AND BECOME SOLELY PREDATORS. WOMEN BECOME WILLING PARTICIPANTS, HOPING ONE MAN WILL EVENTUALLY COMMIT TO THEM.

So much of what occurs in the world's dating system is based on lust. Many guys approach relationships the same way Amnon did. They see an attractive gal, lust after her, figure out a plan to conquer her, and then satisfy their sexual desires on her. Soon after, they abandon that girl for another conquest. Many men lose any pretense of being protectors and become solely predators satisfying their sexual lusts. Women become willing participants, hoping one man will eventually commit to them. In the process, men and women become more and more distanced from their God-ordained roles — men give way to their lower nature of lust and depravity, and women surrender their purity, become wounded, and harden their hearts. Lives are broken, and hopes of healthy marriages and families in the future become more and more an unattainable goal apart from God's grace and restoration.

God has a better way.

Let's look at a completely different approach to relationships. Deuteronomy presents us with a unique Scripture that explains the rules for taking the spoils of battle. *When you go out to battle against your enemies, and the Lord your God delivers them into your hands, and you take them away captive, and see among the captives a beautiful woman, and have a desire for her and would take her as a wife for yourself, then you shall bring her home to your house . . .* (Deuteronomy 21:12). This story begins much like our first story. A soldier sees a beautiful woman among the captives and desires her, but in our last story, the initial attraction quickly turned to lust and rape. What were God's instructions as to what to do with the initial attraction in this instance? *You shall bring her home to your house, and she shall shave her head and trim her nails. She shall also remove the clothes of her captivity and shall remain in your house, and mourn her father and mother a full month; and after that you may go in to her and be her husband, and she shall be your wife* (Deuteronomy 21:12-13).

I call this the "relationship Scripture." It contains God's instructions to young Hebrew soldiers on how to initiate a relationship that could end in marriage. The normal components for a relationship were present as in any relationship. The soldier sees a beautiful woman. That is a normal part of life. As I often say to the students in the schools in which I teach, if this were sin, they would be sinning all day long as they observe the uniquely beautiful, young ladies in their school. Noticing an attractive member of the opposite sex is not sin. Again, it is what we do with those initial thoughts that determine if those thoughts become sin or not.

The next component we notice is that this soldier has a desire for her. Now that must be wrong, right? Desire! That is probably connected to sex in some way. Yikes!

Well, desire is normal, and it is directly connected to the next component.

He wanted to take her as a wife for himself. The sexual "desire part" and the "take her for a wife part" are connected. That is how God-ordained relationships move forward — initial attraction, progressing to desire, desire fulfilled in marriage. Simple.

However, God then cleverly inserted the next steps, ensuring that the relationship progressed in a manner that would honor Him and all those involved. The young man was first to take her into his home, where his parents were invariably present since young adults did not live alone in apartments or condos in their culture. It looks as though their relationship was to begin in the context of family. In the midst of that context, the couple would not be alone but would be working with and interacting with the family on a daily basis. The people who knew and loved him the most would observe their developing friendship. Being in the context of the family would also ensure that the Hebrew morality of purity would be upheld. According to this Scripture, Hebrew soldiers treated their captives completely differently than other nations treated their captives. It is said of the other nations that they cut open the bellies of the pregnant women they took captive. We can only wonder how they treated the young virgins. God next instructed the woman to shave her head completely (probably including her eyebrows) and cut off her seductive fingernails. Finally, she was to undergo a "modesty upgrade" by removing her outfit and exchanging it for the more modest Hebrew garments offered to her by the soldier's family.

THE WORLD'S FOCUS IN RELATIONSHIPS EMPHASIZES PHYSICAL ATTRACTION, OUTSIDE BEAUTY, HORMONES, AND IMMEDIATE GRATIFICATION OF SEXUAL DESIRES.

On top of all that, she was mourning her mother and father and the loss of everything dear to her. Her spirit was probably consumed by sorrow and grief. In *that* state, the man was told to evaluate his future wife and decide if he wanted to marry her. God's plan for relationships is quite the opposite of the world's way. The world's focus in relationships emphasizes physical attraction, outside beauty, hormones, and immediate gratification of sexual desires. God knows every one of those things is a poor foundation upon which to build a relationship and future marriage. The Deuteronomy formula de-emphasizes every one of those things and forces men and women to discard outer beauty and attraction to get to the core of what really matters.

What conclusion can we draw from this set of directives from the Lord? Perhaps, God is saying through this story that He doesn't want any relationships based on the passion of the moment. Said another way, God isn't interested in hormonal or glandular relationships. Behind His commands is the knowledge of a daughter's heart. I believe God never wanted a woman to wonder why a man wanted her. Using the formula in Deuteronomy, she would know for certain that she was wanted for who she was as a person, not for her sexual and physical qualities alone.

TO THE SAME EXTENT A YOUNG WOMAN EMPHASIZES HER EXTERNAL BEAUTY, TO THAT EXTENT SHE WILL ATTRACT YOUNG MEN WHO ARE PRIMARILY ATTRACTED TO HER FOR THOSE REASONS.

Today, no young woman is commanded to do these things. However, it would be to every young woman's benefit to de-emphasize her external beauty in her relationships with young men and cultivate the internal qualities of her heart and character. To the same extent a young woman emphasizes her external beauty, to that extent she will attract young men who are primarily attracted to her for those reasons, thereby contributing to her own future unhappiness. On the other hand, if a young woman primarily emphasizes her internal qualities, she will attract young men who are primarily attracted to her for who she is as a person, thus fulfilling her deepest desire. This will contribute to her future happiness and the success of a future marriage. When you strip away everything external and are forced to look at the internal core of a person, you are much more likely to make a wise decision regarding a future marriage partner than if you don't do so. Of course, this counsel from Deuteronomy was directly applicable to the spoils of war, but I believe its principles have much wisdom for us to apply in our relationships today.

LIES AND DECEIT

I notice different aspects of our story about Amnon that occur today on an ongoing basis. First, Amnon and his friend cooked up a scheme and cultivated a lying and deceitful spirit in order to take advantage of a daughter. Their ploy was to get her alone so Amnon could violate her. Men today have their favorite "lines" they use on girls. They deliberately fill up empty-hearted women with deceitful words of love and with empty

> **IT IS THE JOB OF FATHERS TO DISCERN THE SPIRITS OF THE YOUNG MEN WHO WANT TO SPEND TIME WITH THEIR DAUGHTERS. THIS IS PART OF THEIR PROTECTION.**

promises in order to take advantage of them. Many women are desperate for love and attention and will ignore warning signs, choosing to believe the words are true and sincere. It is the job of fathers to discern the spirits of the young men who want to spend time with their daughters. It is part of their protection.

Not all young men are emissaries from the nether world when it comes to sexual motivation. However, apart from Christ, their relational practices with young women often end up mirroring those of Amnon and Jonadab with Tamar. When I preach in Russia, I often invite a young man to role play with me. I point to a young man in the audience and have him stand up. Then I say to him, "So, you are interested in beginning a friendship with my daughter?"

He looks a little confused, but eventually he plays along with me and says, "Yes, I think so."

I nod and answer, "Well, that's great, but I want to let you know that she is very, very important to me, and if you ever do anything to take advantage of her or say anything that would hurt her in any way, you are going to have to answer to me. Do you understand me?" His face usually turns red and everyone laughs. I smile and say, "Well, I bless you now. You can sit down."

"If I had had that protection in my life, I wouldn't have ended up in so many of the situations that have caused me pain."

When I do that in an audience of women who have had an average of six abortions and mainly have experienced predatory relationships their whole lives, I can feel their hearts and literally hear them sigh in unison. Collectively, they seem to be saying, "Oh, is that possible? That wasn't there for me. I wish it could have been. If I had had that protection in my life, I wouldn't have ended up in so many of the situations that have caused me pain." That is the kind of protection God wants fathers to provide for their daughters — not an abusive kind of control, but a loving involvement that provides safety and security. It is a place of blessing and safety in which a father says, "I love you and want the very best for you. I want to stand between you and anything that might want to harm you." Most women would gladly receive that kind of protection.

Failed Fatherhood

I believe David failed as a father in this situation. In believing Amnon's line, he showed a lack of discernment and sent his daughter into a situation that was not safe, or at best, was without supervision. As I

Without much thought, we send our daughters off with young men we hardly know.

mentioned in the last chapter, without much thought, we send our daughters off with young men we hardly know. We listen to the guy's few courteous words at the door and don't take the time to go below the surface and see what the young man is really all about. It is as if our generation suffers from moral amnesia, forgetting what we were thinking about and what we were doing with young women when we were younger. I know what I talked to my friends about and what I boasted about when I was a young man. I am not proud of that; in fact, it is something from which God has delivered me. How can we forget so quickly what it was like to deal with this area as a young person? If we care about our daughters as God intends for us to care about them as fathers, we will take the time to discern the motivations and intentions of any young man who comes calling. I don't know if David was preoccupied or disinterested or distracted — whatever the reason or reasons, he did not discern the deceitful spirit behind Amnon's words, and, as a result, David sent his daughter into an extremely harmful situation. Again, I think I would be correct in laying the blame for Tamar's loss of purity at her father's door.

Abraham was instructed to command his children to follow the Lord. *For I* (God) *have chosen him* (Abraham), *in order that he may command his children and his household after him to keep the way of the Lord by doing righteousness and justice* (Genesis 18:19). God is looking for fathers who will take seriously the command to train, protect, and guard their children. Adam, the first man, was told to keep the garden. Some of the definitions of "keep" are: *to retain in one's power or possession; to have in custody for security and preservation; to preserve from danger; to protect and guard.* Adam failed in his charge to protect Eve. His failure resulted in devastating consequences for their own lives and the lives of all mankind. There is a lot more to fatherhood than mere procreation. With the responsibility God gave Abraham and Adam and, therefore, to us men as well, we can't afford to be disengaged, absent, or too busy. My family is my responsibility, and my daughters' safety, security, and well-being is my responsibility. In light of that, it would be an understatement to say I am not fond of the world's system of dating. I have seen it wreak havoc in the lives of multitudes of young men and young women. We, as a family, have chosen a totally different means of bringing our children into marriage — one where I, as a father, am involved, aware, and extremely engaged.

MANY FATHERS DO NOT LEAD THEIR FAMILIES SPIRITUALLY OR SPEAK INTO THE SEXUAL LIVES OF THEIR CHILDREN BECAUSE OF THEIR OWN SEXUAL FAILURES AND GUILT.

However, many fathers do not lead their families spiritually or speak into the sexual lives of their children because of their own sexual failures and guilt. David acted horrendously with Bathsheba. He committed adultery with her and arranged to have her husband killed in battle. He later repented of his sins when confronted by the prophet, but I wonder if he ever dealt with his own shame. It is possible that the shame of his failure with Bathsheba disqualified David in his own eyes from (1) training his son as to how to honor women and (2) positioning himself to protect his daughter. Did his shame prevent him from ever talking to his sons and warning them about sexual temptation and the need for self control? Based on what happened with Amnon, I will venture a guess that David never discussed the matter with him. Since both Tamar and Amnon were his children (by different wives), David was responsible to both train Amnon and protect Tamar. When he neglected to look his son in the face, discern his son's heart, and challenge his motives, David silently and unknowingly facilitated the assault.

SHAME PARALYZES US AND DIS-QUALIFIES US FROM LEADING OUR FAMILIES AND PROTECTING THEM.

Shame silences. Men, you cannot afford to hide in your shame and think you will be able and available the moment your daughter needs protection. If you want to fulfill your God-ordained role in your family, you need to walk in repentance, freedom, and purity right now. Shame paralyzes us and disqualifies us from leading our families and protecting them. Shame will render you silent when you attempt to speak to your children about sexual matters. If you are caught in the grip of pornography, get help. Talk to a spiritual mentor, confess your sin, and devise a plan to get free from it. If the shame of past sexual sin paralyzes you, find a place of healing and deliverance. If you are tempted sexually in the workplace, talk to a spiritual mentor and make yourself accountable to someone. Scripture says Joseph *ran* when tempted by adultery. II Timothy 2:22 tells us to *flee youthful lusts*. You might need to take drastic action to free yourself from sexual sin and temptation. Whatever the cost, do what is needed so you can be free to function fully as a father in training your sons and protecting your daughters. The health and well-being of our future families depend on it, as well as the health and well-being of our nation.

THE PROBLEM OF ISOLATION

Sexual intimacy is always conducted in privacy. The only exceptions are when a disturbed individual displays a public act of sexuality, usually resulting in an arrest, or when all moral decency has been ignored and the open display of sexuality is condoned or welcomed, as in a group-sex orgy. Normally, sex is a completely private thing. Amnon was only able to rape Tamar because he isolated her. He got her into his house under the ruse of having her fix him a meal, and once she was there, he sent all his servants away so could be alone with her. That brings up another problem I see with the current dating system — couples tend to isolate themselves from others and spend inordinate amounts of time alone together. Even the most ardent believer in moral purity would find it hard to exercise self control when presented with extended periods of time alone with someone to whom he or she is attracted. That is a perfect setup for sexual immorality. As Christians, we are called to walk in self control. It is foolish to put ourselves in situations where self control would be unduly tested. However, isolation is the setting into which many of us, unthinkingly, put ourselves or our children. Some young people continually expose themselves to the temptation of spending time alone, in isolated settings, with the opposite sex, knowing exactly where it will lead but feigning ignorance. In doing so, they are lying to themselves and to God when they pretend to be an advocate for purity.

> I HAVE TALKED WITH YOUNG WOMEN WHO LOST THEIR PURITY SIMPLY BECAUSE THEY LIVED ALONE AND WERE HIT WITH A BOUT OF LONELINESS.

The issue of isolation should give us pause to think about our current practice of sending our daughters away to school or setting them up in apartments by themselves. I am by no means against the education or emancipation of our daughters. However, I do believe firmly in protecting our daughters' purity. The practice of sending daughters, empty-hearted or not, into a setting where they have little, if any, protection or covering results in devastation to many daughters.

They soon begin to hear things from young men, and the young women want to respond if there are empty places in their hearts. How many times does an empty-hearted daughter need to be "hit on" in a setting where there is no protection or covering before she is taken advantage of? In order for a daughter to be taken advantage of, she has to be unprotected and isolated. Isolation can easily lead to exploitation. If women are to be turned into objects of conquest, they have to be separated from fathers, pastors, and others who are designed to protect and watch over them.

We send our daughters off to school. We send our Christian daughters off to Christian school. We set them up in an apartment alone. Their covering is gone. Then we act surprised if they get into a compromised relationship, lose their purity, become pregnant, confess to the use of the morning-after pill, or admit to a secret abortion. I have talked with young women who lost their purity simply because they lived alone and were hit with a bout of loneliness. In that situation, it takes only one moment for her to ask a young man, "Would you like to come up to my apartment?" In this day and age, that invitation is synonymous with an invitation to sex. Without the continual filling of their hearts with appropriate attention, young women can become vulnerable to the inappropriately motivated attention of young men, resulting in devastating consequences in their lives.

Am I being overdramatic about our daughters' needs for protection? Let me share testimonies of young women whose lives were devastated by this very thing.

In the book *Unprotected*, by Dr. Miriam Grossman, a young woman shares her experiences. Understand more fully a daughter's heart as you see her share about things she desired in a relationship that go beyond mere sexual experience, things she was designed by God to receive in a relationship. In her testimony, she mentions the term, "friends with benefits." That term describes a current practice among young people whereby they engage in sexual activity with the understanding that there is no expectation for any other relational dynamic to occur or any expectation of commitment. The relationship is understood to be purely sexual.

Heather was a 19-year-old studying performing arts. She came in during her freshman year to see a psychologist, due to moodiness and crying spells that came out of nowhere. Normally upbeat and social, Heather was always ready for a good time. But in the past months, she had often withdrawn to her room, feeling worthless — even self-hatred. These episodes were painful and had started to interfere with school and friendships. She tried eating better and practicing yoga, but Heather couldn't get back to herself, and she didn't know why. The psychologist sent her over to me.

As we spoke, she stressed that her moods really didn't make sense, because life was good, and there was nothing to complain about. Heather liked school and had many friends. Her family was supportive. She had enough money. Her health was fine.

"How long has this been going on?" I asked.

"Oh, I don't know. Maybe . . . I guess since the New Year. I've always had low self-esteem, but now it's really bad."

"Did anything happen to you around that time?"

She thought about it. "No, I don't think so . . . I can't think of anything."

There are times when symptoms may appear without any precipitant, but I decided to ask again. "Heather, please think about it carefully. In the fall or early winter, did you lose someone you love, or have a pet die? Did you go through something frightening or dangerous? Did any relationship begin or end?"

She though it over. "Well, I can think of one thing: since Thanksgiving, I've had a 'friend with benefits.' And actually I'm kind of confused about that."

"Really? Tell me more:"

Well, I met him at a party, and I really like
him, but there's this problem. I want to spend more
time with him and do stuff like go shopping or see a
movie. That would make it a friendship for me. But
he says no, because if we do those things, then in his
opinion we'd have a relationship — and that's more
than he wants. And I'm confused, because it seems
like I don't get the 'friend' part, but he still gets the
'benefits.'"

I'M CONFUSED, BECAUSE IT SEEMS LIKE I DON'T GET THE 'FRIEND' PART, BUT HE STILL GETS THE 'BENEFITS.'

She was genuinely puzzled. She had no clue
whatsoever.

"I think many people would feel the way you
do," I told her. "You're giving what he wants, but not
getting what you want."

"Yes," she agreed. "I'm really unhappy about
that. It's hard to be with him and then go home and
be alone."

We talked about her frustration and her
wish that things were different. "Do you think," I
ventured, "that these moods you have, when you are
so unhappy and critical of yourself — do you think
they may be related to this?"

She considered my question. "I don't know . . .
maybe . . . What do you think?"

Heather's story exemplifies the danger young women face when,
in an empty-hearted and unprotected state, they compromise their
dreams and purity for a relationship. We might read Heather's testimony
and say to ourselves that she got into trouble because she didn't have a
relationship with God or attend church. We might think this couldn't

possibly happen to any of our church girls. So, let me share another testimony that will clear up the misconception that our Christian girls are not at risk.

> Growing up as a good Christian girl in an amazing family, I have always had a relationship with Jesus. All through high school, I was on fire for the Lord. My passion was constantly fueled by my church, my youth group, and my family. I left home to pursue my dreams at nursing school. In the process I also left my spiritual foundation, not realizing I did not have a strong foundation within myself. I walked onto campus with lots of passion but no stability. It took only three days for me to notice the attention of several guys and only one more day to begin compromising my standards. Shame, guilt, and condemnation immediately smothered me. Even though I tried to repent, it felt like I was trying to put toothpaste back into the tube. Compromise led to compromise. And doing "everything but" never saved me from any pain or guilt. I knew I was selling out, and I knew there was better. Shame sank deeper and deeper within me, and I started believing the lie that even if I could leave all this behind, no godly man would ever want me. I saw myself as broken goods. All the guys I hung around saw me as a sensual opportunity.

IF WOMEN ARE TO BE TURNED INTO OBJECTS TO BE PURSUED AND TAKEN ADVANTAGE OF IN OUR CULTURE, THEY HAVE TO BE ISOLATED FROM THE PROTECTION THEY WERE DESIGNED TO HAVE.

Fortunately, this broken daughter found a place of repentance, healing, and restoration. Notice her problems began when she left home and entered a sphere where she was alone, apart from protection and covering. I wish I could say her story is rare. It is not. If women are to be turned into objects to be pursued and taken advantage of in our culture, they have to be isolated from the protection they were designed to have.

THE MATERNAL SPIRIT

So Tamar went to her brother Amnon's house, and he was lying down. And she took dough, kneaded it, made cakes in his sight, and baked the cakes. And she took the pan and dished them out before him (2 Samuel 13:8-9). Amnon was supposedly sick, and Tamar did what was natural for a woman to do — she went to minister to him and meet his needs. God put a beautiful spirit of nurture in women, a spirit that desires to give to and bless others. We see that in Jesus' life. Jesus was surrounded by women who constantly provided for Him and gave to Him. Both Matthew 27:55-56 and Mark 15:41 list Mary Magdalene, the mothers of James and Joseph, and the mothers of

> IF THE MATERNAL SPIRIT IS DAMAGED OR SUPPRESSED IN A NATION, THE UNTAMED, BARBARIC, PREDATORY MALE SPIRIT CAN EASILY BECOME THE DOMINANT FORCE.

James and John among the group of women who followed Jesus and served Him. The nature of a woman, by God's design, is to nurture and release blessing. If there is proper protection in a woman's life and she doesn't have to fear, she is free to release that maternal spirit, first on her family, then on others, releasing healing in her nation. A strong maternal spirit in a nation contributes to healthy children and families, which in turn contributes to a strong, healthy nation. God intends the male and female spirits to balance one another in a society. If the maternal spirit is damaged or suppressed in a nation, the untamed, barbaric, predatory male spirit can easily become the dominant force. The female, maternal spirit civilizes the unredeemed, barbarian male spirit and brings balance into society. However, if women are not protected, if they do not feel safe, if their hearts are wounded, the beauty, healing, and nurture of their spirits is not released to be a blessing in their homes, communities, and nations.

MANY WOMEN ENTER INTO DESTRUCTIVE RELATIONSHIPS TRYING TO HEAL A "BAD BOY."

Unfortunately, through deception and guile, Amnon took advantage of Tamar's giving nature in order to satisfy his own lusts. When Tamar heard Amnon was ill, he requested her ministrations. It was natural for her to be willing to go. That is what a daughter's heart is created to do. I can hear her thinking, *He's a son of the king, a man of God, my brother. I want to bless him. He's ill, and I want to encourage him. I want to help this sick prince get well. He needs me.* There is something in a woman's heart that is designed to be wanted and needed. Being sexually assaulted was, undoubtedly, the furthest thing from her mind. Yet a woman's maternal spirit can be the very thing that can get her into serious trouble. Many women enter into destructive relationships, trying to heal a "bad boy." Many young women have progressed from *trying to mother* someone to literally *becoming a mother* in one, fatal moment. I have talked to countless women who have entered into relationships with men who would make less than desirable future mates in the hopes that they can help them become the men they are supposed to be. So many are drawn to men who have potential but also have some serious character flaws. In their desperation for a man, they willingly overlook his flaws and the honest concerns of others, thinking they can help him overcome his weaknesses. The bad boy is usually not healed, and the woman is typically "burned" in the process. Ever heard of missionary dating? Once in a while, there might be a success story, but I believe it is the rare exception. Many times, a young man in pursuit of a young woman in this kind of situation will "reform" or respond to her attempts to heal him, even to the point of claiming conversion to Christ. Only after they have gotten what they wanted will their true colors show. Five years later, the young mother attends church alone with her children while her husband stays home watching a sporting event on television. In such a situation where a "sick prince" suddenly seems to be healed due to the attention of a godly nursemaid, it is beneficial to have the presence of a wise father or other counselors to discern the true motivations of the young man — again, not to control the young woman's life, but to secure her best interests.

THE ULTIMATE VIOLATION

When Tamar took the cakes to Amnon, he grabbed her, and said, *"Come, lie with me, my sister." But she answered him, "No my brother, do not violate me, for such a thing is not done in Israel; do not do this disgraceful thing!"* (II Samuel 13:11-12). The assault is on. Like Tamar, because of the irresponsibility of men who operate out of selfishness and self interest, many daughters are put in a slap-his-hand situation where they are the ones trying to raise the standard of righteousness. She continued, *As for me, where could I get rid of my reproach? And as for you, you will be like one of the fools in Israel. Now therefore, please speak to the king, for he will not withhold me from you* (II Samuel 13:13). Far from saying, "Sex is disgusting. Just stop it!" she graciously reasoned that his desire for her was not dishonorable, but that there was a correct way to go about it. She told him to ask her father for her hand, indicating that he most probably would not withhold her from him and would grant his request. Then the blessing of God would be on their relationship. She even wanted to ensure his honor by preventing the reproach that sexual sin would bring upon him. *However, he would not listen to her; since he was stronger than she, he violated her and lay with her. Then Amnon hated her with a very great hatred; for the hatred with which he hated her was greater than the love with which he had loved her. And Amnon said to her, "Get up, go away!" But she said to him, "No, because this wrong in sending me away is greater than the other that you have done to me!" Yet he would not listen to her. Then he called his young man who attended him and said, "Now throw this woman out of my presence, and lock the door behind her"* (II Samuel 13: 14-17). Scenarios similar to this are enacted time and time again in our culture. Men take from a daughter with no intention of committing to her or caring for who she is as a person. It is solely about the man's personal satisfaction. Tamar pleaded, as women today do also, "Wait a minute. You can't send me away after you've done this. You need to make a commitment to me. It's the honorable thing to do. You still need to go and ask for me. Anyone with any kind of honor . . ." Yet he would not listen to her. Again, a man satisfies his desire, and the woman is violated and then abandoned.

A SPIRIT OF COMPLICITY

One of the critical elements in the story is Jonadab, Amnon's friend. He is almost as guilty as Amnon is for hatching the plan and promoting an exploitative spirit. Suppose Jonadab was of a different spirit and had suggested different things to Amnon? What if he could have been, at least, neutral? That would have been a better alternative. Yet, neutrality in the face of evil is complicity. As we have already said many times over, there is an assault being perpetrated against the daughters of our nation on the airwaves and through advertisements and film. When we pay to watch a film, read a magazine, or patronize a store that depicts exploitation and sexuality without commitment, we are complicit in feeding and releasing that spirit. It is not realistic to think we can totally avoid those images, messages, or products, but I believe God honors our

AFTER SEEING IMAGE AFTER IMAGE, IT'S DIFFICULT FOR OUR DAUGHTERS NOT TO THINK THEY NEED TO BE SEXUAL IN ORDER TO ATTRACT MEN.

attempts to do so. As much as possible, we try to avoid the things that specifically promote that agenda. Additionally, we talk frequently with our children about what they are seeing and hearing all around them in the culture. The sexual messages are ubiquitous; we can't afford to *not* talk about them with our kids. After seeing image after image, it's difficult for our daughters *not* to think they need to be sexual in order to attract men. We need to warn our sons not to emulate the predatory spirit of the men in the culture. We need to openly discuss these issues with our sons and daughters and counter the culture's influences with God's truths.

As men, we can't be neutral. We need to take a proactive stance against that cultural spirit of sexual assault. One day, a missionary friend boarded a subway in Japan. He saw a businessman fondling a young lady in the middle of the crowded car. Chris could not believe his eyes. "Take your hands off her," he said. The man looked incredulously at Chris but didn't stop. "Take your hands off of her now!" Chris demanded. The man stopped. What was surprising was the astonished look on the young woman's face — obviously, no one had ever intervened before. The perpetrator stopped because a Chris, a father, was not willing to be neutral and uninvolved but was willing to intervene and rescue a daughter. That is exactly what we are called to do as fathers.

CHAPTER 11

IDENTITY THEFT

The obvious has been stated; we are under a cultural sexual assault. We are constantly inundated with false ideologies about God's wonderful gift of sexuality. As a result of that assault, an entire generation of young people has experienced "identity theft" — allowing their true, God-given identity to be stolen and instead adopting the false sexual identity of the age. This theft subtly occurs in our lives over time when lie after lie is thrust upon us and we offer no rebuttal or resistance. Over time, those lies or ideas create patterns of thinking that become entrenched in our minds. Those patterns of thinking become spiritual strongholds that determine the choices we make and how we live. Identifying and confronting the initial lies and resultant strongholds is part of the prophetic work the reformer is called to do. Financial experts tell us it can take up to 300 hours to recover from identity theft when bank accounts have been compromised, credit card numbers have been accessed, and personal information has been stolen. Restoring your credit history is relatively easy compared to restoring a daughter's purity, innocence, and dreams – or a son's sense of godly honor. However, that is what we are called to do as leaders and reformers. So, how do we help restore a daughter or son who has experienced demonic identity theft?

RESTORING YOUR CREDIT HISTORY IS RELATIVELY EASY COMPARED TO RESTORING A DAUGHTER'S PURITY, INNOCENCE, AND DREAMS — OR A SON'S SENSE OF GODLY HONOR.

That same serpent who whispered lies to Eve in the Garden is whispering lies into the ears of a generation. He is whispering about one of the most critical areas of their lives — God's gift of sexuality. His lies must be identified and exposed before we can dismantle the resultant strongholds. What are some of the common lies regarding sexuality that need to be exposed and torn down in today's culture? What lies are affecting the identity of a generation of young men and women, and, as a result, their choices and lifestyles? Let's identify some of those lies, and then I will present God's corresponding truths with which to counter them.

OUR TRUE IDENTITY

One of the lies perpetrating identity theft is that the most important part of who we are is our sexuality. Therefore, it is imperative we cultivate and exercise that part of our being. Dirty Girl Cosmetics tells girls, "Release the dirty girl within you," and "Think dirty-girl thoughts." Jane cosmetics tells girls, "Inside every sweet baby Jane is a high-drama diva just waiting to reveal her dark-image side."

> **IF THE ENEMY CAN GET A WOMAN TO MAKE THE PHYSICAL AND SEXUAL PART OF HER BEING THE CHIEF PART OF HER IDENTITY, HE CAN THEN DESTROY HER LIFE AND PLACE HER IN A LIFELONG PRISON OF UNFULFILLED DREAMS.**

Cosmopolitan bursts with sex articles. Thong underwear is marketed for 11-year-olds. Sex-saturated movies and advertisements are part of the strategy of darkness to create a false, destructive identity in a generation searching for their true identity. If the enemy can get a woman to make the physical and sexual part of her being the chief part of her identity, he can then destroy her life and place her in a lifelong prison of unfulfilled dreams. From her earliest years, this demonic spirit attempts to stamp his identity on her to achieve that end. Much of the assault, as we have mentioned, is against a woman's personhood. A woman will not "release the dirty girl within her" or "think dirty-girl thoughts" unless her identity has been bludgeoned by the culture to the point that her innocence and natural inhibitions have been eroded by the constant bombardment of false ideology.

The sequence of the Garden of Eden has not changed. Just as Eve's deception led to Adam's fall, when a woman gives way to the lies of the enemy, she tends to access the lower nature of the men in the culture and cause them to forfeit their true identity and worth as well. The serpent brought temptation to Eve. She gave into temptation and offered the fruit to Adam. At that critical moment, Adam should have refused her offer and led her back into obedience to God. Instead of protecting Eve and resisting temptation himself, he gave in to her offer and accepted the fruit. As a result, they both fell and were separated from their true identities in God.

Counter that lie of false identity with God's truth: Who you are as a person is the most important part of who you are. Your sexuality is only one part of your identity and is only to be expressed within God's protective boundary of marriage.

RELATIONAL CONNECTING POINT

Part of the identity-theft scheme is to create a connecting point between members of the opposite sex that is physical/sexual rather than relational/personal. What do I mean by that? For years I have watched the younger generation utilize social networking tools in their longing for connectedness. Facebook, texting, and similar social-networking tools were created and are used in an attempt to create a sense of community and authentic relationship. For some, these tools allow them to experience a sense of intimacy without the risk of rejection. They don't understand that part of life is moving toward intimacy and that risk is inherent in building true relationships. One of the reasons people connect on a physical/sexual level is because it affords a sense of instant, deep closeness and connection where, at least initially, there is no risk of rejection. Closeness without rejection, instant intimacy — how wonderful! Unfortunately, that connecting point of sexuality leaves people feeling empty and sorely disappointed because they were designed by God for *true* intimacy. The physical connecting point can only deliver a sexual experience, not God-ordained intimacy.

WHEN A YOUNG WOMAN GETS INTO THE HABIT OF CONNECTING TO YOUNG MEN BY USING HER SEXUALITY, SHE SOON DISCOVERS SHE DOESN'T HAVE THE COURAGE TO RELATE ANY OTHER WAY.

If the enemy can get a young woman to adopt sexual contact as her primary connecting point with men, her life will be chaos. When a young woman gets into the habit of connecting to young men by using her sexuality, she soon discovers she doesn't have the courage to relate any other way; she can't trust God with her future because she has been in charge of securing her own future by the power of her seduction. She becomes increasingly afraid to attempt to relate on a personal, non-sexual level because she fears she will not be loved for who she is as a person —her personality, her likes, and her dreams. Unfortunately, she fails to realize that relating to people based on her "power to attract" leaves her empty and does not result in relationships based on reality.

SHE WAS IN THE PAINFUL PROCESS OF DISCOVERING THAT LIFE IS MUCH MORE THAN SEXUAL ENCOUNTERS.

I was acquainted with a young woman who had a history of continuous immoral relationships. Each relationship began with excitement, promise, and hope. With each new beginning, there was the possibility this new relationship would be different and permanent. Because of the fear she had of relating solely on a personal/relational level, sexuality quickly became a major part of those relationships, increasing the sense of excitement and instant closeness. All too soon though, relational incompatibility surfaced, especially as she was honest with herself about what they had — a relationship based on sex. We discussed that pattern in her life and talked about her making a commitment to relate to young men only on a personal/relational level, embracing God's standard of sexual purity as part of the courtship philosophy she now wanted to embrace. With this revelation, she began a new relationship and soon complained that their relationship didn't have the passion and excitement that characterized so

many of her immoral relationships. In fact, she bemoaned the fact that
the relationship seemed unnatural and awkward because of the absence of
those elements of instant intimacy to which she had grown accustomed.
When I inquired about the reason for her feelings, she shared that relating
sexually was much easier than relating on a personal level and almost
guaranteed results, though usually very short-lived. She admitted she was
actually afraid to attempt a relationship on a personal/relational level.
She was in the painful process of discovering that life is much more than
sexual encounters. In other words, there is a tremendous amount of life
that occurs outside of the bedroom. Furthermore, it is depersonalizing to
have your body be the essence of your value. Personal relationships must
be built on more than physical connection alone. For her to experience
relationships as God designed them to be experienced, she needed to find
the courage to learn a new way to relate. We need to remember her story
as we seek to bring healing, both inside and outside our churches, to
countless young women trapped in such destructive cycles of relating.

WE NEED YOU, DADS.

I cannot overstate the power of a father's love and presence in his
daughter's life to create a healthy identity in her. God's beautiful
developmental design in the formation of a daughter's identity through
her father gives us great reason to value and encourage the strengthening
of this father-daughter bond. God took all that into consideration when
He made the blueprint for the family. That identity formation begins
during those important early years in a young girl's life when she is
"female but not sexual." In that season, God intends for her to be filled
with a sense of self-worth and value by words, non-sexual touch, and
attention from her father. The three A's that must be employed by a father
in his daughter's life are:

- Affirmation — the power of his words.

**I CANNOT OVERSTATE THE POWER
OF A FATHER'S LOVE AND PRESENCE
IN HIS DAUGHTER'S LIFE TO CREATE
A HEALTHY IDENTITY IN HER.**

- Affection — the power of his touch.
- Attention — the power of his time and his heart's focus.

Of course, a mother contributes greatly, too, but the father's source of these things is critical to the formation of a daughter's self-identity, especially as it relates to her future relationships with men. During her early years, there should be an overwhelming sense that she is a princess, a special flower, and an irreplaceable daughter to her father. That is not to say she should be a *prima donna* or that she should not also receive correction and discipline. I am simply saying that affirmation and blessing from her father, none of which is linked to her sexuality, creates a foundation for her identity that becomes rooted in her personhood, not her sexuality.

THE POWER OF A FATHER'S LOVE IN THE CREATION OF HIS DAUGHTER'S IDENTITY ENSURES THAT HER HEART IS FILLED; IT PROTECTS HER FROM ADOPTING AN IDENTITY BASED ON SEXUALITY.

Later, when she matures and changes from being a young girl to a young woman, she will not be tempted to make her emerging sexuality her primary identity. Instead, the emerging sexual part of her identity will become incorporated into her already firmly established identity. The power of a father's love in the creation of his daughter's identity ensures that her heart is filled; it protects her from adopting an identity based on sexuality.

Unfortunately, we are witnessing a generation of young women whose fathers have been absent or who have neglected this important responsibility. The result is daughters who are desperate for male attention, blessing, and affirmation, and those daughters tend to use their sexuality to attempt to have their needs met. Young girls who do not have fathers need men in the church who can function as Mordecai did in Esther's life. They need dads who can function as (but not take the place of) their absent, natural fathers.

IT IS CRITICAL THAT MEN IN THE CHURCH BE FREE FROM SEXUAL SIN AND SHAME. ONLY THEN WILL THEY BE IN POSITION TO MINISTER TO THE NEEDS OF HURTING DAUGHTERS.

I want to be very careful here. I do not believe the place of the natural father or mother should ever be replaced in the life of a young person by a spiritual mother, father, or mentor! Honor that is due to natural mothers and fathers should never be bestowed upon spiritual mothers and fathers, and if it is and is accepted by them, I believe it is illegal. Having said that, I cannot overestimate the importance of natural and spiritual fathers in the formation of a young woman's identity. This is why it is critical that men in the church be free from sexual sin and shame. Only then will they be in position to minister to the needs of hurting daughters. In the following letter, listen to the cry of daughters' hearts to have fathers actively involved in their lives.

THE TRUTH BE TOLD, DADS HAVE A RIDICULOUS AMOUNT OF INFLUENCE IN OUR LIVES.

Sometimes I just don't like to talk about it. It's a little bit vulnerable and frightening. Then, at other times, I wish I could explain to every dad on earth what really was in the heart of his daughter. The truth be told, dads have a ridiculous amount of influence in our lives. I think a lot of dads have backed off, though, because modern-day daughters appear so independent, capable, intelligent, and strong. I imagine the thought behind this is, "Look at her. She's fine. She doesn't need to hear from me." And she is. But, she isn't.

I think it is crazy God calls himself "Father." If I were a dad, I might find that title and the corresponding expectations more than a little intimidating. But maybe it's a good comparison, and maybe we could learn something from it. Think about how needy we are before God. How many times do you (dads and everyone else) need to hear you're doing a good job, you've made the right choices, you're valuable, you're . . . and the list goes on. We constantly need God's reassurances. God calls Himself and our dads, Father, and we need to hear from both. Interesting.

THERE'S JUST SOMETHING ABOUT US DAUGHTERS...WE HAVE THIS BUILT IN NEED TO KNOW WE ARE CARED FOR, PROTECTED, APPRECIATED, AND KNOWN.

There's just something about us daughters . . . we have this built in need to know we are cared for, protected, appreciated, and known. I think all those things are connected, because when I say protected, I don't mean locked up in an ivory tower and insulated from life. I think it simply means being known and cared for. That might not sound like protection, but I think it is. There is safety in knowing that because someone is well acquainted with (knows) your heart (who you are), they are ready to jump into action in order to protect you (show they care) at any moment.

Whenever Pastor Jim returns to a place he has ministered in before, there is always an informal line up of daughters who just want a hug. It's hilarious to watch as everyone stands there awkwardly waiting. I've seen people wait over 15 minutes; they just won't leave. Sure, Pastor Jim is unique. But either daughters are waiting in lines to be hugged by men who are willing to be dads, or they're leaving in droves to find guys who have empty arms and are willing to say at least a few things that register somewhere close to a girl's heart. It's how we're made. I have to believe the revelation of what a father, mother, daughter, or son is comes from God and is available to all of us. If God can change me (a girl who would rather die than admit that I need fathers and brothers to speak into my life and surround and protect me), then surely, by the power of His Holy Spirit, He can teach men to become brothers and fathers after His heart. And, there can never be too many brothers and fathers.

I guess it must be intimidating, though. I've heard stories of guys who have been yelled at for opening doors for women, or slapped when they have kindly offered to lift something heavy for a lady. Or maybe those guys received glares or hostile verbal jabs, or the feeling that what they have to offer isn't important or even desirable. Or maybe you dads received a blank stare after you said something nice about what your daughter is wearing, or you tried to hug her, and she went stiff and cold — as if you committed an unpardonable sin against your teenage daughter by invading her personal space. I've never slapped or yelled, but I've surely been hostile. We're just insecure. We're not sure. At least that's been my story. We all have different reasons for the ways we behave.

WE ALL NEED OUR DADS TO PURSUE US AND WORK AT KNOWING US.

Nevertheless, we all need our dads to pursue us and work at knowing us. Possibly, we're mean because we don't know our own worth, and we're looking to see if you will endure our immaturity and rejection and still pursue us. Yes, it is work. And there is tons of spiritual warfare (spiritual tension — like a tug of war between heaven and hell). And no, it won't be comfortable. But if you could actually look into our hearts and

see the power you have to bless our lives, our
understanding of ourselves, and shape how we
relate to men, I think you'd be utterly shocked
and overwhelmed. Dads, God gave you to us
on purpose. You have an incredible amount of
influence in our lives. Our hearts never grow old.
It really is true that in the heart of every woman is
a little girl. Ask God for a revelation of a daughter's
heart, and watch the women in your life change
before your eyes as you reach out to bless and affirm
them.

DADS, GOD GAVE YOU TO US ON PURPOSE. YOU HAVE AN INCREDIBLE AMOUNT OF INFLUENCE IN OUR LIVES.

A healthy father-daughter relationship is the major factor in providing
protection for a daughter. Protection is not so much about creating walls
or prohibitions around a daughter's life, but more about a deposit a father
makes into the spirit of his daughter that protects her from immoral
relationships, her needs having already been met. I like to think of it as a
father-created, invisible force field that wonderfully protects a daughter's
heart wherever she goes.

DESIGNER GENES

Another area in which the enemy lies to us is that of our "design"
as men and women. This lie says women don't need safety, security,
permanence, or commitment. It says they, just like men, are primarily
sexual in nature. It says they can be as unattached as the young men
in our culture when it comes to participating in sexual experiences. In
other words, the enemy lies and tries to erase any differences between
the sexes. In truth, God made men and women very different from each
other. Women are designed by God to need safety, security, permanence,
and commitment. That is why marriage is the God-given context for
sexuality. Unlike men, women are primarily relational and secondarily
sexual. They can safely and fully open up the sexual part of their lives to

a man only when he has first fulfilled their need for safety and security. That is accomplished by making a public, covenantal commitment to her called marriage.

The first indication regarding our God-intended design as men and women is found in Genesis: *God created man in His own image, in the image of God He created him; male and female, He created them* (Genesis 1:27). This verse shows the distinction of identity between male and female. Both are in the image of God but are distinctly unique. This was never meant to be a statement of value denoting one as better than the other, but rather of differing function and design. Interestingly, the woman was taken from the rib of Adam. The symbolism of this deliberate act of creation cannot be overlooked. God did not take the woman out of Adam's calf or foot, but from his rib, which protects and is associated with his heart. That represents nurture, affection, and intimacy. By using the rib in the creation of the woman, God deals with the issue of proximity; He places the woman by her husband's side to be his teammate. By taking her from the rib near the heart, He also sets the issue of priority because the heart is the source from which the issues of life flow. God intends husbands to keep their wives close to their hearts, a priority and a focus in their lives.

> AS MUCH AS THE CULTURE WANTS TO ERASE DIFFERENCES BETWEEN THE SEXES, GOD SAYS THEY ARE DIFFERENT, AND I HAVE OBSERVED FIRST-HAND, THEY ARE, INDEED, VERY DIFFERENT.

As much as the culture wants to erase differences between the sexes, God says they are different, and I have observed first-hand, they are, indeed, very different. I have watched those distinctive God-given characteristics and identities develop naturally in my sons and daughters. My girls have not had to be told to dress up like Mom and pretend to be princesses. They have not had to force themselves to play "Mommy" as they cared for dolls and set up houses with little families inside. Contrastingly, my sons did not have to be told to go out and dig for worms or to punch, poke, and wrestle each other. They did not have to be encouraged to fight the imaginary dark forces in the great, cosmic struggle between good and evil. I often wondered what our neighbors and passersby thought when our youngest son James was on our front lawn dressed up as a pirate, a ninja, a cowboy, or a medieval warrior in imaginary life-and-death struggles, repeatedly throwing himself to the ground and then leaping to his feet in mortal, hand-to-hand combat. Always victorious, James would then disappear from sight, return to his math or reading, and resume his epic struggle during his next break. That just didn't happen with our daughters.

The differences between men and women can be explained by using the analogy of an electrical-breaker box. A man is wired with circuits, each individual circuit representing different areas of his life—work, hobbies, car, physical health, finances, reputation, and sexual desires with his wife. These electrical circuits, representing different areas of his life, function quite independently of each other. For example, in one day he could lose his job, have his golf clubs stolen, total his new pickup on the way home, break his leg in the process, limp up the stairs on crutches, collect his mail and find he is being sued, glance at the local newspaper reporting the same, and then want sex with his wife. When one area short-circuits in a man, the others keep functioning quite well. Each of those circuits could have clicked off, but that didn't mean the sex-with-his-wife switch did — that circuit still worked quite well!

A woman's circuits, on the other hand, are fully integrated. Her breaker box contains electrical circuits representing different areas of her life, including the presence of a main power switch linked to each of these circuits. In other words, when one circuit goes down, they all go down. What happens in one area of her life affects all other areas of her life. For example, if she is mourning the death of a loved one, her sorrow will affect all of her other relationships and activities. If she is worried about finances, that worry will color all of her life. To illustrate further using our previous example, the man arrived home, and his wife informed him that the basement had flooded and all the photos of their children had been destroyed. The flooding immediately switched off the family-memory circuit in her breaker box which is linked to the main switch. Subsequently, the main switch shut down, and with it, all the rest of the circuits, including the have-sex-with-your-husband circuit. (Although the news of the basement flooding might have irritated the husband, he still wanted to have sex.) Real life is not as black and white as my illustration would suggest, but if we are honest with ourselves, we have to admit it is a fair depiction of men and women.

Researchers have found that the brain of the male fetus *in utero* is washed by chemicals. As a result of that wash, the left- and right-brain functions of the male are quite separate from each other. Because the female brain is not washed by those chemicals, the integration of the left and right sides of a female brain are much more pronounced. As a result, women process life's events very differently than do men. Perhaps it explains why negative sexual experiences have profoundly affected a generation of young women much more than they have young men.

WHILE MANY A YOUNG MAN CAN EASILY WALK AWAY FROM A CASUAL SEXUAL ENCOUNTER — HAVING JUST GIVEN HIS BODY — A YOUNG WOMAN DID NOT *JUST* GIVE HER BODY.

It may be the reason that memories and relationships seem to take on such a higher level of importance for women than for men. That difference could explain why young women will often weep uncontrollably for several hours after I pray for healing for them from sexual sin and shame. While many a young man can easily walk away from a casual sexual encounter — having just given his body — a young woman did not *just* give her body. She gave her integrated being—the entirety of who she is. Sex is never a casual thing for a woman. Women are not wired that way. God designed a woman to receive a memory imprint upon her heart through sexual experience, which is intended to be a positive memory, allowing her heart to draw closer to her husband. That wonderful memory then becomes a curse when a woman's sexual experience is not with her husband. Instead of positive memories with her husband in the context of a secure atmosphere of commitment, she can be hounded by memories of fear, shame, guilt, and regret over experiences with other men. And, as I mentioned earlier, those memories cannot be conveniently hidden away in a little box, nor will they simply disappear when she walks down the aisle to the sound of romantic wedding music in the presence of friends and family. Instead, she will carry those memories around with her daily.

IF A WOMAN IS ENGAGED IN SEXUAL ENCOUNTERS BEFORE MARRIAGE, IN BETWEEN SEXUAL EXPERIENCES, SHE ASKS THE "COMMITMENT QUESTION."

God's design for the sexes has profound consequences in the sexual arena. Every cell in a woman's body is wired by God to need safety, security, permanence, and commitment. We see this in the nesting instinct of a woman about to give birth. She hurries around with a burst of energy, cleaning, and preparing to make the atmosphere and environment safe and secure for her new little one. Out of her own desire for safety and security, a woman will create an atmosphere of safety and security for her children. That is why a woman was never designed for casual sexual encounters. If a woman is engaged in sexual encounters before marriage, in between sexual experiences, she asks the "commitment question." She may not ask in words, but she will ask it in body language and facial expression, "When will you commit to me?"

Remember my trip to the store for milk where I was visually assaulted by the magazine covers? Interestingly, the last article on that *Cosmopolitan* cover was entitled, "How to Get Him to Commit." That seems to be an out-of-place article in a magazine that supports the cultural philosophy that women don't need the security of commitment. The marketing department must have discovered that, in order to sell more magazines, they can't completely ignore what is in a daughter's heart.

CHAPTER 12

TRUE INTIMACY

Let's examine another lie of the enemy: True intimacy is achieved through the physical act of sex. God's truth is that true intimacy is composed of three sequential parts:

- spiritual oneness
- progressing to soul/friendship oneness
- completing itself with physical oneness in marriage

THAT COMPLETE DEFINITION OF *YADA* IS WHAT WOMEN YEARN FOR IN A RELATIONSHIP, TO KNOW AND BE FULLY KNOWN AND CARED FOR.

The Bible describes the intimacy of the first married couple on earth with this phrase, "Adam knew Eve." You might say, "Well of course he knew her; she was his wife. He had to know her." Interestingly enough, the word "knew" is a word that goes far beyond our common understanding of the word. The Hebrew word here is *yada* which means "to know and be known." In addition to sexual union, other meanings of *yada* include: sharing love — dedicating ourselves to a person so we can engage them with our love and affection; showing mercy — understanding the needs of those around us and taking care of them; and acting justly — faithfully living out our covenant relationship with the Lord in every area of our life. To apply those definitions in our context, we can say Adam fully knew Eve, and she fully knew him. They did not simply experience a physical union, but knew each other fully — body, soul, and spirit oneness. The word *yada* tells us Adam dedicated himself to Eve and poured out his love and affection on her. He understood her needs and attended to those needs, and he faithfully lived out his covenant relationship with her. That is a far cry from the men who "hook up" with young women for one-night stands! That complete definition of *yada* is what women yearn for in a relationship, to know and be fully known and cared for.

I want to share with you a beautiful example of *yada* lived out in a relationship. As I have shared previously, I have a strong dislike for the current system of relationships found in the world. I liken it to a refrigerator factory that sells refrigerators which have a 50 percent failure rate. In spite of that high rate of failure, most everyone still chooses to patronize the company and buy their products. That is exactly what is occurring in the world's system of relationships. This system is producing a 50 percent rate of failure in marriages, leading to the devastation of men, women, and children. Ironically, no one calls this system to account, and we unthinkingly continue our participation in this broken system. As a result, we get hurt, and our loved ones get hurt. My wife and I have chosen a different route with our children, a route some people call courtship. Unlike traditional dating, courtship employs the principles of purity, protection, communication, honor, and witness or testimony as a couple gets to know each other with an eye toward marriage.

Let me share with you from the courtship of our third-oldest daughter Julie and her now-husband Lee. We will do so in a question and answer format.

~ How did you honor your parents and spiritual authorities in your relationship? ~

Both of our dads are in full-time ministry, so our parents functioned both as parents and spiritual authority figures in our lives. We honored them in two different ways — by honesty and involvement. We were open and honest both individually and as a couple with our parents about our desires, frustrations, and feelings. We set guidelines for each stage of our relationship as it progressed and honored our parents by letting them be a part of the whole process. They have so much wisdom from past experiences, mistakes, and many years of marriage, that it would have been foolish not to welcome their input in our relationship. We respected their advice, and they, in turn, trusted we were hearing from the Lord as we made decisions regarding our relationship. They knew we each had a strong relationship with the Lord, and they allowed us the freedom to seek the Lord for ourselves. We were able to follow what God led us to do for our courtship, as courtship is not a set list of rules. It is unique and different for every couple, just as every one of us is unique and different.

~ How did you learn to communicate with each other,
and what tools did you use? ~

Lee and I had a long (2 ½ year), long-distance relationship, spanning the Atlantic Ocean and the American continent. Most of that time Lee lived in Germany or North Carolina, while I studied fashion design in Seattle or lived at home in Spokane. Lee pursued me by writing letters, with my dad's permission, as a way of our getting to know each other on a friends-only basis for 1 ½ years before our courtship even officially started.

DURING THE DURATION OF THEIR COURTSHIP, LEE LEARNED TO STABILIZE HIS EMOTIONS AND MAKE SURE THE CENTER OF HIS LIFE WAS JESUS CHRIST, NOT JULIE RUTH.

At this point, I, Jim, would like to step in and explain the reasons behind a lot of what happened in Lee and Julie's courtship. Of course, I have Lee and Julie's permission to do so! I do this to help you understand we did not arbitrarily slow down their courtship process. There were reasons behind everything we did. Lee and Julie first met when she and I visited my son Luke in North Carolina. Lee was the bass player, and Luke was the drummer in their band, Cannon Hill. When Lee came home with Luke for Thanksgiving that same year, he began to feel that Julie could be his future wife. Several months later, days before their band left for a 1 ½ year stint in Germany, Lee convinced Luke to drive to Spokane with him on an unplanned cross-country trip, three days before Christmas. They showed up unannounced at our doorstep at two in the morning, having driven 48 hours on treacherous winter roads, only to drive back 36 hours later. Lee wanted to see this possible future wife one more time before he left for Europe. During their brief stay at our home, Lee pulled me aside to say he was interested in Julie. Knowing Julie's cautious nature, we knew she would not agree to court someone she did not know. As a result, we did not use the word "courtship" initially with Julie, but asked if she would be open to getting to know Lee through letter writing. She agreed. Months later, after a lengthy time of letter writing, and later, phone calls, Julie's heart was ready to officially begin a courtship with Lee.

Not only did we keep their relationship moving at a slow pace for Julie's sake, but we also saw things in Lee's life that prompted us to allow things to move ahead slowly. Lee is a sensitive, emotional guy — as am I. I could see he would have a tendency to make Julie too important in his life, and that he often allowed his emotions to rule him. I knew that neither of those things would make for a healthy relationship or marriage. During the duration of their courtship, Lee learned to stabilize his emotions and make sure the center of his life was Jesus Christ, not Julie Ruth. He and I were in frequent communication over issues in his life and the courtship. The fruit borne from their lengthy courtship is good in both of their lives. Julie is a blessed wife, and Lee is a better husband as a result of the pace we took.

THERE HAVE BEEN NO POST-MARRIAGE SURPRISES WHERE SHOCKING TRUTHS CAME OUT OR WHERE THE PERSON WE HAD COMMITTED TO SPEND OUR LIFE WITH FOREVER TURNED OUT NOT TO BE THE PERSON WE THOUGHT THEY WERE.

Now, back to their story. Julie: The long distance and time differences—nine-hour time difference when he was in Germany — were challenging, but in the midst of all the hardship of separation, short phone calls, conversations getting cut short, and missing each other's calls, we really gained something valuable we will have the rest of our lives — we learned how to communicate. That was all we had. We didn't get to see each other on a regular basis, go out for coffee, or hang out on the weekend. We didn't get to do any of the normal things two people do when they are trying to get to know each other. All we could do was talk. And talk we did! We talked about life, dreams, fears, goals, family, past, future, friends, strengths, weaknesses, love languages, communication, personalities, food, all the way down to our smallest likes and dislikes. I can honestly say we truly knew each other when we got married. There have been no post-marriage surprises where shocking truths came out or where the person we had committed to spend our life with forever turned out not to be the person we thought they were. We took the time beforehand and made communication a priority. I speak for both of us when I say it was *so* worth it!

JIM ASSURED ME DURING THE ENTIRE PROCESS THAT WE WOULD BE BLESSED IN THE END. HE WAS TOTALLY RIGHT. WE ARE SO BLESSED!

Lee: I was not allowed to talk about things that would unnecessarily pull on Julie's emotions during that entire season. We could speak as friends, and we could get to know each other, but we could not be romantic in any way. That was difficult for me, a romantic and expressive guy, because I desired to express my deep feelings for her. However, Jim assured me it was best for us both to not let our feelings loose before it was time. I needed to die to those desires every day. That protective strategy allowed us to truly learn about each other. Jim assured me during the entire process that we would be blessed in the end. He was totally right. We are so blessed! Now I can say everything I want to say and buy her flowers anytime I want. Now she gets all the romance she could desire, knowing it is real and comes with a life-long commitment from me.

~ What resources were helpful to you in getting to know each other? ~

Julie: My parents directed us to some amazing resources that helped us work through things and talk about important things we didn't know were important to talk about. We read *Telling Each Other the Truth*, by William Backus, *The Five Love Languages*, by Gary Chapman, *Love and Respect*, by Emerson Eggerichs, and *The Act of Marriage*, by Tim LaHaye — we read this last one only shortly before our marriage. We also worked through personality tests, a strength and weakness test, and talked through a list of questions that progressed from simple "get to know you" questions to deeper, more intimate topics as our relationship progressed. We both admit that at times these resources seemed silly to us when they were first presented. However, by the time we had completed each book or test, we were very grateful for how valuable they had been in helping us know one another and deal with life issues.

Lee: In the beginning of my pursuit of Julie's friendship, I read the books Jim and Lisa had written. They helped me to know the family better and also opened my eyes to know more truth about women and family. Jim and Lisa also gave me a courtship manual I used throughout our relationship. The manual gave me direction and understanding as I led the courtship. It also gave me questions to discuss with Julie that I would never have thought about on my own. Most people never talk about a lot of important areas before marriage. Those questions and topics were important in helping us really know each other. Some topics were fun to talk about, and others were uncomfortable because we were afraid to have differing opinions.

WE FELT AS THOUGH WE HAD JUST DISCOVERED SECRET KEYS PEOPLE DON'T USUALLY DISCOVER UNTIL THEY'VE BEEN MARRIED FOR 30 YEARS.

Julie: I think one of the most helpful, eye-opening books that blessed our friendship, and now our marriage, was *Love and Respect*. As we read, we felt as though we had just discovered secret keys people don't usually discover until they've been married for 30 years. We learned a woman's basic need is love, and a man's basic need is respect. The book gives the reader the keys to understand who God made you to be, who He made your spouse to be, and how to most effectively meet each other's needs.

~ What steps did you take to keep yourselves pure
in your relationship?~

Julie: We set some protective guidelines at the beginning of our relationship that helped us remain pure and honoring towards each other throughout our courtship. We didn't hold hands or have any physical contact at first. We focused mainly on getting to know each other and becoming friends. While we did spend some time alone together, we also spent a lot of time with the whole family, enabling Lee to get to know my family and vica versa. It created a very safe atmosphere in which our friendship could blossom. I felt safe and secure with the covering of my parents over our courtship, allowing me to open my heart slowly to Lee.

As our relationship progressed, so did our desire for one another. I remember talking to my parents about wanting to hold hands at some point. They were fine with it and asked us to pray and hear what the Lord had to say. We both felt an, "OK!" from the Lord and were able to do that on our next visit. We chose not to kiss until we got engaged. We loved the season of engagement in our relationship. We got to experience kissing (within boundaries), but still had to be really careful in guarding our hearts and protecting one another because any physical contact whets the appetite for more physical contact. We had to keep ourselves open to the Lord and His leading. We never wanted to make anything harder for one another than it had to be.

IF YOU FORCE A FLOWER OPEN BEFORE ITS TIME, IT WILL NOT BE AS BEAUTIFUL AS IT WOULD HAVE BEEN IF IT HAD BEEN ALLOWED TO BLOSSOM AT THE PROPER TIME.

Lee: This whole area of sexuality was so hard! We guys always want to go further — always! I felt like I died physically sometimes. I held tight to Jim's analogy about Julie being a flower. If you force a flower open before its time, it will not be as beautiful as it would have been if it had been allowed to blossom at the proper time. In fact, a lot of flowers have been killed that way. I chose, throughout the whole process of courtship, to prepare the ground, water the flower, and serve all the needs of the flower (to use Jim's terminology) so she would have the opportunity to become the most beautiful flower she could be. Now I am blessed way beyond what the devil entices us men to experience prematurely. My wife is now free to respond to me and my love without any of the shame or guilt she would have experienced if we had been morally impure before marriage. All of my self control and waiting were well worth it!

MY WIFE IS NOW FREE TO RESPOND
TO ME AND MY LOVE WITHOUT ANY
OF THE SHAME OR GUILT SHE WOULD
HAVE EXPERIENCED IF WE HAD BEEN
MORALLY IMPURE BEFORE MARRIAGE.

~ What kind of accountability did you have in place? ~

Julie: Our parents were our main source of accountability. My parents
were over our courtship, primarily because Lee's parents and church
offered very little teaching about it. His parents trusted my parents to
help us along in the process. Lee was in communication with my dad
the whole time. Dad regularly checked in with Lee to see how we were
handling physical temptation. Instead of talking to me about something
important, Lee would first go through my dad. Dad was my covering,
and he was there to make sure I felt safe the whole time. As a result,
I always did feel safe because I knew if Lee brought something up for
discussion, he had already gone through my dad.

~ What goals did you have in your courtship? ~

Our goal in courtship was to discover if this was the person God
intended us to marry and spend our life with — and do so in a safe and
protected way. We weren't just playing around, wanting to have fun.

Julie: One of my desires had always been to marry my best friend.
When Lee and I first started courting, we were only acquaintances. I take
a very long time to get to know people to the point where I can open up.
As a result, our courtship process was very slow. I am very grateful to Lee
that he let it progress at the rate I felt comfortable with. He allowed me
the time I needed to begin to open up. And I can say, I really did end up
marrying my best friend.

~ What benefits do you see in your marriage as a result of courtship? ~

I HAD NEVER DATED ANYONE BEFORE.
I NEVER FELT DEPRIVED BY THAT
BECAUSE, AS MY DAD PREACHES,

HE HAD FILLED MY HEART WITH HIS LOVE AND I WAS NOT NEEDY, TRYING TO MEET THAT NEED BY MEN.

Julie: I had never dated anyone before. I never felt deprived by that because, as my dad preaches, he had filled my heart with his love and I was not needy, trying to meet that need by men. I had never held a boy's hand or never kissed anyone until Lee. He was the first for me, and I'm so glad it happened that way. I think there are so many benefits to courting before marriage. We honored God, our parents and one another throughout our whole courtship up until the time we said, "I do!" at the altar. When you do things God's way, by following His principles and staying pure, God is setting you up for a very blessed marriage. God honors you when you honor Him with your purity, wait for His blessing and perfect timing, and enjoy His gift within marriage.

Lee: I dated quite a bit before I met Julie. Dating is all about emotion and doing what feels good. People tend to get blinded by the emotions and feelings involved, and they never get to know the other person. You spend the entire time trying to be the person you think the other person wants you to be. Those emotions lead to less and less communication, and the physical part of the relationship becomes greater and greater. Eventually, you are left with emptiness, hurt, and guilt. I know there are happily married couples who never knew about courtship or used its principles, but I assure you they would now tell you that courtship would have been a better and wiser way for them to start. For parents: You wouldn't let your kids touch the hot stove when they were younger. I am sure they would thank you for that today. Dating can be a hot burner. Start talking with your kids about the issue now. Be honest about your past mistakes. Share with them that God has a much better way.

~ What would you say to your generation about courtship? ~

It is worth waiting to have sex until you've made a commitment in marriage to one another. God's way is always best. Courtship is such a useful tool in helping singles of all ages prepare for marriage, because it creates a strong and deep relationship in a protected, safe environment. It's so wonderful to have the covering of pastors, parents, and/or mentors leading and guiding you along in the process. If your parents are unable or unwilling to do it, seek out another godly couple who will. It's wonderful to have knowledge and advice from people who know lots of things you don't know from a lot of years of experience. It is special getting to know the person you intend to marry and what God has put inside of them — their dreams, their passions, their goals — and to see if they fit with your own God-driven dreams, passions, and goals. The best part of all is seeing the blessing of the Lord time and time again as you honor Him with your relationship. We've really learned to appreciate everything in His timing. When you can't do everything you want to all at once, you really cherish the sweetness of those things when you are finally able to experience them. We still cherish every hand held, every kiss, and every moment spent together because we didn't have those for so long.

♥ ♥ ♥

SEXUAL KNOWING ALONE CANNOT SUSTAIN OR MAKE FOR A HEALTHY RELATIONSHIP.

Julie and Lee are not perfect people; we are not perfect parents, and courtship is not a perfect process. Does their testimony sound incredibly old-fashioned? You bet it does! However, since we, as parents, wanted better for our daughter than the world had to offer, courtship offered a wonderful alternative that helped Lee and Julie get to know each other well before they married — in a *yada* kind of way. They also progressed through the three stages of knowing each other in way that honored God and formed a firm, healthy foundation for their marriage — first getting to know each other on a spiritual level, secondly on a friendship level, and finally on a sexual level once they were married. The world's way in relationships starts with the sexual and often does not backtrack at all to include the other levels of knowing. Sexual knowing alone cannot sustain or make for a healthy relationship.

IT'S MORE THAN PHYSICAL.

The world has it all wrong. Sex is not solely a physical act as the world would have us believe. Unfortunately, our current sex-education classes reflect that belief — they offer "how to" lessons in sexuality and contraception to the exclusion of dealing with any of the spiritual or emotional ramifications. Because we are integrated people, what happens to us physically, and therefore sexually, has ramifications in our spirits, minds, and emotions. Listen closely to this truth through the testimony of a brokenhearted daughter after the breaking up of a relationship in which she had given herself. This story is also from *Unprotected* by Dr. Miriam Grossman:

"WHY DO THEY TELL YOU HOW TO PROTECT YOUR BODY — FROM HERPES AND PREGNANCY — BUT THEY DON'T TELL YOU WHAT IT DOES TO YOUR HEART?"

Olivia, 18, is also a freshman. She was valedictorian of her senior class and hopes to go to med school. But, Olivia just told me that she's been vomiting up to six times a day . . . Olivia originally developed bulimia in the ninth grade. With therapy, she did well, and she thought that the bouts of binging and vomiting were over, until she got to college. It's not the academic pressure — she is doing well in all her classes. No, it was the end of a romance that precipitated the relapse and brought Olivia to our center for help. Her therapist recognized Olivia's depression and eating disorder and referred her to me for evaluation. During our initial meeting, Olivia described the short-lived relationship, her first experience with intimacy. "When it ended, it hurt so much," she said, weeping. "I think about him all the time, and I haven't been going to one of my classes because he'll be there, and I can't handle seeing him. I was so unprepared for this. . . . Why, Doctor," she asked, "why, do they tell you how to protect your body — from herpes and pregnancy — but they don't tell you what it does to your *heart*?"

In Olivia's case, as in the case of many other young women I have talked with, sex was not solely a physical act devoid of any other consequences. A sexual relationship had dire consequences for her heart, mind, and emotions.

YOU CAN BE SEXUALLY INTIMATE WITH ANYONE AT ANY TIME, AND, ACCORDING TO SOCIETY'S DEFINITION, IT IS NOT WRONG, NOR WILL ANYONE GET HURT.

In contradiction to God's boundaries surrounding sexuality, the world puts no limitations on our sexual appetites or desires. Anything goes. You can be sexually intimate with anyone at any time, and, according to society's definition, it is not wrong, nor will anyone get hurt. Unfortunately, I see tragic devastation occurring in young people's lives — in their bodies, minds, and spirits — as a result of sexual immorality.

TO THOSE MOLESTED, VOICES OF DARKNESS SPEAK DAILY SAYING, "YOU ARE DIRTY. YOU WANTED THIS TO HAPPEN; IT'S YOUR FAULT. SOMETHING IS WRONG WITH YOUR SEXUALITY."

Let's apply this "current wisdom" to some modern-day scenarios and see how true it rings. If sex outside of God's boundaries is not wrong, and if it is indeed just a physical act with no further ramifications, then molestation and incest should have no harmful effects on people; being touched by someone in a sexual manner should not bother a little boy or girl. But as I have seen clearly in my many years of ministering in the area of sexuality, when the door of innocence is torn off the hinges through premature sexual experience, it awakens sexuality way before its proper time. The powers of darkness then use that violation to stamp an improper identity (based on sexuality) on those molested. In addition to the sexual images being perpetuated through the media, it is one of the causes of destructive identity theft. To those molested, voices of darkness speak daily saying, "You are dirty.

You wanted this to happen; it's your fault. Something is wrong with your sexuality." We have seen the effects of these illegal and immoral sexual experiences plunge people into self-hatred, early promiscuous behavior, and same-sex experimentation. In fact, many young men and women who struggle with feelings of homosexuality were molested at a young age. Obviously, in those cases, sex was not merely a physical act with no lasting consequences.

We have observed that some young women who were molested later allow themselves to become overweight and begin dressing in an unfeminine manner as a subconscious defense mechanism to deflect male attention. Young women have shared with me that they determined to never again be attractive to any man because the fear and pain that resulted from being a female was great and had led to unwanted and inappropriate male attention. This is very self-defeating behavior, as they often develop a "global distrust for men," yet deep in their heart they desire a *safe* male to want them. However, because of their fear, they consciously or subconsciously sabotage nearly every chance they have for a relationship.

> I HAVE SEEN AND HEARD TOO MUCH
> OVER THE YEARS TO BE ABLE TO
> AGREE WITH A CULTURE THAT SAYS
> SEX IS MERELY A PHYSICAL ACT
> DEVOID OF ANY CONSEQUENCES.

We also see marriages where early childhood molestation or immorality has stained the sexual experience for one or both spouses, leaving them hating God's gift of intimacy that is meant to bond husband and wife together. For those who have not been healed from such sexual violations, the result is significant loss in their lives. Unhealed men and women become accomplices to the destruction of their own dreams because of the resultant shame and fear they carry. I have seen and heard too much over the years to be able to agree with a culture that says sex is merely a physical act devoid of any consequences. After many years of ministering healing and restoration to those wounded by sexual sin, I can testify to the fact that sex outside of marriage in any form has significant negative consequences physically, emotionally, and spiritually. To say anything otherwise is a lie.

EVEN MEN DESIRE MORE

In our own wisdom, we have replaced true intimacy with sexual experience. Men especially have been susceptible to the lie that true intimacy and sexual experience are one and the same. When I speak at men's conferences or retreats, I declare, "Men, God created you for intimacy." Then I emphasize God's three-dimensional reality of intimacy — body, soul, and spirit oneness.

MEN, ONE OF THE GREATEST TRUTHS YOU COULD WALK AWAY FROM THIS BOOK WITH IS THAT SEX WAS NEVER DESIGNED TO FULFILL YOU.

Men, one of the greatest truths you could walk away from this book with is that sex was never designed to fulfill you. Believing otherwise is one-dimensional thinking and will lead to intense frustration and a lack of fulfillment in your life. I recently saw a smiling picture of an aging Hugh Hefner attired in a silk smoking jacket with a Playboy Bunny on each arm. As the founder and head of Playboy International, many would assume that he is the most satisfied man alive, having had unlimited sex with an unlimited number of partners his entire adult life. I can guarantee you that is not true. The reason I can declare that is I know God did not create sex to be our ultimate source of fulfillment. Only *He* can ultimately fill the hunger in our souls, and only *He* can adequately satisfy us. True, sex is one of His great blessings, but it was never meant to be the focus of our lives.

Additionally, if we only focus on one of the three parts of intimacy, we will never achieve true intimacy. The mafia guy with a hooker on each arm is not experiencing intimacy as God designed it; he is just having sex. He is operating with a one-dimensional definition of intimacy that cannot satisfy, because physical intimacy was never designed to be experienced apart from the two other aspects of intimacy. No wonder so many men are frustrated! They are on an endless search for the right sexual experience in an attempt to experience true intimacy and are only looking within the bounds of one part of intimacy, the physical part. Ask any married man about this truth when he has had a fight with his wife. If they have sexual relations before they have truly reconciled, he will not experience much intimacy with his wife — only sex. That husband will readily say he did not experience true intimacy with his wife, because she was mad at him and still withholding her spirit and emotions from him. After they have asked each other for forgiveness and re-established relationship, most men could report that they then experience a whole new level of intimacy with their wife. After reconciliation, the wife is willing to give herself to her husband in body, soul, and spirit, resulting in true intimacy.

ONLY THE MULTI-DIMENSIONAL VIEW OF INTIMACY WILL SATISFY MEN AND WOMEN.

In the uni-dimensional view of intimacy society espouses, men hope to find fulfillment. When they don't, they are increasingly frustrated; as a result, they attempt to add to the experience. They may add pornography, another person, or keep their wife but cheat on her. I believe that is why many men leave their wives when they experience a midlife crisis. If a husband has looked to their physical relationship as their main means of connectedness and his main means of fulfillment to the exclusion of their friendship and spiritual oneness, he will become increasingly dissatisfied with his wife as they grow older and her physical responsiveness wanes. He may hope a new, younger wife will satisfy him sexually and bring him the fulfillment he desires. However, as we have discussed already, only the multi-dimensional view of intimacy will satisfy men and women. And, ultimately, only God can satisfy the deepest longings and desires of our souls.

Similar to the husband and wife in the above scenario, a young man who is having sex with a gal outside of God's covenant of marriage will not experience true intimacy with her. Why is that? His lack of commitment to her in terms of marriage will prevent her from completely giving herself to him. She may yield her body to him, but she will withhold portions of her soul, hindering true intimacy. He gets sex

HE GOES ON AN ENDLESS SEARCH, MOVING FROM ONE WOMAN TO THE NEXT IN SEARCH OF INTIMACY, BUT ONLY EXPERIENCES SEX.

but misses out on body, soul, and spirit oneness. In the dissatisfaction that comes from that, he may think, "The problem must be the person I am with. I need to find a new girl who has read the latest edition of *Cosmopolitan* and knows all the new sex tricks. Then I will be happy." He goes on an endless search, moving from one woman to the next in search of intimacy, but only experiences sex. In his confused search for intimacy, he is looking in all the wrong places. He could experience hundreds of women, as some men have, and still be empty. As we saw earlier, King Ahasuerus had beautiful Queen Vashti as his wife and probably, also, the promise of a great sex life. When he banished her from the throne and went on the search for a new queen, it appears he was looking for something more than a sex partner. I think he discovered true intimacy with Esther.

King Solomon was the wisest man on the earth, but he was a fool in this area of his life. Even this man of supreme revelation from God apparently got trapped into thinking about intimacy in a one-dimensional way. Seven hundred wives and 300 concubines did not fulfill him. He must have been looking for fulfillment in all the wrong places.

THE ENEMY'S LIES VS. GOD'S TRUTH

We need to recognize the following lies of the enemy:

- Our identity is primarily sexual. Therefore, we need to cultivate that aspect of our lives and use that as a means to attract and relate to the opposite sex.

- Since men and women are similar, they are both primarily sexual in nature. Therefore, women can be as casually involved as men in sexual encounters.

- Sex is a uni-dimensional physical act with little or no bearing on the other aspects of our nature. Therefore, any expression of sexuality will not harm us.

- Intimacy is achieved through sexuality.

We need to arm ourselves with these truths:

- Who you are as a person is the most important part of your identity. Your sexuality is only one part of your identity and is only to be expressed within God's protective boundary of marriage.

- In our God-given design, men and women are different. Women need safety, security, permanence, and commitment; they are primarily relational, not sexual; sex is never a casual encounter for them as it can be for men.

- Sex is a multi-dimensional act that has bearing on all the other aspects of our nature. Therefore, any expression of sexuality outside of marriage will have a detrimental effect on our body, soul, and spirit.

- True intimacy is achieved through body, soul, and spirit oneness. All three of those aspects need to be cultivated and present in a relationship to achieve true intimacy.

With a clear awareness of both these lies and truths, we are positioned to halt the identity theft being perpetrated on this generation and recover our true, God-given identities.

CHAPTER 13

IT'S A LEADERSHIP ISSUE

I was preaching at a young adult gathering when I saw that "look" — the kind of look that haunts a father, especially a father like me with a broken heart for what is happening to the young women in our culture. The look came from a couple of young women in the audience. It was an expression I have seen in every nation in which I have ministered — on the face of the Bulgarian waitress, Daniella; in the eyes of daughters on the big-city streets of New York, Washington D.C., Moscow, and Kiev; on the faces of women in the smaller towns of Guatemala, Canada, Western Europe, and America. That look sends two different messages.

One message is, "I am doing what the culture has told me to do to get the love I want to have. I am sophisticated and independent. I make my own decisions about relationships with men. I decide about their character and how involved I will get physically with them. I am a self-made, independent woman of the 21st century. I don't need protection."

"I AM AVOIDING THE GROWING REALIZATION THAT I AM NOT CHERISHED BY THE MAN I AM GIVING MYSELF TO."

However, the second message is saying something quite different. "If you look a little bit closer, you will see the other part of me. I have concealed it as best as I can, as it is not politically correct to mention it, but I have doubts about having sex with my boyfriend. I am avoiding the growing realization that I am not cherished by the man I am giving myself to. He only pays attention to me when he wants to get physical, and I don't get the communication and true intimacy I want and need. The commitment from him that I constantly think about has yet to

appear. I tell myself everything is fine. However, my heart cannot lie
to my face, and that is what you are seeing — my heart is fearful, and
I am very conflicted inside. I am doing everything the culture has told
me to do, but the promises the culture has made to me are not coming
true. I am not happy. I do not feel loved and cherished; I feel taken
from. Someone is lying to me. The current relationship I am in may
end, and for a little while there will be the excitement and hope of a new
relationship beginning. Unfortunately, it will probably end as all the
others have, and I will feel used. I am trapped in this destructive cycle
that repeats itself over and over again."

> ## "I AM DOING THINGS I DON'T REALLY WANT TO DO AND HAVE BECOME SOMEONE I DON'T REALLY WANT TO BE IN ORDER TO GET THE LOVE I KNOW I WANT TO HAVE."

That look is a mixture of seduction and confusion. It combines the
sense of awareness a young woman has in knowing her sexuality can
influence young men, but also the awareness that that influence has cost
her so much. She feels pain, confusion, fear, shame, and regret. Many
women have said to me, "I am doing things I don't really want to do and
have become someone I don't really want to be in order to get the love I
know I want to have."

I continued to preach my message as I watched those young women.
The message I was preaching was one the Lord had used many times to
bring freedom to young people in this generation. I was expecting God's
truth to bring similar freedom to those young people — to set the captive
free and bind up the brokenhearted. It was then the Lord spoke to me
in a still, small voice that said, "Those girls you noticed are not going to
repent." That was strange and difficult to hear. Immediately, I began a
micro-conversation with God telling Him that many men and women
had repented after the preaching of this message and found healing and
deliverance from the shame and guilt of sexual sin. I continued preaching
with a little less anticipation for the response time at the end of my
message than I usually felt. Next, I heard the words, "They can't repent."
I began to argue with the Lord. I pointed out to Him that He was the

One who gave every man a free will, and that I was a man who believed in repentance. I reminded Him that the history of revivals is filled with the spirit of repentance. I told Him my whole ministry and message involves repentance. I was indignant — other people had heard this message and were able to repent, so why could these girls not repent? I knew repentance would bring restoration and healing for them, which in turn would lay a good foundation for strong, healthy marriages in their futures.

THEY WERE NOT GOING TO GIVE UP WHAT LITTLE ATTENTION THEY WERE GETTING FROM THE YOUNG MEN IN THEIR LIVES...TO DEPEND ON A RELIGIOUS SYSTEM THAT WOULD NOT MEET THEIR NEEDS.

The Lord then began to give me understanding. These young women were intuitive, as is the heart of every daughter God has made; they analyze the atmosphere they are in and adjust their behavior accordingly. For that reason, they were making choices. They were not going to give up what little attention they were getting from the young men in their lives — with all the pain, fear, shame, and guilt that accompanied it — to depend on a religious system that would not meet their needs. In other words, this is a church-culture issue that needs to be addressed by leaders.

Part of the solution to the healing of daughters in the nations of the earth has to do with leaders and the decisions they make. When church leaders begin to develop strategies to address the needs of a daughter's heart and intentionally seek to alter or create atmospheres where their needs can be met in Christ in a healthy and pure way, young women will more readily repent and be willing to take on a new identity in Christ.

What we have failed to recognize is that when we call a young woman to follow Christ and forsake her worship of the false gods, we are asking her to assume a new identity. We are asking her to forsake the image the powers of darkness have worked tirelessly to impress upon her from the time she was a little girl. That image is what I call a "woman"

GOD ALLOWS WOMEN TO BE A "WOMAN" IN ONLY ONE RELATIONSHIP IN THEIR ENTIRE LIVES — WITH THEIR HUSBANDS.

— a female who acts sensually and seductively in all her relationships with men. God allows women to be a "woman" in only one relationship in their entire lives — with their husbands. In contrast, God calls women to walk in all other relationships with the opposite sex as pure mothers, pure sisters, and pure daughters. That is why I use the term "daughter" so often in my writing and speaking; "daughter" signifies a woman who is walking in purity and a posture of trust before God, trusting that He will meet her needs and take care of her future. What a relief it would be to many women to take off that primary identity as a sexual being and walk simply as a pure sister to brothers in Christ, or as a mother to young men in the Lord, or as a daughter to fathers in the Lord! But how can a woman take on those new identities if we do not offer that possibility? What if there are no pure fathers for her to relate to? How will men walk as fathers in the Lord if they are not trained and called to be that? How can a daughter of the Lord trust her brothers in Christ if they have not been taught to walk in purity and be protectors instead of predators?

I KNEW I WAS NOW ALSO CALLED TO ENCOURAGE LEADERS, FATHERS, AND YOUNG MEN TO... CREATE NURTURING, SAFE ATMOSPHERES IN THEIR CHURCHES SO THE NEEDS OF YOUNG WOMEN COULD BEGIN TO BE MET IN THE CHURCH.

That meeting came to a close. Those particular girls did not respond to the altar call, though some others did. However, I left the meeting knowing I had been issued a challenge from God. I was to continue to minister to young men and women in the churches and schools, as I had been doing. However, at that point, I saw clearly that part of Adam's sin was his abdication to the enemy. He allowed the serpent to have his way with his wife. He did not maintain an atmosphere in which Eve was safe from the lies of the enemy and the consequences of giving in to those lies — lies that would alter her image, her world, and her view of God. Instead of recognizing the effect of the enemy's lie in her life, he joined her, allowing the offer of the fruit to bring destruction to him as well. I knew I was now called to encourage leaders, fathers, and young men to avoid the abdication of Adam and instead create nurturing, safe atmospheres in their churches so the needs of young women could begin to be met in the church.

My South African Experience

On my first trip to Africa, I encountered almost the same response as that of those two young women. I was preaching at a conference in South Africa where there was absolutely no response from the women. In their hardened faces and spirits, I could see they were not going to reveal their pain to God or any minister of His in a public setting. Wondering and meditating on this uncharacteristic response, I began to sense the Lord telling me that the women in that meeting would not respond, once again, because of the atmosphere. They heard my revelation on the heart of a woman, that I loved my daughters, and that I served and cherished my wife — which was all nice and wonderful.

> ## The predatory, wealthy older men — "sugar daddies" — had propositioned their daughters, offering to pay for school, clothes, and food in exchange for sex.

Unfortunately, I was going to get on a plane in a week and leave Africa, and the Africa they knew - and the men they knew - were going to remain the same. The men of Africa were the ones who had abused them, raped them, molested them, and in some tribes, allowed ritual female circumcision to occur. The predatory, wealthy older men — "sugar daddies" — had propositioned their daughters, offering to pay

for school, clothes, and food in exchange for sex. Their husbands had
betrayed them, and their fathers had molested or abandoned them. The
beatings would continue. The devaluation of the female gender would
continue. The demonic cultural and tribal philosophies which propagated
those behaviors had not been altered. The potential transformation of a
nation through the Gospel had begun, but it had not reached the depths
of these areas yet. The women knew that, and because they sensed the
atmosphere and the reluctance or refusal of the African church leaders to
address those issues, they chose to stay in their pain. They would function
but not thrive as God's daughters. The church meetings will continue.
Conferences will be held. Evangelism will take place. In the midst of all
that, those women will be some of the most significant contributors to
the success of these ongoing endeavors. However, as we mentioned earlier,
women with wounded hearts tend to live as slaves who are trying to earn
favor with God by their service. They are not fully free to release the
beautiful female gifts within them that we desperately need. As a result,
their marriages, their families, their churches, and their communities are
impoverished.

BUILDING THE KINGDOM OF GOD WITH SLAVES IS NOT AN OPTION IF WE ARE TO BE AUTHENTIC LEADERS.

My example comes from Africa, but it is true for our Western
churches as well. Building the Kingdom of God with slaves is not an
option if we are to be authentic leaders. Jeremiah lamented repeatedly in
his book that leaders . . . *heal the brokenness of the daughter of My people
superficially, saying, "Peace, peace." But there is no peace* (Jeremiah 8:11).
Or, as *The Message Bible* so clearly says, *My people are broken —shattered!
— and they put on band-aids, saying, "It's not so bad. You'll be just fine."
But things are not "just fine"!* We would do well as leaders to seek the
complete healing and wholeness of the women in our midst. If we don't,
more than half of our members are crippled, suffering, and not whole,
which means the whole body is crippled, suffering, and not whole. A true
leader will not heal the wound of the people superficially, but will seek for
their complete healing.

Because women are integrated ... unhealed shame, guilt, and remorse over sexual sin affects their whole being.

Let me say it again — because I believe what I am saying is important enough that it bears repeating. Shame and brokenness from sexual sin and immorality can make any daughter into a slave. She may try to make up for the things she believes are unforgivable by trying to be the best church person she can be. Our church programs will run, the conferences will be held, and the books will be published, oftentimes with the contribution of half-healed women in our churches. Because women are integrated, meaning what happens in one part of their lives affects all the other parts of their lives, unhealed shame, guilt, and remorse over sexual sin affects their whole being. Men, on the other hand, can compartmentalize the issues in their lives and live quite effectively with guilt and shame neatly tucked away inside a little box. Women are not wired that way. Shame and guilt over a past abortion colors all that a woman thinks and does. Guilt and wounding over past sexual sin or molestation continually hangs like a cloud over a woman's spirit. These things, if not dealt with, will not only hinder her relationship with God, but will also put her relationship with her husband at risk. This may lead to another broken marriage and family, resulting in hurting children who doubt the reality of the Kingdom of God.

A Leadership Decision

Every leader has a decision to make. Do we want to be like one of the leaders of old who built the pyramids and canals with slave labor? Will we do the same with our churches and build with modern-day slaves? Will we be content to evaluate our success with numbers and well-oiled programs? Or will we become those true reformers who choose to take time to seek deep healing for the people for whom we are called to care? That means dealing head on with people's sexual pasts, lives, and choices. A choice for deep healing has an eye toward the future relationships and marriages of the young people, blessing for those already married, and restoration for those whose brokenness has left them divorced and alone. It will take

IT WILL TAKE DELIBERATE EFFORT ON
OUR PART AS LEADERS TO CREATE AN
ENVIRONMENT IN WHICH OUR WOMEN
CAN RECLAIM THEIR TRUE IDENTITY. IT
WILL TAKE WORK TO HELP OUR MEN
WALK IN AUTHENTIC MANHOOD.

deliberate effort on our part as leaders to create an environment in which
our women can reclaim their true identity. It will take work to help our
men walk in authentic manhood — reflected by sexual purity and a
posture of honor toward the women in their lives. Too often, we don't
deal with these issues and then wince each time we hear about another
marriage in our church that has failed or a young man or woman living
an immoral lifestyle in secret. Or we may grieve and even weep when we
discover that someone made a trip to the abortion clinic or is pregnant out
of wedlock. Those kinds of sexual experiences and failures set stumbling
blocks in the foundations of the next generation of marriages. This next
generation of marriages must be whole and strong if we are to see the
church restored to be the city set on a hill we know God has called it to
be. Without a strong church, made up of solid marriages, whole families,
and secure children, we will not see sustained spiritual awakening and the
resultant reformation in our land for which we long. Healing from sexual
sin is a key ingredient in attaining those goals, simply because sexual sin
has such far-reaching ramifications in people's lives.

SEXUAL SIN IN THE CHURCH

Lest you think I am blowing things out of proportion in my call for the
need for sexual healing in our people, let me share some startling statistics.
I was teaching my seminar at a church in California that had electronic
touch-sensitive buttons installed into the arms of each of the 400 chairs
in their auditorium. I could ask a question and give options, *A* through
D, as a response. Fifteen seconds after the people responded, their answers
were tabulated and expressed in the form of percentages which I could
see. I wanted to find out how many people were dealing with shame. I
asked, "Who is dealing with shame from a sexual experience? (It could be
old shame or new shame.) If yes, press *A*, if not, press *B*." Moments later,

Most of our people need to be freed from shame resulting from sexual sin, and a good percentage need to deal with current sexual sin.

I was looking at some surprising results. Eighty percent had answered "yes." Eighty percent of the people in that auditorium were dealing with shame from old or current sexual experience — 320 of the 400 people present! Next, I asked if they were dealing with old shame or current shame. Seventy-five percent reported it was old shame they were carrying. Twenty-five percent — 80 people — indicated they were experiencing new shame over current sexual sin, things they had not brought into the light yet. Eighty people *in church* that day were dealing with *current* sexual sin! This occurred in a charismatic, life-filled church. And with people who were motivated enough to sign up and attend a seminar on sexuality! We are naïve, as leaders, if we think we can shepherd our people effectively without dealing with the pervasive issue of sexuality. Most of our people need to be freed from shame resulting from sexual sin, and a good percentage need to deal with current sexual sin.

When I go to the airline counter to board a flight, a friendly attendant inquires, "How many bags will you be checking today?" I am often reminded of what shame does and what young people face when they come to the "marriage counter." They are asked what baggage they are bringing into their marriage. A lot of young people have to stand back, point to a long line of bags, and ask, "Is there room for this much stuff? I have so many bags; I have a lot I am dragging into this relationship. I am afraid of men. I have been deeply hurt and have not forgiven my own father. I have negative associations with sexual experience. I carry memories from the multiple relationships I've had. I am currently dealing with pornography or lust. I am full of shame and guilt from my past. Can there be some help for me? Is there any healing for me?"

Yes, there is healing in Jesus Christ. We do not need to carry our sexual history and shame with us into our future. We, as leaders, would be wise to give requisite attention to these issues that profoundly affect the large majority of our sheep.

NEHEMIAH'S EXAMPLE

Nehemiah was one such leader. Note his response when he heard of the devastation of the city of God and the condition of God's people: *When I heard these things, I sat down and wept. For some days I mourned and fasted and prayed before the God of heaven. Then I said: "O Lord, God of heaven, the great and awesome God, who keeps his covenant of love with those who love him and obey his commands, let your ear be attentive and your eyes open to hear the prayer your servant is praying before you day and night for your servants, the people of Israel. I confess the sins we Israelites, including myself and my father's house, have committed against you* (Nehemiah 1:4-6, New International Version). He repented of sin on behalf of himself and his people, but he then took further action: *And I said to the king, "If it please the king, and if your servant has found favor before you, send me to Judah, to the city of my fathers' tombs, that I may rebuild it"* (Nehemiah 2:5). Nehemiah did not stop with a broken heart for the condition of the people but made a plan to see the broken places restored. He made an honest evaluation of the condition of God's people and then devised a plan that promised restoration.

CHANGING THE TOXIC, SEXUAL ATMOSPHERE OF A NATION OR GENERATION WILL ONLY BE ACCOMPLISHED BY LEADERS WHO MAKE THE CHOICE TO BE INTENTIONAL AND DETERMINED ABOUT CHANGE.

Changing the toxic, sexual atmosphere of a nation or generation will only be accomplished by leaders who make the choice to be intentional and determined about change. King Josiah, in tearing down the high places, must have understood the prophetic, apostolic formula for change. As I mentioned earlier in discussing the obituaries of the kings, tearing down the high places was the first thing that reformer-revivalist king did. And remember, those high places represented the worship of the false sex-gods. It took him a full six years to tear down the high places and purge the land of idolatry and the resultant harlotry and sexuality that accompanied it. Six long years! The length of time it took to eradicate idol worship demonstrates to what degree that false worship had permeated the culture. Then, and only then, did he give orders for repairing the house of the Lord. One might think, as leaders, that all our energies must first go toward the goal of stabilizing and strengthening the house of the Lord. Here, though, the work of healing and restoring the church began with first dealing with the high places. It is almost as if we will not see the healing of our land take place unless tearing down the high places is part of our blueprint for building. Just as with Nehemiah and Josiah, we are not going to see atmospheric changes in our churches in one week, or as the result of one conference or one visit of a special speaker. All of those things may be part of the package God puts together to see the strongholds come down, but leaders implementing an ongoing strategy is the key to atmospheric change. Leaders must see the need, get a blueprint from God, and then doggedly pursue the goal over a lengthy period of time. I believe the lives of the next generation are worth it. I believe the dreams of our sons and daughters are precious enough to ask nothing less from us.

Confronting Sexual Sin

As I meditated on the need for reformers of this sort, the Lord brought to mind John the Baptist. John announced the coming of the long-hoped-for One, Jesus; he was preparing the way of the Lord. But he also tore down the modern-day sexual strongholds, the high places of his day, even though most of us would not think of him in that context. We see this in the following Scripture: *For Herod had seized John, and bound him, and put him in prison on account of Herodias, the wife of his brother Philip. For John had been saying to him, "It is not lawful for you to have*

Calling for sexual purity while at the same time announcing the coming of the Savior went hand-in-hand for John.

her." (Matthew 14:3-4). John was a New Testament reformer after the Old Testament pattern of Josiah and Hezekiah. Calling for sexual purity while at the same time announcing the coming of the Savior went hand-in-hand for John. Declaring the eternal truth of the person of Jesus and

creating an atmosphere of honoring God's sexual standards were part
and parcel of the same mission for John. His confrontation of Herod's
sexual sin was no momentary whim of intolerance on his part that would
result in an embarrassment to the true cause of Christ. Instead, it was
a compatible conviction for which he was willing to risk his life and
ministry. His confrontation of the sexual sin of the ruler, ultimately, led
to his beheading.

WHO WILL WE TRUST?

While I was reading about the life of King Hezekiah, I noticed a
Scripture that helped me understand how that king brought revival to
his nation: *They feared the Lord and served their own gods according to the
custom of the nations from among whom they had been carried away into
exile* (II Kings 17:33). It goes on to say . . . *So while these nations feared the
Lord, they also served their idols* (II Kings 17:41). In other words, God's
people were attempting to live out some kind of commitment to the One
True God, but at the same time served the false gods of the day, the idols
of the land. Hezekiah called the people of God out of the multi-god
worship, which was the custom of the nations. He had the courage to
confront their duplicity, calling the people to trust God and God alone.
Obviously, that meant calling them out of the sexual immorality and
child sacrifice involved in the worship of those false gods, and ushering
them into the moral purity which marks the worship of the One True
God.

It did not take long for Hezekiah's trust in God to be tested. Early
in his reign, his nation of Judah came under siege from the barbarian
nation of Assyria. It was not an idle threat. The Assyrian army had
already conquered most of the world's nations. Furthermore, they were
known as a brutal, merciless people. The Assyrian emissary mocked
God and His ability to deliver them (recorded in II Kings 18). However,
Hezekiah held firm and told the emissary they would trust God and
God alone and not look to any other gods for deliverance. The emissary's
mocking continued, and he made pronouncements to the people on the
city wall. *"Nor let Hezekiah make you trust in the Lord, saying, 'The Lord
will surely deliver us, and this city shall not be given into the hand of the king
of Assyria.' Do not listen to Hezekiah, for thus says the king of Assyria, 'Make*

*your peace with me and come out to me . . . until I come and take you away
to a land like your own land, a land of grain and new wine, a land of bread
and vineyards, a land of olive trees and honey, that you may live and not
die'''* (II Kings 18:29-32).

THE WORSHIP OF THE ONE TRUE GOD DEMANDS THAT WE WALK IN SEXUAL PURITY AND TRUST HIM SOLELY TO MEET OUR NEEDS.

The enemy of God's people taunted them with fear over and over
again and then promised blessing if they would give themselves to him.
The enemy uses the same tactic today with God's people — taunting them
about trusting in God, assaulting them with fear, and then promising
them all they desire if they will give allegiance to him. It is the exact same
tactic he uses against daughters today. God calls young women to submit
their beauty to Him, to walk in purity, and to trust Him. The enemy wars
against them by assaulting them with unrelenting fear regarding their
future and their prospects for marriage. He ridicules their trust and faith
in God's wisdom and ability to provide for them. He lies to them and
promises great blessing if they will only follow and serve him. As it did for
Hezekiah, it takes great courage and faith to stand against that assault,
refuse to listen to the lies, and place the entirety of our life and future
in God's hands. Countless women capitulate to the enemy and resort to
using seduction, manipulation, and their physical beauty to attempt to
capture a man and secure their future. As always, the enemy promises
life but delivers only death — a reality most daughters discover too late.
King Hezekiah placed his whole trust in the Lord. We have that same
decision to make on a daily basis: Who will we trust to meet our needs?
That is why moral purity is so important, especially for a young woman.
By choosing to walk purely and not employ her sexuality and physical
beauty to seduce a man, she trusts God to move on her behalf to meet
her desires and fulfill her needs. What she does with her sexuality is truly
a worship issue. The worship of false gods demands we give ourselves
away sexually. The worship of the One True God demands that we walk
in sexual purity and trust Him solely to meet our needs. Just as with
God's people in the Old Testament, we cannot worship God *and* the

false idols simultaneously; it is not acceptable to attend church and then live a sexually impure lifestyle. The two are diametrically opposed. Either we worship God and walk in purity, or we worship the false idols whose worship involves sexual immorality.

THE WORK OF A LEADER

We see in the enemy's taunts one of the job descriptions of a true leader and reformer: *Nor let Hezekiah make you trust in the Lord, saying "The Lord will surely deliver us . . ."* (II Kings 18:30). A leader will help the people he is serving to trust in the Lord in every situation. Hezekiah did not voice feigned trust in God, and then, in secret, look for another avenue of deliverance. All the other polytheistic nations had already fallen to that vicious army. He knew their only hope was in God's help and deliverance. Later, in Hezekiah's prayer for deliverance, he declared his trust in God and used the language of monotheism as he cried out to God. Hezekiah prayed before the Lord and said, *"O, Lord, God of Israel, enthroned between the cherubim, You alone are God over all the kingdoms of the earth . . . Now, O Lord our God, deliver us from his hand, so that all kingdoms on earth may know that You alone, O Lord, are God"* (II Kings 19:15, 19—New International Version). Notice how he declared God to be the true God? The beautiful phrase, "You alone," is used twice in this prayer. He was reminding his people that we cannot serve and trust God and other gods simultaneously. In that very real life-and-death situation, he chose to trust God.

> YOUNG AND OLD PEOPLE ARE
> INVOLVED IN CHURCH MEETINGS
> AND ACTIVITIES, YET MANY WORSHIP
> AT THE SEX ALTARS THAT PROLIFERATE
> IN OUR MODERN-DAY CULTURE.

Today, life-and-death choices are occurring daily in people's lives. Young and old people are involved in church meetings and activities, yet many worship at the sex altars that proliferate in our modern-day culture. The enemy relentlessly taunts people with fear and then offers blessing and fulfillment if they will give him allegiance. Daily, young women are faced with the life-or-death decision of whether to follow and trust the True God or the sex-gods of our modern culture. We often don't understand the demonic pressure a young woman faces when she is waiting to be married and walking in purity. She lives in the midst of a culture that worships the false gods of sexuality where "everyone else" is exercising their sexuality in an attempt to meet their needs. Her life-and-death situation is just as real as the Assyrian siege around Jerusalem that faced Hezekiah. Either she can trust God for her future and say no to sexual temptation, or she can give in to the supposed shortcut to blessing and see her purity stolen and her dreams destroyed. Many do not have the faith and courage to trust God alone. I have prayed with thousands of young women who have paid a high price for walking in the modern-day duplicity of giving lip service to Jesus and then bowing down at the altar of sexuality. For young men, the same duplicity has caused them to give in to the habit of feeding their lower natures, resulting in enslavement to lust, pornography, and a predatory posture in relationships. It is our job as leaders to help them trust and follow the Lord in these situations and then support them as they live out their commitment to walk in purity.

THEY NEED US

Most leaders want to leave a lasting legacy. I believe the greatest legacy we could leave would be the transformed lives of the next generation, complete with hearts for God, strong marriages, and godly families. The most important decision a young person will ever make is their decision to follow Jesus Christ. What is their second-most important decision? It is the decision concerning whom they will marry, to whom God will join them in order to see His kingdom purposes go forward in the earth. The proper selection of a spouse will greatly determine a person's ability or inability to fulfill the will of God in their lives. Too often we see the devastating effect on the lives of those who do not follow God's clear plan to be equally yoked in marriage. Establishing a goal of strong marriages for the next generation is a good objective for leaders to make. Helping them practically to get there is quite another issue. The disparity between our stated goal of strong marriages and the help we offer to make that become a tangible reality is greater than we often want to admit. It is an issue that begs our attention as leaders in the church.

> I BELIEVE THE GREATEST LEGACY
> WE COULD LEAVE WOULD BE THE
> TRANSFORMED LIVES OF THE NEXT
> GENERATION, COMPLETE WITH
> HEARTS FOR GOD, STRONG
> MARRIAGES, AND GODLY FAMILIES.

We need to have answers for the myriad questions young people are asking in the area of sexuality and relationships:

- What do I do with my unmet needs for attention and affection as a young woman if I grew up without a dad, or my dad didn't meet those needs?

- What do I do with "my power to attract" as a young woman?

- How can I be healed from the memories that torment me from my past sexual experiences?

- How can I learn to trust men again and even hope to be married when I have a distrust of men based on my past experiences?

- As a man, how can I get rid of the sexualized images of women I have become accustomed to and learn to honor women in the right way?

- What do I do with the shame I am carrying from my past sexual sins?

- How can I be healed from the need to have the opposite sex respond to me in order to feel good about myself?

- How should I relate to the opposite sex in a God-honoring way?

- How do I start a relationship that can lead to marriage?

- How do I know what is emotionally and physically appropriate in a relationship?

- How do I overcome old habits and patterns of relating to the opposite sex that, in the past, have brought destruction to my life?

- What do I do with the gender confusion that remains in my heart and spirit because of sexual experimentation?

- The dating system seems so broken, but what is there to replace it?

- How can I have a relationship that is not based on emotional fantasy, but on reality?

- How do I go into a future relationship when I have so much baggage from past relationships?

- What can I do about the sexual assault in my life that has made me dislike God's gift of sexuality?

- What can I do about the sexual molestation I experienced that makes me hate being a woman or a man?

- How do I get healed from years of pornography that have altered how I see women?

- How can I deal with the fact that my parent's divorce has given me a fear of commitment regarding marriage?

These are all pertinent questions and issues young people face today. Often they have no one to look to for answers. Ideally, the church should help young people find answers to these questions. I suggest, though, that means we need to focus on the issue of sexuality more than once a year in our youth or young adult groups. If this issue is truly the second-most important issue young people will deal with in their lives, and the ramifications of their decisions in this area will affect their future and destiny in major ways, then we would be wise as leaders to give the issue the requisite attention it deserves. I believe it should be a major part of our blueprint in caring for God's people.

PROVIDING HELP

Not long ago I heard of a young couple whose marriage had failed. I remember having had questions about their relationship from the beginning, wondering if their pasts and their views of sexuality and intimacy would cause a bumpy road for them in marriage. I remember wondering if they were going to be able to deal with the old issues sufficiently to lay a strong foundation for their future and the inevitable tests that come to every marriage. There is a chance they never received the answers and help they needed for their marriage to have the possibility of success. Seeing the warning signs and hoping against hope that a young couple will succeed is not good enough. Providing answers for a generation desperate to be successful in marriage and helping them deal with real-life issues surrounding sexuality is a modern-day version of dealing with the high places.

> PROVIDING ANSWERS FOR A GENERATION DESPERATE TO BE SUCCESSFUL IN MARRIAGE AND HELPING THEM DEAL WITH REAL-LIFE ISSUES SURROUNDING SEXUALITY IS A MODERN-DAY VERSION OF DEALING WITH THE HIGH PLACES.

Let's look at some of the practical ways in which we, as leaders, can help God's people deal with sexual issues:

- Expose the enemy's lies around sexuality and present God's truth — in men's meetings, in women's meetings, in youth and young-adult meetings.

- Talk about sexual temptation and pornography at men's meetings and offer opportunities for repentance and accountability.

- Talk about molestation and incest with our men. In many cases, a horrifying 30 percent of young people in the discipleship schools I minister in have been molested. I am not insinuating that fathers are always the culprits. However, if men are called to be like Adam and protect those under their care, then our protection is remiss, according to these statistics.

- Teach fathers about the importance of their words of blessing, appropriate affection, and time and attention in their daughter's lives — the keys to protecting the purity of their daughters.

- Teach our men about the importance of being sincere, humble men of God in their homes with their families. Men are called to protect their daughters, but many daughters are not willing to come under their father's protection if he has not built relationship with them over the years, or if he is a hypocrite in his own walk with the Lord.

- Train our fathers in how to train their sons in purity.

- Talk to our young people about sex — a lot. Much more than once a year we need to talk about sexuality and relationships because it occupies their focus multiple times a day. It did ours, but we forget that it did.

- Talk about the broken system of dating and present godly alternatives.

- Regularly talk about sex from the pulpit and provide opportunities for healing from sexual sin and shame.

"Breaking the sound barrier" — talking about these issues — in these ways and in these settings will help set a generation free and contribute to the success of their future marriages and families.

GOD IS LOOKING FOR MODERN-DAY JOSIAHS WHO UNDERSTAND THAT THE NATIONAL REVIVAL AND REFORMATION WE ARE LONGING FOR IS DEPENDENT ON OUR TEARING DOWN THE MODERN-DAY ALTARS OF BAAL.

In King Josiah's time, God's strategy for deliverance included an understanding of what needed to be addressed first before the rest of God's victory strategy could be employed. Josiah first tore down the altars of idol worship and then built for God. The worship of the god of sexuality, complete with the shedding of innocent blood through abortion, is the modern-day equivalent of idol worship. I believe the same strategy that worked in Josiah's day is the principle we have overlooked today in our struggle against cultural and spiritual strongholds. I believe God is looking for modern-day Josiahs who understand that the national revival and reformation we are longing for is dependent on our tearing down the modern-day altars of Baal.

We would do well to begin where Josiah did, with the destruction of
the worship of the sex-gods and everything involved in that, and *then*
commit ourselves to creating an atmosphere of sexual purity in which
our sons and daughters can grow up.

In the book of Jeremiah, the prophet received his calling from God
with a specific set of directions and a prescribed sequence of actions
that were to follow. *See, I have appointed you this day over the nations
and over the kingdoms, to pluck up and to break down, to destroy and to
overthrow, to build and to plant* (Jeremiah 1:10). The first function of
the prophet is to pluck up and break down, to destroy and overthrow.
Jeremiah was involved in twice as much tearing down and uprooting as
he was in building and planting. God is helping us see that part of the
positive work of reformation involves the destroying of strongholds. Of
course, reformation will involve building and planting, but only after we
have done the uprooting and casting down of demonic ideologies and
entrenched cultural strongholds that, if left unaddressed, will destroy
people's lives. That reminds me of Paul's challenge to us. *And do not
participate in the unfruitful deeds of darkness, but instead even expose them*
(Ephesians 5:11). Part of building for God is first identifying the work of
the enemy, exposing his schemes that work destruction in people's lives.
Our job is to identify and tear down the broken systems that destroy a
generation and leave them no hope, and then to build new life-giving
structures based on God's truth.

> IF THE FALSE GODS ARE WORSHIPPED
> BY SEXUAL IMMORALITY — WHICH
> THEY ARE — AND THE TRUE GOD IS
> WORSHIPPED BY PURITY — WHICH HE
> IS — THEN THE ISSUE OF SEXUALITY
> IS NOT A SIDE ISSUE IN THE CHURCH
> BUT AN EXTREMELY IMPORTANT ISSUE
> TO BE DEALT WITH.

What we do sexually is a worship issue; we cannot condone
duplicitous worship in the church. If abortion (the shedding of innocent
blood) and sexual immorality bring a curse on the land and invite

God's judgment on our nation — which they do — then we need to eradicate those things from our midst. To do so, we must address the root causes, not only the resultant fruit. We will never eradicate abortion and reverse the curse unless we recognize that abortion is simply at the end of the conveyor belt in a culture that worships sex. When we expose the cultural sexual assault, tear down the high places, deliver and heal those wounded by sexual sin, teach fathers to train their sons and protect their daughters, and lead our sons and daughters into their true God-given identities, *then* we will be part of the fulfillment of Malachi 4:6. *And he will restore the hearts of the fathers to their children, and the hearts of the children to their fathers, lest I come and smite the land with a curse.* Then, and only then, will we truly see the curse lifted off our land. *That* is the legacy I want to leave my children and grandchildren.

Contact Information and Resources

Lifeline Ministries
P.O. Box 8071
Spokane, WA 99203

509-325-2852

info@lifeline-ministries.org

www.lifeline-ministries.org